Goethe's Path to Creativity

D1696491

Goethe's Path to Creativity provides a comprehensive psycho-biography of Johann Wolfgang von Goethe, a giant of modern German and European literary, political, and scientific history. The book brings this influential work by Rainer Matthias Holm-Hadulla to the English language for the first time in a newly elaborated edition.

Goethe's path to creativity was difficult and beset by a multitude of crises, beginning with his birth, which was so difficult that he was initially not thought to have survived it, and ending with an infatuation that left him, at the age of 74, toying with the same kind of suicidal thoughts he had entertained as a 20-year-old. Throughout his long life, he suffered bitter disappointments and was subject to severe mood swings. Despite being a gifted child, a widely recognized poet, and an influential scientist and politician, he spent his entire life loving and suffering; nonetheless, he had the exceptional ability to endure emotional pain and to transform his sufferings creatively. The way in which he mined his passions for creative impulses continues to inspire modern readers. Readers can apply the lessons they have learned from his life and use Goethe's strategies for their own creative art of living.

Goethe's Path to Creativity: A Psycho-Biography of the Eminent Politician, Scientist and Poet will be of great interest to all engaged in the fields of creativity, literature, psychoanalysis, psychology, psychotherapy, and personal growth.

Rainer Matthias Holm-Hadulla is Professor for Psychiatry, Psychosomatic Medicine, and Psychotherapy at Heidelberg University, Germany. He is a Training Analyst (IPA) and teaches at universities in Buenos Aires and Santiago de Chile and at the Pop-Academy, Mannheim. Professor Holm-Hadulla is the author of over 100 scientific papers, as well as six books on creativity, counselling, and psychotherapy, including *The Art of Counselling and Psychotherapy* (Karnac 2004) and *The Recovered Voice: Tales of Practical Psychotherapy* (Karnac 2017). Previous versions of his *Psycho-Biography of Johann Wolfgang von Goethe* have been published in German, Spanish, Italian, and Persian.

"Among the numerous books on Goethe, the work of Rainer Matthias Holm-Hadulla takes an exceptional position. It provides reliable information about Goethe's life and work and unlocks the secrets of his creativity. Goethe is understood as a personality who was able to overcome individual crises in artistic creation. A book not only for Goethe friends, but also for those seeking guidance in today's world."

Jochen Golz, *President of the Goethe Society in Weimar, Germany*

"Holm-Hadulla's psychobiography of Goethe offers a psychology of creativity that is pleasantly devoid of any psychoanalytic or psychologic dogmatism. This is already apparent in the author's approachable language, which steers well clear of jargon and mumbo-jumbo. The book provides perspicacious insights into the peaks and troughs of Goethe's creativity, insights that one frequently seeks in vain in purely literary biographies."

Dieter Borchmeyer, *Senior Professor of German Literature at Heidelberg University, Germany*

Goethe's Path to Creativity

A Psycho-Biography of the Eminent
Politician, Scientist and Poet

Rainer Matthias Holm-Hadulla

Translated by Deanna Stewart

Routledge
Taylor & Francis Group

LONDON AND NEW YORK

First published in English 2019
by Routledge
2 Park Square, Milton Park, Abingdon, Oxon OX14 4RN

and by Routledge
52 Vanderbilt Avenue, New York, NY 10017

Routledge is an imprint of the Taylor & Francis Group, an informa business

English edition © 2019 Rainer Matthias Holm-Hadulla

© Vandenhoeck & Ruprecht & Co. KG, Rainer M. Hadulla,
Leidenschaft: Goethes Weg zur Kreativität, 2. bearb. Auflage,
Göttingen, 2009

Translated by Deanna Stewart

British Library Cataloguing in Publication Data
A catalogue record for this book is available from the British
Library

Library of Congress Cataloging in Publication Data
Names: Holm-Hadulla, Rainer Matthias, 1951- author. | Stewart,
Deanna, translator.
Title: Goethe's path to creativity : a psycho-biography of the
eminent politician, scientist and poet / Rainer Matthias
Holm-Hadulla ; translated by Deanna Stewart.
Other titles: Leidenschaft, Goethes Weg zur Kreativitèat. English
Description: Abingdon, Oxon ; New York, NY : Routledge,
2018. | Includes bibliographical references.
Identifiers: LCCN 2018013722 (print) | LCCN 2018013755
(ebook) | ISBN 9780429459535 (Master e-book) |
ISBN 9781138626027 (hardback) | ISBN 9781138626041 (pbk.)
Subjects: LCSH: Goethe, Johann Wolfgang von, 1749-1832--
Psychology. | Authors, German--18th century--Biography. |
Authors, German--19th century--Biography. | Creation
(Literary, artistic, etc.)
Classification: LCC PT2051 (ebook) | LCC PT2051 .H57513 2018
(print) | DDC 831/.6 [B] --dc23
LC record available at https://lccn.loc.gov/2018013722

ISBN: 978-1-138-62602-7 (hbk)
ISBN: 978-1-138-62604-1 (pbk)
ISBN: 978-0-429-45953-5 (ebk)

Typeset in Times New Roman
by Integra Software Services Pvt. Ltd.

MIX
Paper from
responsible sources
FSC
www.fsc.org FSC® C013056

Printed and bound in Great Britain by
TJ International Ltd, Padstow, Cornwall

Contents

Acknowledgments

I would like to thank Dover Publications for permission to use multiple poems from *103 Great Poems/103 Meistergedichte: A Dual Language Book* (Johann Wolfgang von Goethe; New York: Dover, 1999).

Introduction
Goethe's path to creativity

The gods, the infinite ones, give everything
to their favorites, entirely,
all joys, the infinite ones,
all pains, the infinite ones, entirely.[1]

Goethe's path to creativity was difficult and beset by a multitude of crises,
beginning with his birth, which was so difficult that he was initially not thought
to have survived it, and ending with an infatuation that left him, at the age of 74,
toying with the same kind of suicidal thoughts he had entertained as a 20-year-
old. Throughout his long life, he suffered bitter disappointments and was subject
to severe mood swings. Despite being a gifted child, a well-loved poet, and an
influential politician, he spent his entire life seeking, erring, and suffering; nonetheless, he had the exceptional ability to endure emotional pain and to commute it
into his own creative development. The way in which he mined his passions for
creative impulses continues to inspire modern readers, and even from a distance
of more than 200 years, readers can apply the lessons they have learned from his
life and work to their own creative development and their own art of living.

Goethe's life and work is of particular interest to psychologists because he
had a unique ability to describe his personal development and the crises he
experienced. He developed strategies to solve emotional problems that are of
practical use still today. In his works, he describes a wide variety of personal
and social conflicts; his letters, diaries, and recorded conversations are also full
of problem-solving inspirations. Although this constant preoccupation with
himself may seem off-putting to some, it does provide one main advantage to
researchers: We know almost everything about his life, from his earliest childhood to his death. Moreover, the style of these self-narratives is more nuanced
than we could imagine possible of today's authors. A vocabulary of less than
1,000 words suffices for many communicative situations today, including the
reporting on Facebook, Twitter, and in tabloid newspapers. More challenging
conversations and more sophisticated texts, though, use a vocabulary of around
10,000 words. Goethe, on the other hand, expended a vocabulary of over 90,000
different words to fully describe his personal experiences.

Not just himself, but also those around him – first his mother, father, and sister, and later his friends, lovers, and colleagues – also provided detailed accounts of his personal development. This was made possible by the age in which he lived; at that time and in that society, impressions, ideas, and emotional experiences were chronicled to an extent that has not been practiced before or since.

His own writings, though, are the best testimonies to his path to creativity. While these always included his hopes and longings, they also described his disappointments and mortifications. This mode of writing allowed him to discover human truths that are otherwise inaccessible to mundane understanding or to scientific reasoning. His work, therefore, remains not only actually relevant, but also universally valid.

Goethe's ability to remain dedicated to life and to his creativity, despite severe emotional crises, is of special psychological interest. His frequently self-flagellating preoccupation with memories and fantasies stabilized him throughout his life. Self-reflection, political and scientific work, as well as poetic writing were indispensable for him to overcome emotional turmoil, relational conflicts, and mood swings. His creative striving to come to terms with adverse life events began with the death of his brother Hermann Jakob when Johann Wolfgang was ten years old and was reinforced by emotional crises and awareness of political conflicts in his adolescence:

> And thus began that habit from which I could not break away my whole life through – the habit of turning into an image, into a poem, whatever delighted or troubled, or otherwise occupied me, and thus of coming to some definite conclusion with regard to it, so that I might both rectify my conceptions of external things and satisfy my inner cravings. To no one was the faculty for so doing more necessary than to me, for by nature I was constantly carried from one extreme to the other.
>
> (Smith, vol. 1, p. 252)

It was through reflection, fantasy, and literary creation that Goethe was able to perceive, to endure, and to overcome his conflicts. Although he was dealing with his own personal anxieties and difficulties, he also found generally applicable strategies for solving both social conflicts and individual conflicts. Throughout his long life, he suffered bitter disappointments and was subject to severe mood swings. Many people – not only his mother, father, and sister, but also numerous friends, both men and women – helped him to cope with psychological crises in a creative way. During his childhood and youth, he exhibited a strong desire to be noticed, acknowledged, and validated, a need that he was fortunate enough to have complied with by those around him.

Psychology has made great strides since Goethe's day, and the new field of neurobiology has given us revolutionary insights into the human mind. Using modern medical imaging techniques, we can see which locations in the brain are activated when someone is in a good or bad mood, and also which biological processes are involved in human behavior, perception, and thought. Nevertheless, even leading neuroscientists believe that complex psychological experiences can only be understood with the aid of appropriate verbal methods (see Andreasen 2005). There are many things that cannot be learned from brain scans; the only way to learn why a Mozart sonata elicits memories of a lover's smile in one person and the boredom of a Sunday afternoon in another is through the power of words.

This highlights the necessity for understanding human beings by delving into everyday and literary narratives. In doing this, we all make use of our own prior understanding, an understanding influenced by our life experiences. The philosopher Hans Georg Gadamer, one of the most important thinkers of the twentieth century, has convincingly argued that it is important to consciously apply this prior understanding when approaching a text. Gadamer has also pointed out that although understanding is a natural human ability, it nonetheless requires constant practice. It is in the act of understanding that we experience ourselves and the world around us, and it is only through understanding that we are able to find firm ground on which to stand in a sea of impressions and experiences. Rational encounters with other people, with experiences, and with texts can give rise to something new, something that can expand our horizons and help us to find our bearings. But understanding is more than just the mental structuring of experience. It is also an all-encompassing journey that includes both sensory and practical experiences, one that allows people to become their true selves and to meet their own potential. I would like to take you on just such a journey.

The first part of this book is an examination of Goethe's life and work, which gives rise to important insights I will share with you, with a special focus on Goethe's passionate striving to achieve a creative life. An investigation of Goethe's path to creativity from a psychological perspective does not entail a detective-like search for problems and disorders, but rather an exploration of the circumstances that allowed him to lead a productive and creative life. The second part of this book begins with Goethe's conceptualization that life itself is the result of creative realization, followed by an examination of his life and work from the perspective of creativity research. Of particular interest is the way in which he was able to deal with emotional disturbances. The third part of the book provides a summary and draws further conclusions by the interpretations of three of Goethe's elementary works: his poem *Legacy*, his last letter, and the second part of the tragedy *Faust*.

Note

1 Unless otherwise specified, translations of source materials (excerpts from poems, plays and letters) are our own. *Trans. (DS) and author (HH)*.

Part 1

Goethe's life and work

Chapter 1

Childhood and youth

Frankfurt, 1749–1765

Now through my navel-string
I suck nourishment from the world.
And splendid all around is Nature,
holding me to her bosom.

Johann Wolfgang, the first-born son of Catharina Elisabeth and Johann Caspar Goethe, came into the world at noon on 28 August 1749. The conditions under which he was born seemed favorable, as Goethe was later to record in his memoirs: "The aspect of the stars was propitious: the sun stood in the sign of the Virgin, and had culminated for the day; Jupiter and Venus looked [at each other] with a friendly eye" (Smith, vol. 1, p. 1). But the birth was very difficult, and it was initially thought that the infant had not survived. Echoes of this threat of death will be found throughout Goethe's life and work.

Goethe's mother, Catharina Elisabeth, came from a wealthy family of scholars and jurists. Her father, Johann Wolfgang Textor, had been the mayor of Frankfurt, the highest municipal office in Frankfurt, since 1747. Catharina was the oldest of four siblings and had a relatively unconventional upbringing. Looking back on her childhood, she wrote that she thanked God "that, even in youth, [her] soul had never been corseted and that it had been allowed to grow and flourish to its heart's content and to spread its branches wide, not like the trees in a dull ornamental garden, which are pruned and mutilated into unnatural shapes" (Koester 1923, p. 78: DS).

Although lacking in education, she was rich in worldly wisdom, as is evident in the letters she wrote to Duchess Anna Amalia. At the time of Goethe's birth, she had just turned 18 years old and was "as yet almost a child", as Goethe wrote in his autobiography, *Poetry and Truth* (Smith, vol. 1, p. 200). She was healthy and experienced no problems during her pregnancy. Goethe's father did not see any reason for concern, and both he and his wife looked forward to the birth of their offspring. Goethe's father was financially comfortable, thanks to his own father's success as a merchant, enough so that he could dedicate himself to the life of an independent scholar and study those things that interested him.

Johann Wolfgang's birth was beset by many complications: his mother was in labor for three days, and the family could not help but remember the tragedy of his grandmother's first three children, who were all stillborn. After many different attempts to revive the child, his grandmother was finally able to announce to her daughter-in-law that he was alive.

We know today from research in the fields of neurobiology and psychology that experiences during birth and even prenatal sensations can leave behind unconscious traces in the "embodied mind". Even when there are no complications, both mother and child undergo many hours of stress during childbirth. The newborn experiences overwhelming fear and a sense of impending doom, which are stored in its unconscious mind. Nevertheless, the child copes with this mortal fear, which it is freed from by its first cry, in much the same way as the mother is relieved of her physical pain by her feeling of joy at the birth of her child.

Goethe places great significance on his birth experience in his autobiography, *Poetry and Truth*; he returned to the themes of birth and personal growth accompanied by pain and the threat of death again and again throughout his life. He conceived of his own self-actualization as a continuous process of "dying and becoming", i.e. a continuous process of creation and destruction. Being aware of this conception allows us to understand the lines of verse that he included in a letter to Auguste zu Stolberg, in which he states that he had been given everything entirely, "all joys, the infinite ones,/all pains, the infinite ones, entirely" (HA 1, p. 142: HH). For Goethe, joy and despair were often conjoined: at the time he wrote these lines, his living situation would have been the envy of many, but he had also just received news of his sister's death.

Goethe's creativity helped him to find solace in his relationships with other people and in his zeal for nature and culture. For example, after experiencing a crushing romantic disappointment, he composed the poem quoted at the beginning of this chapter while on a hastily arranged journey to Switzerland. In this poem, he draws "sustenance from the world" and feels as if he is being held "to Nature's breast", as if born anew. His writing allowed him to overcome crises and to create himself anew again and again. But we can also see in his work, from *Werther* to *Faust*, that this creative act of self-creation was accompanied by anxiety, despondence, and painful feelings of inferiority. In *Faust I*, he says:

> Alas! Our deeds as much as our passions
> Hamper the course of our lives. [. . .]
> What gave life to us, the glorious feelings,
> Congeal in the earthly turmoil. [. . .]
> Sorrow nests right away into the heart,
> There it causes secret pain [. . .]
> I am not like the gods! Too deeply it is felt:
> I am like the worm that rifles through the dust [. . .]
> (Vs. 632–653: HH)

These verses are similar to rhymes the 17-year-old Goethe shared with his sister, in which he confessed the deep despair he felt during the crises of his student years. An incessant struggle for the vitality of the self could be considered one of the guiding motifs throughout Goethe's life, but he also conceived of individuation in a general sense as a process of changing and dying; for this reason, self-actualization and a creative life cannot occur without pain and danger. These ideas led Goethe to choose the following motto for *Poetry and Truth*: "He who is not flayed does not learn" (qtd. in Wiethölter, p. 75).

Even after little Johann Wolfgang survived his difficult birth, his family continued to worry about him. He seems to have reacted to the dangers of his first few weeks of life with intense emotions and active attempts to cope mentally. Bettina von Arnim described

> [how] in his ninth week he had already had troubled dreams; when grand-mother, grandfather, and mother and father, and nurse, had stood around his cradle, and listened, what violent movements showed themselves in his mien, and upon wakening, changing to a most afflicting cry, — often, too, shrieking so violently, that he lost his breath, and his parents feared for his life; — then they procured a bell. When they observed that he became restless in his slumber, they rung and rattled violently, that, upon waking, he might immediately forget his dreams.
>
> (Arnim 1861, p. 311)

Although Bettina's description is not a completely reliable source, it is not inconceivable that little Johann Wolfgang was plagued by fears and anxieties that he, like any other child, attempted to assuage by means of intense psychological activity. Thanks to neurobiology, it is now possible to confirm this psychoanalytical supposition. During their first few months of life, babies are already starting to actively process internal and external stimuli, which allows them to reach a level of emotional stability.

Goethe's relationship with his mother, even after their shared experience of his difficult birth and first few months of life, was not completely free of frustrations and threats. Catharina Elisabeth became pregnant again only six months after his birth, and when he was 15 months old, she devoted herself completely to the care of his newborn sister, Cornelia. It is likely that Goethe's father and grandmother assisted him in his attempts to cope with the relative loss of his mother; nonetheless, this loss left scars in the form of separation anxiety and creative attempts at coping. It is possible that this early separation from his mother, although not a complete separation, caused him pain while also fostering his imagination.

Johann Wolfgang was also prone to disturbances in his later development. Bettina von Arnim recorded that he was easily overexcited and tended to react with anger. If something was damaged or was not in its usual place, he was prone to respond with an angry outburst. Even as an old man, he had difficulty dealing with anything that disrupted his usual routine, such as illness in those around him. He also avoided coming into contact with sick people and even the dead. He did not attend the funerals of either of his closest friends, the poet Schiller and the Grand-Duke Karl August, and he could not bring himself to see his wife, Christiane, during her final illness. For all of his avoidance of defectiveness, illness, and death in real life, Goethe dealt with these topics repeatedly in his writing, which became his approach to coping with any issues that he found difficult in real life.

Even as a child, his response to an unpleasant experience might be an angry outburst, but it might also be an attempt to understand the chaos of his emotions to use his creativity to transform them, in which he was aided by his ability to transform negative experiences into a reality that he found more acceptable. His mother, Catharina Elisabeth, described how he listened carefully to the fairytales she read to him:

> There I sat, and there he soon devoured me with his great black eyes; and when the fate of any favorite did not turn out exactly according to his notion, I saw how the passionate veins swelled upon his forehead, and how he choked his tears. He often caught me up, and said, before I had taken the turn in my tale: "Mother, the princess won't marry the nasty tailor, even if he does slay the giant, will she?" When I made a stop, and put off the catastrophe to the next evening, I might be sure that, during that time, he had put everything in good order; and so my imagination, when it could reach no further, was often supplied by his.
>
> (Arnim 1861, pp. 313–314)

Goethe's mother

Catharina Elisabeth loved her son dearly and called him her "little pet" (*Hätschelhans*), even as a grown man. Nevertheless, there was always a certain distance between mother and son. Goethe wrote the following observation on one of the manuscript pages of *Poetry and Truth*:

> Children's moral character does not develop out of their relationship to their parents. The distance between them is much too great; gratitude, affection, love, and respect prevent these young and needy creatures from expressing themselves in their own ways. Every act of resistance is a crime. Privation and punishment quickly teach the child to turn away from the parent and towards itself, and because the child's wishes seem very reasonable, it will soon be clever and manipulative.
>
> (HA 9, p. 844: DS)

After the death of her husband in 1782, Catharina was to live another 26 years, during which she followed her son's development with lively interest. It does not seem to have pained her, though, that Goethe only visited her a total of four times after moving to Weimar in 1775. She never complained, and at the age of 55, she even wrote to her son:

> My life is flowing peacefully along like a clear stream … my body is at rest, but my thoughts are all activity. I am able to spend the whole day alone and still find myself taken by surprise at the onset of evening. I am as cheerful as a goddess – and in this world, happiness and satisfaction are all that is really necessary.
>
> (HA Letters 1, p. 93: DS)

Even with the physical distance between them, mother and son maintained an intimate rapport that lasted their whole lives. As Catharina Elisabeth (now 76 years old) wrote to Bettina von Arnim, "and on Wolfgang I must think for hours together; how, when he was a little child, he played before my feet, and then, how prettily he played with his brother Jacob, and made stories for him" (Arnim 1861, p. 36). Her son found few opportunities to visit and care for his mother after relocating to Weimar, but he remained connected to her in his work. He was relieved, though, when other people maintained close relationships with his mother. Bettina von Arnim wrote to the elderly Mrs. Goethe:

> He has said, that I shall supply his place with you, and show you all that love which he cannot; and must be to you as if you had shown to me all that love which he can never forget. – When I was with him, I was so silly as to ask, if he loved you? Then he took me in his arms, and held me on his heart, and said: "Touch a string, and it will vibrate, even if it should long have yielded no tone".
>
> (Arnim 1861, p. 38)

Even though Goethe never invited his mother to visit him in Weimar, or never seriously, they nonetheless maintained a lively correspondence. He considered Weimar to be his world, and Catharina Elisabeth accepted the parent's inevitable fate, to be left behind while her children move on. The deeper dimensions of Goethe's relationship with his mother can only be determined by analyzing his writings and his approach to mother–child relationships in general.

Throughout his life, Goethe grappled with the relationship between mothers and their children and dealt with this topic in his writings, especially the tragedy of mothers murdering their children shortly after birth. While a student in Leipzig, he was preoccupied by the story of Catharina Maria Flindt, who had been sentenced to death for the murder of her illegitimate child. Her lover freed her from prison, but she returned of her own free will, tormented by her conscience. Goethe was even more affected by the fate of the maidservant Susanna Margaretha Brandt, whom he learned about while studying in Strasbourg in 1770. Susanna Margaretha was a 24-year-old woman of good character who lived in Frankfurt. She was seduced and became pregnant, and after secretly giving birth, her fear and desperation led her to kill her child. Goethe followed the trial until her execution. This event seized hold of Goethe's imagination and led him to include the Gretchen tragedy in his play *Faust*.

In this tragedy, he examines the destructive aspects of the relationship between mother and child. After giving birth, Gretchen kills her child, the fruit of her love for Faust, and is executed like Catharina Maria Flindt and Susanna Margaretha Brandt. One main theme of these tragedies is that mother and child destroy each other, an idea that can be found throughout Goethe's writings. We repeatedly draw "fresh nutriment, new blood" from Mother Nature, but she takes as well as gives life. In *The Sufferings of Young Werther*, the protagonist's suicide allows him to become united with Mother Nature, she whom he had previously experienced as "a fearful monster, for ever devouring its own offspring" (*Works* 6, p. 54). In the first draft of his play *Goetz von Berlichingen*, the antagonist Weislingen says to Adelheid: "Such is woman's favour! At first she fosters with maternal warmth our dearest hopes; and then, like an inconstant hen, she forsakes the nest, and abandons the infant brood to death and decay" (*Works* 11, p. 284).

While it is clear that Goethe idealized mothers, we can also see that he was aware of the contradictions inherent in their life-giving and threatening aspects. In the novel *Elective Affinities* (*Die Wahlverwandtschaften*), Charlotte gives her own child into the care of her niece Ottilie because there is no room for it in her life. Through her carelessness, Ottilie, herself still basically a child, allows the child to drown. This is another instance of Mother Nature, symbolized by the water, reclaiming her offspring. The fullest expression of Goethe's holy awe of mothers can be found in the "Dark Gallery" scene in *Faust II*.

Faust must descend into the dark gallery of creation to fulfill his promise to the Emperor to bring to life the ideal couple, Paris and Helen. Mephistopheles resists Faust's plan to enter the realm of the Mothers and of female fertility.

Mephistopheles.	Such secrets I'm reluctant to betray –
	Goddesses enthrone remote in solitude,
	No space, even less time around them;
	To name them is embarrassment:
	They are the mothers!
Faust (terrified).	Mothers!
Mephistopheles.	You are shuddering?
Faust.	The Mothers! – Mothers! – Yes, it sounds so strange.

(Vs. 6212–6217)

Mephistopheles wishes to avoid all contact with the Mothers, and Faust is filled with a sense of religious awe. Nevertheless, they are unable to create real humans without the Mothers. Like his characters, the poet must also enter the dark world of unconscious, maternal phantasms as part of his creative process. The realm of the Mothers is a taboo zone, though, and no paths lead there.

> *Mephistopheles.* There is no way to this
> Untrodden void where none may tread, this sphere
> Where none has asked, and none may ask to go.
> (Vs. 6223–6225)

The path to the Mothers is blocked by more than social taboo; a meeting with them can only occur outside of time and space.

> *Mephistopheles.* No locks or bolts are here;
> You are adrift, alone. Can you conceive
> What solitude and desolation mean?
> (Vs. 6225–6227)

Mephistopheles invokes another world, one that Faust has no knowledge of and cannot know, but Faust refuses to accept that this world is denied to him.

> *Faust.* You don't impress me with such make-believe;
> It reminds me of that dismal scene
> Inside the witch's kitchen long ago.
> Was my whole life not burdened and constricted?
> Was it not emptiness I learned and taught?
> (Vs. 6228–6232)

Faust hopes that his experience of the real world and his philosophical examination of the emptiness "where none may tread" mean he has already done everything humanly possible, but Mephistopheles counters with the following:

> *Mephistopheles.* If you had swum across the furthest ocean,
> And seen the vastness of infinity,
> Though dread of death might seize you, you'd still see
> The rolling waves in never-ceasing motion.
> You would see *something* . . .
> (Vs. 6238–6243)

This is not the case in the realm of the Mothers, though.

> *Mephistopheles.* You will see nothing in that void all round,
> You will not hear your footstep where you tread,
> Beneath your feet you'll feel no solid ground.
> (Vs. 6246–6248)

Mephistopheles describes an unconscious experience that cannot be recalled or consciously comprehended afterwards, but that is nevertheless real. This is reminiscent of the infant's bodily experiences in utero and during the first few months of life. Neurobiological and psychological studies have shown that a fetus's experiences of temperature, movement, and sounds in utero are stored at the neural level, but can never be consciously recalled. Feelings of agitation, disquiet, and pain are also said to leave behind unconscious traces in memory. One could argue that it is this dimension of human experience – which is only one of many possible dimensions, not least of is the artistic dimension – that is being addressed in the "Dark Gallery". But how might it be possible to gain access to an experience that cannot be recalled? Faust, who refuses to accept any limitations, insists on experiencing this unconscious dimension of life, one existing outside of time and space, fully expecting that it will give him a comprehensive understanding of the world.

> *Faust.*   Come then! I will explore this mystery,
> And in your Nothing hope to find my All.
>   (Vs. 6255–6256)

The knowledge Faust has laid claim to, though, cannot be acquired by earthly means; he needs a magic key, which once again is provided by Mephistopheles.

> *Mephistopheles.*   Here is a key, now take it, hold it tight;
>   Respect its power, and you will understand.
> *Faust.*   This tiny thing!
> *Mephistopheles.*   First seize it and do not disrespect.
> *Faust.*   It's growing in my hand! It glows and flashes!
>   (Vs. 6259–6262)

What is this key to recognition that is growing in Faust's hand? It brings to mind an alchemist's magic wand, but in the context of sexuality, motherhood, and creativity in which it is mentioned, it is also reminiscent of the male genitalia. Here, sexuality and creativity are considered two sides of the same coin. This idea touches on an existential taboo when it comes to the Mothers, though.

> *Mephistopheles.*   That key will sense the way that you must go,
>   And lead you to the Mothers far below.
>   (Vs. 6263–6264)

This is the point at which Faustian striving meets an impenetrable barrier, and he shrinks from it.

> *Faust (shuddering).*   The Mothers! Still it strikes me like a blow!
>   Why do I shudder when I hear that word?
>   (Vs. 6265–6266)

But now something unusual happens, something that characterizes both Faust and his creator, Goethe. Faust's fear does not paralyze him, like Lot's wife looking back on Sodom and Gomorrah, rather, it drives him to seek a creative solution.

> *Faust.* I shall gain nothing if I'm numb with fear;
> Our highest self is in our sense of awe.
> Though in the world our feelings cost us dear,
> Such dread can move us to our inmost core.
>
> (Vs. 6271–6274)

The poet's work is the key to warding off the fear and paralysis caused by the Mothers.

> *Mephistopheles.* Descend – or rise, it's all the same –
> but flee
> Beyond the extant world into the free
> Untethered realms of forms
> unfashioned, see
> And marvel at what long since ceased
> to be.
> Like clouds they'll drift around you on
> your way –
> Hold out the key to keep the wraiths
> at bay.
>
> *Faust (with enthusiasm).* Ah yes! Grasping it tightly I feel
> new power,
> My breast is broadened to go on this
> great quest.
>
> (Vs. 6275–6282)

Here we see that overcoming feelings of holy awe in the face of female fertility is a recurring motif of Faustian creativity. Goethe used his writing to dissociate himself from his mother and at the time he created a special closeness to her by his poetry. Thus, art was a way for Goethe to remain in contact with the Mothers while simultaneously keeping his distance from them.

As a rule, most people do not feel the need to delve so far into the mystery of erotic relationships in their everyday lives. For this reason, their sexuality is less complicated and more satisfactory than Goethe's, and less fraught with powerful fantasies. That being said, most people who become involved in intense sexual relationships will nonetheless encounter the unfathomable and find themselves near the "untrodden void where none may tread". It is then up to them to find a creative way of taking the unfathomable and turning it into a vivid partnership.

Creativity allows Faust, and also Goethe in this instance, to touch on the inexpressible.

> *Mephistopheles.*
> You'll see a burning tripod, and you'll know
> You've reached the deepest depths below.
> The Mothers are reflected in its glow;
> Some sit, some stand, while others come and go
> Just as they please. Formation, transformation:
> Eternal thought's eternal recreation.
> The forms of all created things drift near;
> They cannot see you, all they see is mere
> Abstraction. But the danger here is such,
> You must be bold: you take the key and touch
> The tripod with it!
>
> *Faust. (Strikes a resolute and imperious pose with the key)*
> *Mephistopheles (watching him).*
> That's exactly how!
> It follows you, you are its master now.
> Good fortune buoys you up, you calmly rise,
> And bring it back before they realise.
> Then from the deepest night you can retrieve
> The hero Paris, and fair Helen too –
> And you have had the courage to achieve
> What none before has ever dared to do.
>
> (Vs. 6283–6300)

The creative process is being described here, and it touches on the deepest parts of human existence. The tripod becomes the vessel within which the poet, like the Mothers, creates human figures. For Goethe, art is a type of magic that allows him not only to approximate the female power of creation, but also to cope with the threat inherent in the realm of the Mothers.

In reality, Goethe's creative endeavors were supported by his own mother, probably more unconsciously than consciously. If we look at his relationship with his mother from the perspective of attachment theory (Bowlby 2006), we can safely state that he was securely attached to her. Securely attached children are more able to develop a sense of creative curiosity and to confidently explore the world around them than children who are insecurely attached. Despite this, there was still a certain amount of ambivalence in Goethe's relationship with his mother. He was able, though, to take the negative aspects of the relationship – the restrictions and dangers – and not merely cope with them, but actively transform them through his creative work. The trust he had in his mother and his secure attachment to her provided him a firm foundation from which he was able to confront and work his way through the more destructive aspects of the mother–child relationship. It was not necessary for him to transform the Mothers into an idealized and remote image; instead, he approached the dangers inherent in every mother–child relationship with a degree of empathy unusual for a man, especially for a man of his time. Reading the tragedy of Gretchen from this perspective, the level of understanding that Goethe was able to develop for the pain involved in motherhood is impressive.

If we start with the psychoanalytical work of Melanie Klein (1957) and Hanna Segal (1991), we can explain this sensitivity to the Lady-of-Sorrows – Mater dolorosa – aspect of the mother–child relationship. A child who is sufficiently psychologically healthy is already able to perceive during his first year of life that his mother is not only the one who meets his needs, but is also the source of his frustrations. He senses that he is developing aggressive impulses and causing his mother pain. This feeling gives rise to the need to "repair" the mother image that has been damaged by his destructive impulses. This desire to make amends goes hand in hand with the development of the child's creative abilities. If the child finds sufficient acceptance of both his loving and his aggressive impulses, it becomes easier for him to use these energies for constructive pursuits. This is what happened with Goethe, whose portrayal of his "awful and repulsive" character Faust, with whom he identified to a great degree, was actually a portrayal of his own worst tendencies. Goethe also said, with himself in mind, that we are all composed of both light and dark, heaven and hell.

According to Jacques Lacan (1949), every child is confronted with a "primordial lack" (*manque primordial*). This lack leads to a lifelong attempt to create completeness and perfection, even if only in their imagination. People are especially successful at this in the arts and in the area of erotic love, although the results may not be permanent. An additional dimension that is important for future artists is the narcissism dimension, which refers to the child receiving sufficient mirroring, acknowledgement, and appreciation from his parents. Goethe probably received this narcissistic recognition from his mother starting from an early age. Heinz Kohut (1971) thought that creativity could be promoted by the "sparkle" in a mother's eyes, a gleam that Goethe most assuredly saw. Freud also believed that Goethe's self-assurance derived from the love of his mother: "If a man has been his mother's undisputed darling he retains throughout life the triumphant feeling, the confidence in success, which not seldom brings actual success along with it" (Freud 1917, p. 26: DS).

Nonetheless, the love Goethe received from his mother was also associated with disappointments. A small child can experience a separation from the mother as a severe setback, even as psychologically damaging. Goethe was separated from his mother due to her preoccupation with her next pregnancy soon after his birth and with the later deaths of his siblings; we will see later that Goethe frequently experienced feelings of existential danger. The sensation of impending doom during his birth and the anxieties of his earliest years left a deep impression on Goethe throughout his life. He invariably transformed these feelings into motifs in his work and used his creativity to cope with his fears. This does not mean, though, that there is a causal relationship between birth trauma and early childhood development and the later development of artistic abilities. Early experiences in life do find expression in moods and fantasies, however; they then become themes that turn up again and again in adulthood, to be experienced and transformed anew. As Freud said, "These examinations are not intended to explain the genius of the poet, but rather to show which motifs awoke it and which subject matter has been assigned to it by fate" (Freud 1933, p. 276: DS).

We can then view the end of the tragedy of *Faust* from the perspective of Goethe's relationship to his mother and women in general. "Mountain Gorges", the last scene in *Faust* and which was most likely written in 1830, shortly before Goethe's death, deals with the human ability to remain intact while simultaneously falling apart. Several characters appear in the scene: the Virgin Mary (Mater Gloriosa), Gretchen, and the Blessed Boys, who died shortly after birth. The "awful and repulsive" Faust, who had wreaked so much havoc and caused so much pain, is redeemed.

> *Angels.*   This noble spirit is released
> From evil and damnation;
> *For those whose striving never ceased*
> *We can lead to salvation.*
> (Vs. 11934–11937)

Likewise, Goethe's relationship with his mother was also redeeming. Both were able to cope with this pain, the pain experienced by every human being, but in their own ways – the mother by means of her active vitality, and the son through his writing. This is where he repeatedly dealt with both the loving and threatening aspects of his relationship to his mother; ultimately, he was able to create a positive internal image of this relationship, one that he was also able to reconcile with his human fate of having to die. This is an essential aspect of the closing chorus in *Faust*.

> All that must perish
> Is but a parable;
> What is unsufficient
> Here becomes efficient.
> The indescribable,
> Here it is done;
> Eternal womanhood
> Draws us all on.
> (Vs. 12104–12111)

Goethe's father

Goethe's father, Johann Caspar, was born in 1710 to a successful tailor who left him a large fortune which was substantially increased through his marriage. After studying law at the University of Giessen and at the University of Leipzig, he went to the Imperial High Court (*Reichskammergericht*) in Wetzlar at the age of 25 and received a doctoral degree three years later. This was followed by an educational trip (*Bildungsreise*) through Italy and France that lasted another three years and which left a lasting impression on him. When he returned to Frankfurt, he was preoccupied by the imperial coronations taking place there. He acquired the title of Royal Councilor from the Bavarian Emperor Charles VII, who was crowned in March of 1742, for the tidy sum of 313 guldens. This title turned out to be more of a curse than a blessing, though, after the tides turned and the Habsburg Francis I was elected Holy Roman Emperor in 1745. Desperate for a position, he even offered to work without pay, but this offer was declined. So it was that he retired from public life at 32 years of age and spent his days as an art lover, collector, and patron of the arts. His desire for social recognition continued unabated, though, leading the 38-year-old to seek a wife from the best circles, taking as his bride the 17-year-old daughter of the wealthy and influential mayor of Frankfurt.

Johann Caspar Goethe compensated for being marginalized in his career by throwing himself into his educational aspirations for his family. He frequently urged his wife to practice her writing, piano playing, and singing, and he insisted she learn Italian. After the children were born, Catharina Elisabeth was spared her husband's efforts to improve her because he was able to direct his educational zeal toward his children. It was only during the extensive renovations on their house that the children were sent to public school, where Johann Wolfgang, then only five years old, was taught reading, writing, and arithmetic. At the school, he discovered a coarseness he had never encountered at home, and he was involved in many an altercation due to his self-confidence (and perhaps even arrogance). Young Goethe's relationship with his peers was not an easy one. We know from Bettina von Arnim that his comportment was frequently precocious and solemn. He boasted about his Grandfather Textor, the head of the Frankfurt municipal council, and was mocked by his playmates for it.

Young Goethe only attended the school for a short while before his father was able to resume teaching the children at home, where he introduced them to Latin and Italian. In addition to the lessons, their father was able to encourage their interests in a wide range of subjects, thanks to the large collection of compendia and atlases in his library. Later, several private tutors instructed Johann Wolfgang in ancient Greek, Latin, and Hebrew. His father undertook to instruct Johann Wolfgang in English, French, and science himself, and his encouragement of the lively boy's interests planted seeds which would later bear fruit. Looking back, Goethe wrote:

It is a pious wish of all fathers to see what they have themselves failed to attain, realized in their sons, as if they were in a manner living their lives over again, and could at last turn their early experience to account ... My father had succeeded in his own career very much as he had wished: I was to follow the same course, only the way was to be easier and go further ... For linguistic forms and usages I had a ready perception; and I also quickly realised what was involved in the conception of a thing ... It was essays such as these that gave my father particular pleasure, and for which he often rewarded me with presents of money, considerable for such a lad.

(Smith, vol. 1, pp. 21–22)

As we can see, Johann Caspar had certain expectations that he wished to see his son fulfill because he had not been able to achieve them himself. What is remarkable about this is that he recognized his son's talent quite early on but repressed his ambitions for himself with relatively few signs of envy. Later, Johann Caspar even relieved his son of much of his day-to-day work as a lawyer so he could follow his literary aspirations. On the whole, the young Goethe's relationship with his father was characterized by obedience and subordination, rather than tenderness and intimacy; nevertheless, his father's strictness did not seem to cause him any suffering. He was able to put the structures his father had set out for him to good use in his emotional and intellectual development. By way of contrast, he believed that his father's strictness and unapproachableness had had a negative effect on his sister's development.

But, after Goethe broke off his studies in Leipzig at the age of 19 and returned to his family home, he found himself in open conflict with his father. Johann Caspar was irritated and did not want "the invalid" to be cared for at home, but rather in a sanatorium. After his recovery, Goethe found life under his father's roof too constricting. Looking back at the year 1770 after having recovered from a long depressive episode he wrote:

By the spring I felt restored to health, and still more to youthful spirits, and once more longed to be out of my father's house, this second time, however, for very different reasons. I had come to hate the charming rooms and pleasant scenes where I had suffered so much, and it was impossible to establish any friendly relations with my father. I could not quite forgive him for having shown an unjustifiable impatience at my relapses and at my tedious recovery; for speaking with cruelty instead of comfort and forbearance, about that which lay in no man's hand, as if it were a mere matter of will-power. And he, too, felt hurt and offended by me in various ways.

(Smith, vol. 1, p. 317)

This description could be interpreted as an expression of the two men's disappointment in each other, but it could also be an expression of the pushing away that naturally occurs between fathers and sons. Later, even though their relationship became somewhat friendlier, it remained rather impersonal and businesslike. Accordingly, there are only a few instances to be found in Goethe's work on the topic of fathers. Unlike his friend Schiller, who placed the conflicts between fathers and sons front and center in dramas such as *Intrigue and Love, The Robbers*, and *Don Carlos*, Goethe depicted in his works bland, colorless fathers who remained in the background. Although the subject of fathers and sons is touched on in works such as *Goetz von Berlichingen*, it is not further expounded on. In *Faust*, the protagonist's father is referred to only fleetingly, as a "decent man". Although Faust himself seems proud to be the father of Euphorion, there is no sense of rapport between them.

It is possible that Goethe's relationship with his father, which, while largely conflict-free, was not particularly close, led him to seek out friendships with older men. It was Goethe's friendship with the private tutor Behrisch – 12 years his senior – that provided him with a sense of security during the psychologically turbulent period of his studies in Leipzig and which gave him the encouragement he needed for his first attempts at writing poetry. He was able to confide in his friend and to take his advice, without jealousy or a sense of rivalry. During his studies in Strasbourg, he embraced Herder as a role model and mentor, and later the care and affection of his friend and benefactor Merck, eight years his senior, was of great benefit to him during the significant years of 1773 and 1774, a period of high creativity for Goethe. Like Behrisch and Herder, Merck was already well-established in his career and in society, and he acted as a fatherly mentor to Goethe, advising, supporting, and guiding him, all of which played an important, positive role in Goethe's personal and artistic development. He acknowledged in *Poetry and Truth* that these older friends had had "the greatest influence" on his life (Smith, vol. 2, p. 53).

Goethe was able to learn from older men without becoming entangled in power struggles; it is possible that his relationship with his own father, in which they had occupied fixed positions since his childhood, was conducive to this. The father supported the son's efforts to fulfill the father's wishes, and the son felt supported and positively mirrored, yet the two never became too close nor too similar to each other. Goethe's father obviously recognized his son's talent early on, encouraging him without envy and calmly accepting his own relative unimportance in the greater scheme of his son's poetry.

Goethe's sister Cornelia

Starting from a young age, Goethe and his sister Cornelia, only 15 months younger, had a very close relationship, and the siblings remained inseparable throughout childhood. Bettina von Arnim reported the following of them:

> For his little sister Cornelia, while she was yet in the cradle, he had the strongest affection; he brought her everything, and wanted to feed and

nurse her alone; and was jealous when any one took her out of the cradle, in which he was her ruler.

(1861, p. 312)

Here, we can clearly see a trait that will later characterize his other relationships: Goethe took possession of the people around him, from Cornelia to Friederike Brion to Charlotte Buff to Charlotte von Stein, with an unconcern that bordered on presumption. He wrote about his early relationship with Cornelia in his autobiography, but cut it from a later draft:

> He already loved his little sister Cornelia affectionately from the time when she still lay in the cradle, and he used to carry bread privily in his pocket which he would push into the child's mouth when she cried. If anyone wanted to pick her up, he became furious, as he was in general likelier to be infuriated than to cry.
>
> (qtd. in Eissler, vol. 1, pp. 71–72)

Judging from this excerpt, he seems to have been a little know-it-all who had a temper and responded with anger whenever someone pointed out his limits. Kurt Robert Eissler (1963) argues that the young Goethe's caring and altruistic behavior toward his sister was actually a distortion of his true feelings of jealousy. Furthermore, he sees Goethe's elevation of himself to the role of his sister's provider as a compensatory measure for the narcissistic injury of having to share his mother's love. As we will see later with the death of his brother Hermann Jakob, he identified more with adults and simply ignored the fact of his own powerlessness. He behaved as if Cornelia were his own child. Even as a small child, Goethe had a notably possessive attitude about everything around him. He viewed his sister as his own property, but he did not stop there; he incorporated many of his female friends into his fantasies in later years. From this perspective, Goethe often appears impertinent and intrusive. But on the other hand, he had the special ability to reach out to people without hesitation, an ability that helped him to overcome many crises. Similarly, he employed his imagination to freely embrace inanimate nature, viewing it as both his possession and his comforter. We will see that this was essential for his creativity.

Cornelia acted like a magnet on Goethe over the course of his childhood, remaining his most important confidant, even into adolescence:

> Only a year younger than I, she had lived my whole life with me as far back as I could remember, and was thus bound to me by the closest ties. To these natural causes was added a forcible motive, springing from the conditions of our family life. There was on the one hand a father, certainly affectionate and well-meaning, but grave ... on the other hand, a mother, as yet almost a child, who first grew up to womanhood with and in her two eldest children ... Under these circumstances it was natural that brother and

sister should be closely drawn to one another ... But since the hours of solitude and toil were very long compared to the moments of recreation and enjoyment, especially for my sister, who could never leave the house for so long a time as I could, the necessity she felt for intercourse with me was further sharpened by the longing with which she accompanied me in my wanderings.

(Smith, vol. 1, pp. 200–201)

Goethe's description of Cornelia, which he wrote more than two decades after her death, is characterized by a deep affection, an affection that none-theless could not overcome his critical eye:

Her features, neither striking nor beautiful, indicated a character that which was not and could not be in unity with itself. Her eyes were not the finest I have ever seen, but the deepest, with most hidden depths, and with an unrivalled power of expressing love and affection.

(Smith, vol. 1, p. 202)

In respect to his erotic relationship with Cornelia, thoroughly analyzed by Eissler (1963), the following excerpt from his autobiography is rather cryptic:

As she shared my universal tolerance for the good and human, with all its eccentricities, provided it was unperverted, there was no need to conceal from her any idiosyncrasy which might mark unusual natural gifts, or for its owner to feel any constraint in her presence; hence our parties, as we have seen before, were always varied, easy, well-behaved, though occasionally somewhat daring in character. My habit of associating with young ladies in a respectful and courteous way, without any resultant feeling of being definitely bound or appropriated, was entirely due to her.

(Smith, vol. 2, pp. 258–259)

Elsewhere, Goethe spoke of "that amazement at the awakening of sensual impulses which clothe themselves in processes of mind, of cravings of the mind assuming sensual images, all our broodings upon these themes, which obscure rather than enlighten us ... the many errors and aberrations springing therefrom", all of which "the brother and sister shared and endured hand in hand. Yet the nearer they wished to approach each other, to draw from one another light upon their strange condition, the more forcibly did the sacred awe of their close relationship keep them apart" (Smith, vol. 1, p. 201).

Reading these lines, it is possible to imagine that Goethe wrestled with a sexual attraction for Cornelia. But although Eissler describes the relationship between Cornelia and Johann Wolfgang as incestuous, the term seems exces-sive. It is natural that Goethe's feelings for his sister, as is the case in many sibling relationships, contained erotic components. Much more important than this sexual aspect, though, was his deep brotherly attachment to Cornelia, which stabilized him emotionally and inspired him artistically for many years. He continued to have a close relationship with Cornelia, even after he had left the family to study in Leipzig. His letters reveal that Cornelia remained his most important confidant and that he remained more attached to her than to any other person during this period, even sending her a flurry of daily letters at different times. His choice of words attest to their closeness:

> Dearest little sister. It would be unreasonable of me not to also think of you. *Id est*, it would be the grossest injustice a student had perpetrated since Adams' children attended university if I were to neglect to write to you ... Rest easy, my angel; I am doing better here than I ever could have imagined ... Farewell, I am going to bed. Tomorrow we will be together again ... It seems as if you, you other girls, have a certain mysterious charm that you use to captivate us, just as you wish.
>
> (FA 28, p. 15: DS)

It seems that Cornelia confided completely in Goethe and continued to feel a close connection with him, despite the distance. He became her teacher, but even this change in their roles could not disrupt their emotional closeness. In May 1777, he responded to one of her letters thusly:

> I am completely overcome by your letter, your writings, your mode of thinking ... Don't believe that I only mean to flatter; my enthusiastic tone, which I could not but assume after reading this entertainment in the form of a letter, proceeding from authentic feelings from the heart, a heart which has long not felt so much pure joy as that arising from the contemplation of a sister who has improved so much ... I thank God, my sister, that there is not one single girl in Leipzig who compares with you.
>
> (FA 28, p. 639: DS)

Unlike her mother, Cornelia became shy and reserved during her adolescence and as a young woman. Goethe lamented her restrictive upbringing and regretted that his father did not allow his sister the freedom she needed to develop her personality. When he returned to Frankfurt in 1768 after almost three years in Leipzig, he was troubled by his sister's development:

> My sister was, and remained, a being who defied analysis, the most singular mixture of sternness and gentleness, of stubbornness and complaisance ... Thus she had, in a manner terrible to me, turned the hard side of her character towards her father, whom she could not forgive for having prevented or spoiled for her so many innocent joys during these three years, and she refused to recognize a single one of his good and excellent qualities. She did all that he commanded or prescribed, but in the most

unamiable manner in the world. She did it according to the usual routine, but not a bit more and not a bit less. She never made any concession from love or a desire to please, so that this was one of the first things of which my mother complained in a private conversation with me. But since love was as essential to my sister as to any human being, she expended all her affection upon me.

(Smith, vol. 2, pp. 301–302)

Goethe ascribed the hardness in Cornelia's character at least in part to the strictness of their father. It is also possible that her inhibitions, which prevented her from reciprocating her husband's uninhibited affection and sexual attraction, were due to her close relationship with her brother: "There was not the slightest sensuality in her nature. She had grown up with me, and had no other wish than to continue and end her life in this brotherly and sisterly harmony" (Smith, vol. 2, p. 258).

Goethe's physical surroundings

Goethe's physical surroundings also played an important role in his personal development. The house he grew up in, full of nooks and crannies, not only provided protection, but also fueled his imagination. Located on the edge of the Old Town of Frankfurt, its rooms were accessible by means of a tower-like staircase. The young Goethe loved to spend time in the spacious hallway on the ground floor, which opened out onto the street by means of a small porch surrounded by a wooden latticework. During the warm months, the women sat there at their work and conversed with each other. This is also where the young Johann Wolfgang came into contact with the other children in the neighborhood. In *Poetry and Truth* Goethe imbued the following memory from his childhood with special significance: One afternoon, he was playing on this porch with his toy kitchenware, and when he became bored, he threw some of it into the street. The three brothers von Ochsenstein, who lived across the street, were delighted with this game and encouraged him to throw more crockery into the street. With their calls of encouragement ringing in his ears – "Another!" and "More!" – Goethe flung not only his toy crockery but also his family's real tableware onto the pavement to the applause of the children from the neighborhood. Freud (1917) interpreted this childhood scene as a reaction to the birth of his brother Hermann Jakob, who was only three years younger. The older child gave vent to his rancor at the arrival of a new rival by throwing things and reacting to things with rage; he feared the loss of his position as his mother's clear favorite. An alternative way of looking at this is that he orchestrated theatrics in order to cope with his emotional turmoil, an idea we will come back to.

From the back side of the house, there was a pleasant view of the neighbors' gardens, and young Goethe loved to spend time in the garden room on that side of the house. From there, he could look out over a fertile plain, and the sunset never failed to entirely capture his attention. He could also watch his neighbors in their gardens and see their children playing, which aroused feelings of loneliness and longing, even at a young age. He found his own house gloomy. The Goethe children were expected to sleep alone from an early age; if they left their beds during the night, seeking the comfort of their parents or the servants, their father would frighten them and send them back to their rooms. Their mother had more empathy for them and instead promised them a reward in the morning if they could overcome their fears during the night by themselves.

Young Goethe was riveted by his father's collection of engravings of the landmarks of Rome, including images of the Piazza del Popolo and St. Peter's Basilica. His father's predilection for Italy and the Italian language made a deep impression on Goethe; for instance, his mother often played the piano while the language teacher Giovinazzi sang, and the young Goethe learned the Italian songs they performed by heart.

Johann Wolfgang's grandmother, Cornelia Goethe, was not only closely linked to his memories of the family home, but she also played an important role in his feelings of security and attachment. She had acquired the house after the death of her husband, and she lived there with her son and his family until her death in 1754. The children played near her, and Goethe remembered her as a gentle, friendly, and benevolent woman. The young Goethe was forever grateful to her for the gift of a puppet theater that left a lasting impression on him (although it was actually a gift from his father (Boyle 1991)). Johann Wolfgang was delighted to be able to enact what his imagination created, and the puppet theater continued to be in his thoughts throughout his life. He considered it the final bequest of his grandmother, as she died shortly after he had received it.

Goethe's rearing and education

We have already touched on the role Goethe's father played in his son's rearing and education. Rote memorization, which is often treated with contempt today, played a major role in his tutelage. The children were already being impelled to recite short poems and to learn songs at three or four years of age. Apparently, Johann Wolfgang enjoyed this so much that it was not long before he took it upon himself to recite poetry and dramatic pieces from memory. He received a great deal of praise for this, but this recognition does not seem to have been the sole driving force behind his diligence. Probably more important was his pleasure in creating an internal world, which saw him through the dull hours and his loneliness:

> My young brain was comparatively early furnished with a mass of pictures and events, of significant and wonderful figures and occurrences, and I never felt time hang heavy on my hands, as I always occupied myself in assimilating, repeating, and reproducing what I had acquired.
>
> (Smith, vol. 1, p. 24)

Figurative thought and imagination were Goethe's constant companions from his earliest days and provided him with the personal continuity and stability he needed to draw on during later periods of crisis. As a whole, he had access to a very diverse array of educational offerings. Not only was he required to apply discipline in learning languages at a young age, but he also had a regimen of physical exercise, including riding and fencing. He had an art teacher for instruction in portrait and landscape drawing, and he received dance and piano lessons, which he did not continue long, and his dancing remained stiff and clumsy (Boyle 1991).

Goethe was not a child prodigy in poetry. His first attempts were childish and uninspired, much like the poems written by hundreds before and after him. In 1757, this "most faithfully obedient grandson" sent his grandparents a poem, and it is conceivable that his father had a hand in its composition:

> Illustrious Grandpapa!
>   A new year approaches,
> Therefore I must do my duty and pay my respects;
> My deep respect commands me to write these verses from the heart,
> Which, however poorly done, are well intended . . .
> Illustrious Grandmama!
>   This year's first day
> Has awakened in me a tender feeling
> That also commands me to bind you to me
> With verses that, perhaps, no connoisseur would enjoy reading . . .
>
>   (HA 1, p. 7: DS)

There is no hint of genius here, but practicing the fine motor skills required for writing was also considered important. Just as Mozart studied musical technique at an early age, Picasso meticulously practiced drawing, and Einstein pondered the movements of the compass needle before he was old enough to attend school, Goethe was practicing, at the age of seven, the art that would become his métier. Five years later, his writing did not sound much different, even though it proved him to be a classically educated youth:

> Grandparents, as this year has its beginning today
> Please accept this offering that I place before you
> And whether Apollo has been kindly to me or not,
> Please do me the honor of reading it, if only once.
>   (HA 1, p. 8: DS)

He was, after all, already 13 years old. We will see that his first authentic poetry appeared only after the storms of life had tossed about the innocent self still evident here. Höfer (2002) describes how Goethe became familiar with the Old and New Testaments through a regimen of daily readings from the Bible and regular church attendance, where he put his excellent memory to use learning the sermon off by heart each Sunday. He found inspiration in Bible figures, leading him to write the first of his more sophisticated poems, "Poetic Thoughts on Jesus Christ's Descent into Hell". This poem shows that the 15-year-old was grappling with religious themes, was patiently practicing meter and rhyme, and was learning mastery of the stylistic elements common to his time. The beliefs of the orthodox Protestantism of his day set the tone of this early work, which portrays Jesus' descent into hell, an event that was only briefly mentioned in the New Testament. In the poem, Jesus appears as the heroic son of God, exacting revenge on the forces of evil:

> He goes–the tempests round Him break,
> As Judge and Hero cometh He;
> He goes–the constellations quake,
> The sun, the world quake fearfully.
> (Bowring, p. 275)

Christ destroys the devil and "the Dragon, trampled down ... grinneth hideously". The throngs of people, "the partners of [Satan's] cursed career", are overcome by the glory of God. Christ descends to those who have been led astray and redeems the faithful. Those who persist in sin, though, remain damned and lost forever:

> Wrapp'd in the sleep of sin ye dwelt,
> Now is My fearful judgment felt,
> By a just doom your guilt requited.
> (Bowring, p. 278)

This poem could be a reflection of Goethe's struggle with his own vices. Shortly before writing the poem, he had made the acquaintance within his circle of friends of a young lady who had awakened erotic longings in him. For various reasons we will touch on later, he considered meeting her to be his "Fall". The poem, however, was written in a very conventional style and did not exhibit any of the personal expression found in Goethe's later poems. The individual of the poet remained hidden behind the ornate late baroque imagery, which would no longer be the case only a year later in the poems written during his time in Leipzig. Nevertheless, if we listen closely, we can just make out Goethe's concern. Gundolf's assessment, though, seems to miss this completely: "It is completely lacking in any personal views, in any particular emphasis, in any personal belief: It is nothing more than a piece of virtuosity" (Gundolf, p. 37: DS). Goethe's personal struggle with sin, sorrow, and redemption is absolutely perceptible in the poem, which he seems to have used to give expression to his conflicted examination of religion. In one point, Gundolf's criticism is correct: Goethe had not yet found his own creative voice when he left Frankfurt and his childhood behind.

Psychological traumata and physical illnesses

The death of five younger siblings was traumatic not only for his mother but also for little Johann Wolfgang. Only his sister Cornelia survived beyond childhood. Two years after Cornelia's birth, Hermann Jakob was born and lived to the age of seven. His death led to the intense reactions of his brother that we will comment on below. Goethe's second sister, Catharina Elisabeth, was born in 1754. She died during her second year of life, and in 1756, another child was stillborn. Johanna Maria was born one year later and Georg Adolf in 1760, but both only lived to the ages of one and two, respectively.

In November 1755, a powerful earthquake struck Lisbon, spreading fear over all of Europe. Goethe took an active interest in the news reports about the catastrophe, and his childhood belief in a benevolent God began to waver. His uncertainty did not lead to a turning away from religion and the world, though; rather, it triggered attempts to come to grips with the incomprehensible and the terrible. His need to connect complex external events to his internal experiences became a central theme of his life and work. Another significant tremor was the Seven Years War. This military conflict between Prussia and Austria, which broke out in 1756, had a direct effect on his family. His maternal grandfather sided with imperial Austria, but his father was a supporter of the Prussian king, Frederick the Great. This caused a rift between the two families; Goethe was dismayed by partisan injustice and began to think about political issues.

His childhood illnesses also brought him face to face with the frailty inherent in being human. Measles and chickenpox made him miserable, and he had a severe case of smallpox that took a long time to clear up, which only increased his tendency toward contemplation:

> I escaped neither measles nor chicken-pox, nor whatever the other torments of childhood may be; and I was assured each time that it was a good thing that this malady was now done with once for all. But, alas! another was already threatening me in the background, and attacked me. All these things increased my propensity to reflection; and as I had often practised endurance, in order to overcome the torture of impatience, the virtues which I had heard praised in the Stoics appeared to me highly worthy of imitation, all the more as they resembled the Christian virtue of patience.
>
> (Smith, vol. 1, p. 26)

When he contracted smallpox, his suffering increased, leaving physical traces that led his aunt to repeatedly exclaim, "Fie, nephew! what a fright you've grown!" (Smith, vol. 1, p. 26).

In *Poetry and Truth*, Goethe's childhood is depicted as idyllic and his mother's nature as cheerful, but this depiction is, at best, only half the truth; for Catharina Elisabeth, the death of five children must have left deep wounds. We know very little about how the young mother handled these tragic deaths, nor the effect they had on Johann Wolfgang. The descriptions found in Goethe's autobiography are rather sparse, but in his poems we can find evidence that the theme of child death never relinquished its hold on him. The only explicit mention made of the subject in *Poetry and Truth* is the following:

> While on the subject of family illnesses, I will mention a brother about three years younger than myself, who was likewise attacked by the same infection, and suffered greatly from it. He was naturally delicate, quiet and self-willed, and we were never great friends. Besides, he hardly lived beyond infancy. Of several younger children, who like him did not live long, I only remember a very pretty and attractive little girl, who also soon passed away; so that, after the lapse of some years, my sister and I were left alone, and were all the more deeply and affectionately attached to each other.
>
> (Smith, vol. 1, p. 26)

There are many ways in which people deal with trauma, but two would become characteristic for Goethe: On the one hand, he might withdraw into intellectual pursuits and self-contemplation, which could appear insensitive, but on the other hand, he might seek alternatives, in this case, his surviving sister, Cornelia. He took a similar approach to his own illnesses: he was able to patiently endure feelings of discomfort and pain, attempting to overcome them with reading, thinking, imagining, writing, and conversations with family and friends.

The death of his brother Hermann Jakob in 1759 was especially significant for both Goethe and his family. Although the people who lived during periods with high child mortality rates dealt with the death of a child differently than we might today, Goethe's mother must certainly have experienced hope, fear, and suffering during Hermann Jakob's long illness. Young Johann Wolfgang must also have been affected, and he began to immerse himself in intellectual activities that would help him to cope with sad experiences. Bettina von Arnim described Goethe's reaction to Hermann Jakob's death as follows:

> It seemed strange to his mother, that at the death of his young brother Jacob, who was his playmate, he did not shed a tear; he rather seemed to feel a sort of irritation at the complaints of his parents, brother, and sisters. When his mother, some time after, asked him if he did not love his brother, he ran into his bedroom, brought out a quantity of papers from under the bed, which were filled with exercises and little stories; he told her he had written all that to teach his brother.
>
> (1861, p. 313)

Here we can see how young Johann Wolfgang was already attempting to cope with feelings of sadness and despair through learning, reading, and writing. From the tragedy of his brother's death arose a coping strategy that influenced the further course of Goethe's life. Sigmund Freud emphasized the hostile aspects of Goethe's reaction to his brother's death and drew attention to Johann Wolfgang's supposed feelings of rivalry and triumph. According to Freud, Goethe's unconscious mind created a certain logic: "I am lucky; Fate has kept me alive, although I was born basically dead. But Fate disposed of my brother so I would not have to share my mother's love with him" (1917, p. 26: DS). Yet the loss of his siblings appears to have saddened and frightened young Goethe. Mothers and women had cared for him, even spoiled him, but now he also experienced them as dangerous. It was only with his sister that he felt secure, and together they coped with the deaths of their siblings.

What he and his sister shared was a refuge from their mother's negligence and father's strictness. He could share with Cornelia his sorrows and anxieties, e.g. about the mentally ill young Balthasar Clauer who lived in their family home for many years under the guardianship of their father. The young man did not take his meals with the family, but he lived in an upper room of the house and was therefore always present. First the father and later Johann Wolfgang and Cornelia wrote reports for the authorities about Clauer's mental illness. This activity may have been Goethe's motivation to occupy himself with psychological disorders until old age. While a student in Strasbourg, he encountered the poet Lenz, who was becoming increasingly psychotic, and during his time in Weimar, he supported Plessing, who was probably also psychotic. In *Wilhelm Meister's Apprenticeship*, Goethe developed realistic therapeutic strategies that are still in use today. He himself unwillingly became an expert in coping with dysthymia and depression. We will return to this issue in a later chapter.

First love: Gretchen

When the 13-year-old Goethe made the acquaintance of the 16-year-old Gretchen, it signaled the end of his childhood. She was the pubescent boy's first love, and he never ceased to cherish the memory of it, even in old age: "This girl's image never left me from that moment; it was the first durable impression made upon me by any woman" (Smith, vol. 1, p. 146). He had been in the practice of writing love letters for his friends, but now he employed that skill on his own behalf. Here we can clearly see his lifelong proclivity for elevating romantic attachments to an ideal:

> The first impulses of love, where youth is still pure and unspoiled, will be free from all taint of sensuality. Nature seems to intend that each sex should find in the other an embodiment of the ideas of virtue and beauty. Thus the sight of this girl, and my love for her, had opened out to me a new world of loveliness and goodness.
>
> (Smith, vol. 1, p. 149)

He was not satisfied with simply idealizing Gretchen in poems, though; he also wished to get closer to her sexually, but Gretchen refused his advances and avoided all physical contact. Within their circle of friends, they spent many evenings together, sharing friendly conversation and perhaps love-struck glances. Gretchen, three years older, did not take him seriously, though, even ridiculing him. Once again, he found solace in his sister:

> As confidants to whom one reveals a love-affair by their genuine sympathy become lovers also, nay, grow into rivals, and at last, perchance, attract the passion to themselves, so it was with us two; for, when my connection with Gretchen was broken off, my sister consoled me the more warmly, because she secretly felt the satisfaction of having got rid of a rival; and I, too, could not but feel a quiet, half-malicious pleasure ... that I was the only one who truly loved, understood, and esteemed her.

Goethe reminded himself, though, that "the confidants are not allowed to change into lovers" (Smith, vol. 1, p. 203).

One day, it was discovered that Goethe's circle of friends, which included Gretchen, was involved in criminal activity. Goethe's father was beside himself with rage and banished Johann Wolfgang to his room for several days. After being questioned, Goethe developed feelings of guilt, afraid he might have said something wrong about his friends, and he declared that he would harm himself if his friends were treated unjustly: "These considerations pressed so over-whelmingly on me, and so sharpened the edge of my distress, that I was half-maddened with grief. I threw myself full length up on the floor, and bedewed it with my tears" (Smith, vol. 1, p. 187).

Goethe's response sounds rather hysterical, yet he does not actually say in *Poetry and Truth* what the charges were. But he was obviously shaken, and neither his mother nor his sister was able to induce him to leave his room, even after his father had rescinded his banishment: "My only satisfaction now was to chew the cud of my misery, and to multiply it a thousandfold in my imagination" (Smith, vol. 1, p. 189). This "thousandfold" increase in his imaginings is something that crops up repeatedly throughout Goethe's life. He spent his days and nights alternating between agitation and exhaustion. His family feared that he would harm himself, so they hired a young man to act as his daily companion. Ultimately, Goethe became physically ill and began to "torment myself by weaving the wildest romance of sorrowful events, all leading to an inevitable and tragic catastrophe" (Smith, vol. 1, p. 190).

After he learned that his closest friends had been released with only a slight rebuke and that Gretchen had left Frankfurt to return to her hometown, he was relieved:

> I ... hastily assured my friend that all was now over. I spoke no more of her, her name never crossed my lips; but I could not leave off the bad habit of thinking about her, and of recalling her form, her manner, her demeanour, though now, in fact, it all appeared to me in quite another light. I felt it intolerable that a girl, at the most only a very few years older than I, should

regard me as a child, while I imagined I passed for a very sensible and clever youth. Her cold and repelling manner, which had before so charmed me, now seemed quite repugnant to me; the liberties which she had allowed herself to take with me, but had not permitted me to return, altogether odious.

(Smith, vol. 1, p. 193)

These are the words of a disappointed and resentful lover, which is completely understandable. But we can also observe a feature of this particular romantic attachment that would become characteristic of later ones: Goethe threw himself into it with his whole being, idealizing the object of his infatuation to an extreme degree, only to turn away from her just as decidedly; this defeat would then provide fodder for his poetry. He drew creative energy from disappointment and rejection, which he then applied to his writing. Women – including Gretchen, but later also Käthchen Schönkopf, Friederike Brion, Charlotte Buff, Frau von Stein, Marianne Willemer, and Ulrike von Levetzow – became screens onto which he projected his feelings and ideas. He sought his reflection in them, registered the sentiments of the objects of his affection, and returned to himself, enriched by the experience. The philosopher Hans-Georg Gadamer (1989) characterizes a real human encounter "as being beyond oneself in another person and returning to oneself as another person" (p. 369). Early on, Goethe adopted this form of relationship for his romantic attachments.

Goethe had some other means of elevating his romantic attachments to the level of the ideal: He associated them with historically significant events. In the case of Gretchen, Goethe interwove his infatuation with her with the ceremonies surrounding the coronation of Joseph II as King of Germany, which took place in Frankfurt in 1764. By creating such connections, he was able to imbue personal experiences with significance, which prevented him from feeling too miserable. Goethe's propensity to dramatize his own emotions is a source of annoyance to some, who might accuse him of overweening narcissism. His strategy of creating significance seems to have been of help to him, though.

The incident with Gretchen remains a mystery to this day. What actually occurred? Was Goethe involved in petty criminal activity, and was there sexual activity among his circle of friends, as has been conjectured by Eissler (1963)? Whatever happened during and after the Gretchen incident, Goethe remained in distress for some time, yet his zeal for learning and activity continued unabated. Despite all the humiliations he had experienced, he assiduously continued reading, conversing on philosophy, and broadening his knowledge, as if the adversities encountered in life were unable to damage his core self: "For my own part, I too had it in my mind to achieve something extraordinary, but in what it was to consist was not clear" (Smith, vol. 1, p. 141).

During the period after the Gretchen incident, Goethe's long rambles in the countryside did their work as well. He became more stable, and his emotional turmoil abated. It took quite a long time, though, before he felt himself sufficiently secure to leave his family home for Leipzig in order to study the law.

Chapter 2

Crises during his student days
Leipzig, 1765–1768

At the insistence of his father, Goethe began in October 1765 to study law in Leipzig. He himself felt more drawn to classical philology and history, but his father prevailed. Goethe experienced his departure for Leipzig as a liberation: "The secret joy of a prisoner, when he has loosed his fetters and rapidly filed through the bars of his gaol-window, cannot be greater than was mine" (Smith, vol. 1, p. 213). Höfer (2002) and Boyle (2000) explain that the University of Leipzig had an outstanding reputation at that time and was considered very sophisticated, especially in comparison to the old imperial city of Frankfurt. While royal splendor was cultivated in Dresden, the seat of royal power in Saxony, Leipzig was characterized by the establishment of a wealthy middle class. University professors were regarded with great respect, and they belonged to the leading ranks of society.

Goethe wanted to make a big splash in this world but was mortified when he was mocked for his antiquated wardrobe. His manners were also an impediment to his entering this cultivated world; his friend Horn ridiculed him in a letter as a coxcomb. Even so, Goethe was not lacking in self-confidence, and he was determined to make a place for himself in the world of Leipzig. Unfortunately, he was soon to suffer embarrassing defeats. He had received a friendly welcome from his mentor, Johann Gottlob Böhme, an expert in constitutional law, but their relationship soon turned sour. Böhme vehemently opposed the philological and literary interests of his mentee, which Goethe responded to by pulling away from his mentor. He found the courses in jurisprudence dull and attended poetry courses despite Böhme's injunction against them. He was enthusiastic about them at first, and his letters to his sister often included exuberant, effusive accounts of his literary leanings.

It was not long, though, before Goethe's mood grew darker and he admitted to his sister that he often felt depressed. At the beginning of Easter Week in 1766, he wrote to his sister, "I frequently become melancholic. I do not know from whence it comes. Then I stare fixedly at those around me like an owl ... And then a darkness comes over my soul, a darkness as impenetrable as October fog" (FA 28, p. 603: DS). He included with his letter "A little poem on my lack of self-confidence", in which he bemoaned his "melancholy" and the "fog of doubt". During such phases, he reported he was unable to find a "spark of worth" in himself. A short time later, though, his letters would begin to sound more cheerful again. In May 1766, he recorded the following: "I am often in a good mood, sister. In a very good mood! Then I visit the pretty women and the pretty girls ... I am hard-working, I am cheerful, and I am happy. Farewell" (FA 28, p. 604: DS). In September 1776, though, he wrote about his bad mood again and ascribed his self-doubts to unfulfilled longings: "Likewise, I have abandoned my foolish idea that I am a poet, and I hardly ever produce verses any more ... Perhaps if I had a beautiful thing by my side, Cupid would allow me to sing more, and better" (FA 28, p. 624: DS).

In the months that followed, he experienced even more disappointments. He made no progress with his attempts at writing, and the courses on poetry demoralized him. The instructor's rigid rules did not provide him the space he needed to express what was in his heart. He began to have doubts about his literary talent and told a friend, the private tutor Ernst Wolfgang Behrisch, that writing made him feel like a "worm in the dust" beholding the "eagle of poetry" soaring beyond his reach. Years later, he would put similar verses in the mouth of his character Faust:

> I am not like the gods! Too well I know
> That I am like the worm that rifles through the dust [...]
> (652–653)

Goethe's friendship with the older Behrisch gave him a degree of inspiring security. In him, he found a sympathetic companion who was not only interested in his attempts at poetry, but also cared about his personal concerns. Goethe entrusted him with some of his verses, which he compiled into a small volume of 19 poems. Encouraged by his older friend, Goethe was able to put his longings into words. He had selected Anna Katharina Schönkopf, whose father kept the inn where Goethe regularly took his midday meal, as the object of his desire, and his erotic yearnings found an outlet in his poems "To Annette":

The Night

I gladly leave this cottage,
Where my beauty lives,
And roam with silent footsteps
This deserted forest.
Luna breaks the night of the oaks,
Zephyr announces her course,
And the birches pleasantly scatter
The sweetest incense on her.

A shudder that makes the heart feel
And brings the soul to melt away

Wanders through the bushes in the chill.
What a sweet, beautiful night!
Joy! Delight! Barely to be grasped!
And yet, Heaven, I would willingly leave to you
A thousand heavenly nights,
If my maiden would give only one of them to me.

As in the other poems in the collection, Goethe uses the conventional imagery of Anacreontic verse, which had found its way into German literature around 1740 and was being used with enthusiasm. Anacreontic poetry embraced a refined attitude toward life that developed around the themes of love, nature, and conviviality. Goethe's early style was influenced by the conventions of these poems, and yet, the tone of "The Night" is very personal and original. The narrator (the "lyrical I") gives voice to Goethe's subjective experiences, without actually being Goethe.

Here I would like to introduce the concept of the "poetical self", which is slightly different from the literary concept of the "lyrical I". It serves to stress the psychological emphasis of my interpretations and will be further developed later in the interpretations of some other of Goethe's poems. Within modern psychology and psychoanalysis, the term "self" has gained acceptance as a way of characterizing the entirety of a person's impressions and experiences that goes beyond the Freudian structural model of the id, ego, and super-ego (Kohut 1971). The self encompasses both conscious and unconscious processes and physical activities that can intrude on consciousness, such as in the form of affects and self-representations. The residue of an individual's relational experiences are also part of the self, and for this reason we can say that the founding of a "poetic self" is intersubjective. Moreover, the concept of a coherent poetic self is useful to integrate philosophical ideas with findings from sociology, psychology, and neurobiology (Fuchs 2016; Holm-Hadulla 2013).

The interaction of social, psychological, and physical factors is fundamental for the coherence of the self, which is considered to be crucial to mental health. Empirical studies have confirmed the importance of a sense of coherence for the development and stability of the self. This sense of coherence is not a static entity, though; it must be actively created over and over again in order to have a salutogenic, i.e. health-promoting, effect (Antonovsky 1987). In conjunction with this, the self must feel both reflected and acknowledged in its actions. In modern psychology, this is referred to as "self-efficacy" (Bandura 1982). I call a self that is engaged in the creative process of self-discovery and self-realization "poetical", in accordance with the Greek idea of *poieīn*, meaning "to make, to form, to be creative". From a psychological perspective, Goethe's poems fulfill exactly this function of poetically bringing forth a coherent and effective self. Poetry takes sensory impressions, physical sensations, and relational experiences and transforms them into something that can be grasped consciously. Thereby, diffuse impressions can gain vivid reality. In the process of poetical creation, the self becomes something which had only been potential up to then. The poetical self will only reach its full flowering if it is perceived, responded to, and acknowledged. We will see that there were many times in Goethe's life when his poetical self-realization helped him to overcome life crises.

In the poem "The Night", it is notable from a psychological point of view that the poetical self[1] only perceives the stirrings of love when it is alone, after the beloved has abandoned it. The poetical self leaves the familiar cottage and wanders the dark, dying woods alone in order to discover what it is feeling. Luna, goddess of the moon, and Zephyr, the god of spring, are the poetical self's traditional companions, but despite that, it is initially unable to ward off the chill of the night. But through a "poetical triumph", it is finally able to overcome its fear of being in love, and the dark night of its emotions. The "shudder that makes the heart feel" is transformed by Goethe into a "sweet, beautiful night". The poetical self speaks in high spirits of pleasure and delight and mocks the superior powers of heaven with a saucy quip.

The reality was more complicated, though. Käthchen Schönkopf had probably given Goethe a friendly glance or two, maybe even a look promising something more, but nothing ever came of it, and there was certainly no sexual relationship between them. It is possible that Goethe required a certain amount of distance in order to be able to express his feelings all the more passionately. He developed within him an effusive world of emotions that did not correspond to external reality. Ultimately, Käthchen Schönkopf did not know what to make of this young man head over heels in love, and she was so vexed by his jealous scenes that she soon avoided even superficial contact with him. This rocked him to the core:

> But it was too late! I had lost her really, and the frenzy with which I revenged my wrong-doing upon myself, by frantic attempts to injure my physical self, in order to inflict pain on my moral self, contributed very much to the maladies which spoilt some of the best years of my life; indeed, I should perhaps have been completely ruined by this loss, had not my poetic talent shown itself particularly helpful with its healing power.
>
> (Smith, vol. 1, p. 253)

It is easy to dismiss Goethe's infatuation as juvenile extravagance, but this point of view fails to notice that this relationship, just like his later relationships, allowed him to give shape to internal tensions. Goethe required a counterpart to be able to experience his wishes and longings, even his personality, as coherent. The objects of his affection served to make him sure of himself and to assure himself of his place in the world. For this to occur, though, he had to love them from afar. In March of 1768, Goethe wrote to that effect in a letter to Behrisch: "I can live without seeing her, but not without loving her ... Listen, Behrisch, I can't, I don't want to ever leave the young lady, yet leave I must, I want to leave ..." (FA 28, p. 122: DS). In addition to

Goethe's "love from a distance" pattern of relationships that occurred throughout his love affairs, there is his remarkable habit of transferring his attentions from one beloved to the next: "She should never feel the pain of seeing me in the arms of another until I have felt the pain of seeing her in the arms of another" (FA 28, p. 122: DS).

This description is oddly touching. Why would Goethe prefer to see his beloved in the arms of another and to relish his own pain? One train of thought says that he found it necessary to experience this self-tormenting passion in order to be able to work creatively. Another way of looking at it is to focus on Goethe's desire to master his feelings and those of others. Even if Käthchen proves herself to be independent of him in reality, he nevertheless wants to understand her feelings and actions from within. During the process of reduplicating his beloved within his imagination, he tries to comprehend his feelings and to cope with the humiliation of being rejected. This means of mastering real suffering using imaginary duplication would become characteristic for him.

What would also become characteristic of his later relationships was the peculiar love-triangle in which he would find himself enmeshed with Käthchen Schönkopf and Behrisch during his Leipzig period. Behrisch had become his most important confidant, whom he had entrusted with all of his feelings for Käthchen, whom he had called "Nette" in his letters. In a letter from April 1768, he poured his heart out to him:

> You will see that I still like you as much as when you were by me, and Nette as much as when she was by me, truth be told, both of you even more, because an ardour that has become more calm is more powerful, and such is mine. Oh, Behrisch! I have begun to live! ... Enough – Nette and I, we have separated, we are happy ... She is the best, the most amiable young lady, and now I can swear to you that I will never stop feeling for her that which constitutes my life's happiness ... Behrisch, we live in the most pleasant company, as you and she do; no longer any familiarity, not a word spoken of love, and so cheerful, so happy, Behrisch, she is an angel ... I love her still, so much, God, so much. Oh, that you were here, that you were comforting me, that you could love me.
>
> (FA 28, p. 122: DS)

In this letter, Goethe initially appears highly agitated and even deranged. This letter and others like it have caused some authors to question Goethe's mental condition. Eissler (1963), a psychiatrist and psychoanalyst, even conjectured that Goethe was suffering schizophrenic episodes. Looking ahead to the chapter on Goethe's emotional disturbances and in light of the letter quoted above, we can say that the letter is an expression of an adolescent crisis of maturation rather than a mental illness. Goethe seems to have been in a frenzy of agitating feelings, and he was seeking a means of expressing diffuse and unconscious impulses. He was only partially successful in this, though; the ambivalence of his feelings remained unresolved. He allowed himself to experience a bewildering passion that, much like the pain of being born, is a prerequisite for creative self-actualization. The emotional roller coaster is where poetry comes into being, and for the first time, his poems are independent, authentic creations. This becomes apparent in "Odes to Behrisch", which Goethe wrote on the occasion of Behrisch moving to another city. In the third ode, which we will use as an example, he portrays his pain over the upcoming separation from his friend:

> Be void of feeling!
> An easily stirr'd heart,
> Is an awful good
> Upon this changing earth.
> . . .
> Death is separation,
> Threefold death
> Separation without hope
> To meet again.
> . . .
> You go, – I stay
> . . .
> Then the bars break, I'm free then as thou!

In this poem, there is no longer any trace of the idyllic, pastoral world of Anacreontic poetry. Goethe is emotionally distressed and seems to have to bow to an event that he cannot consciously control. It is true that there is a slightly pathetic tone to the piece, yet contrived witticisms and laborious self-display give way to personal dismay. When faced with the looming separation from his friend Behrisch, the poetical self exclaims in desperate protest, "Be void of feeling!" This exclamation instantly includes the reader, as well. Doesn't our "easily stirr'd heart" bring more pain than joy? Aren't our intense emotions too reminiscent of the "changing earth" on which we stand? Goethe is advising himself on how to cope with distress and psychological wounds. In some situations, we must sequester our feelings in order to bear our suffering at the hands of the world. The joy we feel at "spring's sweet smile" is nevertheless always overshadowed by "winter's gloomy tempests". Just as we have all been deceived by a "sorrow-engendering breast", we are also all familiar with the "lynx-like" gaze of envy. This jealousy is deceptive and powerful, and it latches onto us like "panther-claws".

"Death is separation": Goethe takes us on a journey whose destination is despair. Suicidal thoughts are clearly evident but friendship tethers us to life. The anger displayed is familiar to many of us, and we have often wished to escape a detested situation and not to let withered "flowery chains" restrain us. Many have said, "Burst them!" Thought is no longer free and cheerful, but trapped "in his dungeon" of desperation. Nevertheless, life goes on, turning "round the smoking axle" until "the bars break" and a new freedom is attained.

In this poem, Goethe shows three ways of escaping from desperation and loneliness: engaging with emotions, close friendships, and creative work. Goethe had already begun to cultivate these forms of coping, but they were not very developed during his Leipzig period. After Käthchen's rejection, he became more and more distraught, as if the foundation of his emotional existence had been pulled out from under him. We do not know how serious his suicidal thoughts were at this time, but we can presume that he would have been at serious risk without his self-therapeutic efforts. By engaging with his contradictory thoughts and emotions, communicating them to people he trusted, and giving form to them in his imagination, he was able to cope with this crisis, at least to some extent.

In his perturbation, Goethe opened himself up to chaotic emotions, transformed them into poetry and found people who listened and responded to him. To Goethe, his affective turmoil was no game, as evident in a letter to Behrisch in November 1767:

> Seven o'clock in the evening. Ha, Behrisch! Now is one of those moments! You are gone, and this paper is a cold refuge compared to your arms. Oh, God! God – Just let me come to myself again. Behrisch, love is accursed. Oh, if only you could see me, if only you could see this miserable person, how he raves but doesn't know against whom he should rave – you would bemoan it. Friend, friend! Why do I only have one? – 8 o'clock. My blood is no longer boiling, I will be able to speak more calmly to you. Whether rationally, only God knows. No, not rationally. How could a madman speak rationally? ... My beloved girl! Ah, she will always be my beloved. Look, Behrisch, the moment she causes me to rave, I feel it. God, God, why must I love so ... This evening, I sent downstairs to have something fetched for me. The maid came and brought me the news that she [Käthchen] had been to a comedy with her mother. Where the minute before my fever had made me shiver with its frost, this news turned my blood to fire. Ha! Attending a comedy when, as she knows, her beloved is ill. God, that was terrible of her. But I forgive her ... I have attempted to cry all evening long, but in vain, my teeth knock against each other ... I believe I have drunk poison from her hand. Forgive me, friend! On my honor, I am writing in a fever ....

(FA 28, p. 106: DS)

Not only did Goethe feel rejected, mortified, and lonely, but he was also in a state of emergency for several months. His letters show how deeply he engaged with these painful feelings and tried to cope with them in conversation with Behrisch and with himself. He also found an outlet for his desperation in his poems:

By the River

Flow away, dearly beloved songs,
to the sea of forgetfulness!
Let no lad sing you again in delight,
no girl in the season of blossom.

You sang of my sweetheart only;
now she mocks my fidelity.
You were written on water,
and so flow away along with it.
(Appelbaum, p. 5)

Here, hope has completely disappeared. The "dearly beloved songs" belong to the past. The "lad [singing] in delight" and the "girl in the season of blossom" are gone. Their love was "written on water" and has now passed by. And yet, there is something comforting in the poem, as if the cycle of nature provides feelings of security. This peculiar form of comfort could be the result of Goethe's three strategies: first, he accepts and embraces melancholic moods; second, he communicates his feelings of desperation to a friend, to a reader, and to himself; and third, he overcomes his desperations by giving authentic form to them. We could call this a "poetical triumph", a creative transformation of sufferings.

Note

1 To prevent confusion, I have elected to refer to the poetical self as "it" rather than "he", which I have reserved for Goethe himself. *Trans.*

Chapter 3

Return to the family home
Frankfurt, 1768–1770

An invalid who seemed to suffer more in mind than in body.

During the summer of 1768, Goethe's already poor state of health deteriorated considerably. In July, he suffered a hemorrhage, probably as a result of a tubercular infection. His Leipzig friends cared for him for several weeks until he was able to begin the journey home to Frankfurt, on his nineteenth birthday. In September, he wrote to his friend Langer:

> My affairs of the heart! What an odyssey it has been! If I only understood it myself, I would gladly tell you; but I don't even understand myself. As coldly tranquil as it is only possible to be when waking in the morning after a good night's sleep, such is now my soul – calm, without longings, without pain, without joy, and without memory ... I know that I love you all; and yet I cannot feel it, I must say it first to myself. And this is how everything is for me. My love, this unfortunate emotion which has cost me much, too much, for me to ever forget, is buried, buried deep in my memory, cold distraction thrown over it; I think about it sometimes, completely indifferent ... My circumstances are otherwise too strange for me to go into, because I am writing now from duty and not from friendship, for I swear to you that even writing makes me cross ....
>
> (FA Vs. 28, p. 124: DS)

In this letter, Goethe portrays symptoms typical of depression: He is both numb and indifferent to his emotions, and he feels listless and enervated. He even finds his daily habits, like writing letters, inexpressibly difficult. He feels hurt and hopeless. But unlike patients suffering from severe depression, he was able to remain productive. He wrote to Käthchen Schönkopf in November:

> No one knows better than I the figure I have cut; and the figure my letters cut I can well suppose. When we remember what has happened with others, it needs no prophetic soul to divine what will happen with us. With that, I

am well content. It is the usual lot of the departed, that those left behind
and those coming after should dance on their graves.

(Bell, pp. 19–20)

What is notable is that Goethe does not retreat in shame, but rather manages
to maintain a certain, rather sarcastic distance from himself in his letters. Upon
Goethe's arrival in Frankfurt, his father was vexed "at finding in the place of a
robust, active son ... an invalid who seemed to suffer more in mind than in
body" (Smith, vol. 1, p. 302). His mother and sister received him warmly,
though, and made his period of suffering more bearable. Cornelia, in particular,
blossomed at his arrival; their strict father had sharply curtailed her personal
sphere while there was no brother at home to supervise her:

My sister at once became my companion ... My father had, after my
departure, concentrated his pedagogic mania upon my sister, and in a house
the doors of which were closed to society, rendered secure by peace, and
even cleared of lodgers, he had cut her off from almost all intercourse with
or recreation in the outer world.

(Smith, vol. 1, p. 300)

Goethe enjoyed the devotion of his mother and sister, and they discovered
that he brought more liveliness into their daily lives. They entertained each
other by reading aloud and reciting to one another, and by having long
conversations. Goethe's physical illness lasted several months, and he had
several relapses. There was a distinct possibility Goethe would die, and this
reinforced his propensity to focus on the metaphysical. He was introduced to a
circle of Pietists by Susanna von Klettenberg, a relative by marriage and a
friend of the family. This group had withdrawn from harsh reality to a place of
introspection, sensibility, and piety. Goethe described Frau von Klettenberg
thusly: "Her serenity and peace of mind never deserted her. She looked upon
her sickness as a necessary part of her transient earthly existence; she suffered
with the greatest patience, and, in painless intervals, was animated and talkative"
(Smith, vol. 1, p. 303).

In his conversations with Frau von Klettenberg and her circle, Goethe found
that his search for meaning struck a chord with them, and he was able to
compose his mind by reflecting on religion. In January 1769, he wrote to his
friend Langer:

Much has happened to me; I have suffered, and now am free again; this
calcination was very profitable for my soul, and my relative circumstances
have thereby also been improved, and if my body – as they claim – now
can really hope to improve because it has discovered the proximate cause
of my illnesses; I don't know of any more fortunate occurrence in my life
than this dreadful one ... The Savior has finally caught me, I ran from him

too long and too fast, but then he caught me by the hair ... I am sometimes nice and calm about it, sometimes when I am quiet, very quiet, and feel all of the good things that have come to me from the eternal source. Even when we go astray, we two, for however so long, in the end, it will work out.

(FA 28, p. 148: DS)

At these religious gatherings he was able to find comfort for and give voice to his sufferings. He read the Bible with fresh eyes, and his mother consoled him with hopeful biblical passages. He slowly recovered from his illness, using his enforced retreat from society to educate himself further. Nonetheless, his long convalescence was not easy for him, and in April 1769 he was still being described as unhealthy in appearance and lethargic. The atmosphere at home had also taken a turn for the worse. Goethe's grandfather Textor had suffered a severe stroke in August 1768 during a meeting of the city council and remained semiconscious and paralyzed until his death in 1771. Cornelia was now 17 years old, and her conflicts with her overly strict father were escalating. Even Goethe's relationship with his father was turning noticeably frosty. While looking back on this period, Goethe assumes a critical tone for the first time in his writing about his father:

My father, for his part, led a life of tolerable comfort. He was in good health, spent a great part of the day in the instruction of my sister, continued to write the description of his travels, and spent more time in tuning his lute than in playing on it ... My mother, by nature very lively and cheerful, led a very tedious life under these circumstances.

(Smith, vol. 1, p. 302)

It is likely that Johann Caspar was also frightened by his son's illness, since he had lost his two brothers to fatal illnesses at the ages of 19 and 23. It appears that his negative reaction to his son's illness was due not merely to impatience and wounded vanity, but also to fear. Johann Wolfgang's own reaction to others' illnesses in later days would also be characterized by impatience, rejection, and ignorance. Despite his troubles, Goethe continued to be productive. He finished his pastoral play, *The Lovers Mood*, in which he grappled with his passion and jealousy. He had begun the one-act piece, written in verse, while in Leipzig and worked on it for some time. As early as October 1767, he was able to write to Cornelia,

I have been working on it now for eight months, but it does not want to obey; I do not allow myself any regrets, because I am not without hope that, with time, it can become a good little piece, because it has been carefully copied from nature ....

(HA 4, p. 470: DS)

In the play, Goethe portrays aspects of himself in the figure of the youthful lover, Eridon, who torments his beloved, Amine, with his jealousy and who can only be cured by means of a trick. *The Lovers Mood* is a typical example of how Goethe came to terms with his injurious relationships with young women. He delved deep into his own feelings and brought his experiences vividly to mind, which allowed him to find his way to himself: "Nothing throws greater light upon ourselves than to see before us what we produced some years before, so that we are able to regard ourselves from an objective point of view" (Smith, vol. 1, p. 308).

Early in 1769, Goethe finished the first draft of his comedy *The Accomplices*. It depicts the noble libertine, Alcest, and Sophie, the daughter of an innkeeper, who meet once again. Sophie is now married to Söller, but she finds herself agreeing to a rendezvous with Alcest. Sophie is able to extricate herself from Alcest's arms before it is too late, but in the meanwhile, her father the innkeeper has crept into Alcest's room to read his correspondence, because he believes Alcest to be an important man. Her husband, Söller, believes he has been betrayed by Sophie and Alcest and steals Alcest's money. The next day, suspicion falls on the innkeeper for the theft, but Söller reveals the truth. In the end, everyone involved feels responsible for what has happened, and they all forgive each other.

Goethe researcher Erich Trunz is of the opinion that few if any signs of autobiography can be found in this farce (HA 4, pp. 474f.), but Goethe biographer Nicholas Boyle sees the conflicts of the Leipzig period reflected in the comedy and surmises that Goethe wanted to exact revenge for his personal defeat in Leipzig (1991, p. 87). Supporting this interpretation is Goethe's conceptualization of the Schönkopfs' inn, with the small-minded father and his unhappily married daughter, Sophie, who bears a resemblance to Käthchen Schönkopf. The respectable Dr. Kanne, who wed Käthchen in 1770, is lampooned in the figure of Söller. Goethe himself identifies with Alcest. Alcest's disappointed love for Sophie is a recapitulation of Goethe's love for Käthchen and of his fear of commitment. In the second version of the comedy, which Goethe penned after his period of suffering in Frankfurt, the innkeeper takes on the characteristics of Goethe's father, and the farce no longer appears to be an act of contemptuous revenge for the humiliation he experienced in Leipzig, but rather a despondent reflection on his own inability to love at that time.

Goethe's first volume of poems, *New Songs*, appeared anonymously in 1769 after his long illness. By this time, he had almost completely overcome both his physical illness and his depressive episode. In the poem "To Luna", we see that Goethe had discovered an entirely personalized language for his emotions.

To Luna

Sister of the first light,
Image of tenderness in mourning!
With a silver shivering, mist floats

About your sublime visage;
The quiet course of your feet
Awakens, from out of caves locked by day,
Sad, departed souls,
Me and night-birds.

Searchingly your gaze looks out over
A wide-ranging expanse.
Lift me to your side!
Give to ecstasy this happiness;
And in rapturous rest
May the knight, driven far from home,
Through the glassy bars
Watch the nights of his maiden.

Twilight, where sensuality is enthroned,
Wafts about her round limbs.
Drunkenly my gaze sinks downward.
What is being veiled from the moon?
But what sort of wishes are these!
Full of desire to savour,
Yet required to hang on high;
Ah, one could peer down until one went blind.

(Krebs)

The poetical self appears calm and relaxed, playful and humorous. The poem still contains Anacreontic stylistic devices, such as the moon being addressed as "sister of the first light" and the theme of the "knight, driven far from home", but Goethe has found an authentic and distinctive form of expression. Nature, as described in the poem, is no longer simply Anacreontic background decoration, but has become a distinct realm of experience. The sister of the sun, the moon is treated as if she were a lady-love. She conveys an "image of tenderness", has a "sublime visage", and moves via the "quiet course of [her] feet". This is quite Goethean, in that something objective is subjectively experienced and transfigured.

The "sister of the first light", with her "sublime visage", creates an erotic atmosphere, in which many remembered images become solid. Here, an image is evoked of his sister Cornelia, who may have awakened in him erotic feelings: "night-birds". In the poem, these subjective remembrances are now being objectivized, and the poet is creating a transfigured image of the erotic night. Decades later, Goethe would put the following verses in the mouth of Philina, a sister figure in *Wilhelm Meister's Apprenticeship*:

Don't sing with mourning sounds,
Of the loneliness of night:

No, you beauties,
it is made for conviviality.

(*Works* 2, p. 46)

In the poem "To Luna", the depressions and fears that tormented Goethe for so long, by day and by night, are still there, but they have been transformed into lyrical "silvery shivers".

The sensual but also fearful mood of the "sad, departed souls" is transformed at the beginning of the second stanza into a detached, even dissociated, attitude. The poetical self identifies with the moon, who disinterestedly surveys a "wide-ranging expanse", but "searchingly". The poetical self also observes itself from the outside as a fantasist, one who pleads without hope, "Give to ecstasy this happiness!" From the safe distance of poetical vision, the poetical self can dream of "rapturous rest", knight-errantry, and a happy homecoming. Its desire for the "nights of [its] maiden" is not expressed plaintively, because it cannot be fulfilled. No, in a poetical triumph, this longing is savored with relish.

At the beginning of the third stanza, where sensuality "floats" around the "round limbs" of the beloved, the poetical self awakens and "drunkenly my gaze sinks downward". With a questioning glance, it looks up again, in order to discover "what is being veiled from the moon?" But recovering itself, the poetical self rises above its desire: "But what sort of wishes are these!" In so doing, it distances itself from its emotions and overcomes the disillusionment of its own unfulfilled longings, "full of desire to savour", by ascribing them to the moon and then mocking her for it: "Yet required to hang on high/Ah, one could peer down until one went blind." This poetical representation of events has turned a defeat into a victory. The poetical self was helped in this by maintaining an ironic distance from itself; on the one hand, it identifies with the moon, who is able to observe erotic desires but not reach them. But on the other hand, the poetical self is able to triumph because it can play with its own wishes.

"To Luna" illustrates an ability of Goethe's, one that characterizes his entire life: He was able to lose himself in his enthusiasms and infatuations and to allow himself to be surrounded by emotions and fantasies, and yet he was also able to remain quite down to earth. Many took exception to his inclination for the conventional; some felt repelled by it. Psychologists might argue that people need clear, even conventional structures in order to be able to delve into their creative fantasies. It is possible that the only reason why Goethe was able to creatively cope with and survive his Leipzig period was because he was able to accept and utilize conventional structures, starting with his cultivation of the personal relationships his father had facilitated for him and ending with his ceaseless work, which he even pursued whenever he felt great alarm or "fluctuated between the extremes of unrestrained gaiety and melancholy discomfort" (Smith, vol. 1, p. 295). Maintaining personal relationships while also treading new emotional territory, patiently learning traditional stylistic devices while discovering, step by step, a completely new language of his own – this was Goethe's creative model. This alternation between employing conventions and discovering originality can be encountered in many creative individuals, whether named Mozart, Picasso, Einstein, or García Márquez (see Holm-Hadulla 2010).

Goethe's recovery from his mental crisis and physical illness while in Frankfurt was certainly reinforced by poetical work, communication, and acknowledgment of his experiences by those close to him. In early 1770, he had reached the point where he was able to leave home once again.

Chapter 4

Flight from love
Strasbourg, 1770–1771

How splendidly glows
Nature for me!
How the sun gleams!
How the field laughs!

Goethe arrived in Strasbourg on a beautiful spring day in 1770 and was immediately delighted. From the tower of the cathedral, he was able to look out over the Alsatian countryside, which seemed to him a paradise:

> And now, from the summit, I saw before me the beautiful country ... it will then be possible to conceive the rapture with which I blessed the kind fate that had appointed me, for some time to come, so beautiful a dwelling place ... Such a fresh glance into a new land where we are to take up our abode for a time, has this peculiar feature, at once pleasant and awe-inspiring, that the whole lies before us like an unwritten tablet. As yet no sorrows and joys which relate to ourselves are recorded on it ... But a presentiment of the future already troubles the young heart.
>
> (Smith, vol. 1, pp. 318–319)

He resumed his study of the law and attended lectures in medicine, history, and philosophy. In September of that year, he was able to successfully complete two oral examinations, and he began work on his dissertation. He also befriended a group of students who regularly dined together. Unhindered by any issues with authority, he came into contact with notable professors of jurisprudence and medicine and was able to befriend them. He may have withdrawn from his first attempt at university life in a depressed state, but he left his family home more mature, with a new, animated social life and a new, stimulating intellectual life.

In addition to socializing, writing, and imagining, Goethe used strategies to improve his well-being. A degree of irritability was a lingering remnant of his emotional crisis; this led him to want to work on himself. He hoped to desensitize his hearing by exposing it to the nightly drumming of the city guard but was unsuccessful. Goethe had more success in conquering his fear of heights. He frequently climbed the stairs to the tower platform of Strasbourg Cathedral, and by gradually edging closer to the balustrade, managed to overcome this phobia:

> I repeated these dreaded and painful sensations until I was quite indifferent to them, and I have since derived great advantage from this training, in mountain travels, geological studies, and on high buildings, where I have vied with the carpenters in running on the bare beams and the cornices of the edifice, and in Rome itself, where similar risks must be run to obtain a nearer view of important works of art.
>
> (Smith, vol. 1, p. 334)

In addition to treating himself for his fear of heights, Goethe took walks through graveyards at night to overcome his fear of the dark.

Of great significance, though, were his meetings with the slightly older Herder, who at this time was already a recognized author. Goethe was inspired by Herder's astuteness and self-assurance and had a high regard, without a trace of envy, for his superior education. He also exhibited a lively interest in the development of Herder's *Treatise on the Origin of Language*, from which he gleaned important ideas. It proposed a direct language that would express the soul naturally and in its pure form. Goethe was able to accept Herder as an authority figure and showed himself to be apt and willing to learn. Herder, for his part, supported Goethe's literary aspirations and pretentious plans. The following old German saying became an important maxim of Goethe's: "The wishes of youth are garnered in age!" (Smith, vol. 1, p. 345). It means that even wishes that appear unrealistic can be expressions of abilities that lie dormant within an individual. With hard work and imagination, this potential, at first only sensed, can be realized in the further course of life.

Driven by an unquenchable love of life, Goethe frequently, and gladly, suspended his studies and his learned discussions. He never passed up an opportunity to dance, and even hired a dancing instructor to improve his technique. This instructor had two daughters, and Goethe took a great liking to the younger one. The three of them danced together and read aloud to each other, and the elder of the sisters fell in love with him. He felt the pull of affection toward the younger sister, Emilie, and the tug of pity toward the elder, Lucinda. Emilie suggested a separation to ameliorate the suffering Lucinda experienced as a result of his frequent visits. When he took his leave of them, there was a horrible scene between the sisters. Lucinda pulled Goethe's head forward and kissed him on the mouth, saying,

> I know that I have lost you; I make no further claims on you. But you shall not have him either, sister! ... Now ... fear my curse! Woe upon woe, for ever and ever, to her who kisses these lips for the first time after me! Dare

to have anything more to do with him! I know heaven hears me this time.
And now, Sir, be gone, be gone as quickly as you can!

(Smith, vol. 1, p. 354)

Goethe was shocked, and he avoided flirtations of every kind for a while. But
in the fall of 1770, he met the Brion family in the Alsatian town of Sesenheim[1]
while out for a ride. He seems to have fallen in love at first sight with the
second eldest of the clergyman's three daughters:

At this instant she actually appeared at the door; and then indeed a lovely
star arose in this rural firmament ... Slender and light, she tripped along
with buoyant step, and her neck seemed almost too delicate to bear the
weight of the thick, fair plaits on the neat little head. The look of her merry,
cheerful blue eyes was frank and free ... and thus, at the first glance, I had
the delight of seeing and appreciating her at once in her full grace and
loveliness.

(Smith, vol. 1, pp. 387–388)

The 18-year-old Friederike Brion returned Goethe's affection, and he visited
her as often as he could, and they spent many happy months together. During
this period, Goethe felt inspired to write new poems and composed the wonderful *Songs of Sesenheim*. They begin with the prophetic, "Whether I love you, I
don't know". The poem "May Festival", which Goethe later renamed "May
Song", revealed the poet reborn.

May Festival

How gloriously Nature
Lights up for me!
How the sun shines!
How the field laughs!

Blossoms press forth
From every branch,
And a thousand voices
From the bushes

And joy and delight
From every breast.
Oh earth, oh sun
Oh bliss, oh delight!

Oh love, oh love,
So golden beautiful,

Like morning clouds
On those heights;

You bless gloriously
The fresh field,
In blossoms' fragrance
The full world.

O maiden, maiden,
How I love you!
How your eye gleams!
How you love me!

Thus the lark loves
Song and air,
And morning flowers
The heaven's fragrance,

As I love you
With warm blood,
You who to me youth
And joy and spirit

For new songs
And dances give.
Be eternally blissful
As you love me!
        (Wellbery, pp. 5–6)

This poem demands to be read with enthusiasm, in the same spirit it was written, some May morning in 1771: "How gloriously Nature/Lights up for me!" Goethe's use of three exclamation marks within the first four lines reveals his high spirits. Here, nature lights up, shines, and laughs. This is pure Goethe: He imbues nature with his feelings, is reflected in it, himself permeates it, and is in turn permeated by it. Nature itself speaks to ardent youth. "Joy and delight" are no longer located within the subject but now fill the entire world, not just the individual. In the fourth stanza, love, "golden beautiful", emerges from the narrow confines of the individual's feelings and unfurls like "morning clouds" between individuals. Happiness and pleasure merge with the "full world". In this mood of delight and elation, "your eye gleams!", and the poetical self's love is reciprocated; it is loved as the lark loves "song and air". The poetical self receives "youth/And joy and spirit" from the lover, and filled with thankfulness, it exclaims, "Be eternally blissful", though a provision is added: "As you love me!"

The poem includes an unbelievably dense concentration of feelings and images, but also psychological insights. The poetical self appears quite unabashed when it wishes its beloved happiness, even if only on the condition that she give it courage, creative energy, and love. As a matter of fact, the poetical self considers itself the center of the universe. This exuberance did not last very long, though. Soon Goethe began to feel troubled by his passionate relationship with Friederike, and the other parts of his life in Strasbourg also began to change. His dissertation was not accepted, and his academic achievements were such that he was only able to receive a lower degree in law. The early stages of his friend Lenz's mental illness had a moderating effect on him. He was working on a folktale about the beautiful Melusine, which he also recited at the home of the Brion family. In the folktale, Melusine's husband is not allowed to see his wife on Saturday evenings, because that is when she assumes a horrible form with a long, snake-like tail. The tale creates a melancholy and depressing atmosphere that Goethe responded to. "May Festival" shows us only his euphoric side at that time, but he was full of anxieties about a close relationship, self-doubts, and ill humors. In his letters, he spoke of "deep unease", without being able to give a reason for it. But the story of the beautiful Melusine and poems such as "A Gray, Gloomy Morning" (later renamed "To Friederike Brion") explain his moods:

A Gray, Gloomy Morning

A gray, gloomy morning
covers my beloved field,
hidden deep in the fog,
the world lies all around me.
O sweet Friederike!
If only I were allowed to return to you!
In just one of your glances
there is sunshine and happiness.

The tree, in whose bark
my name stands next to yours,
is turning pale from the harsh wind
that blows away every pleasure.
The green luster of the meadows
is turning gloomy like my face;
They never will see the sun,
and I never will see Friederike.

Soon I will go among the vines
And harvest the grapes;
All around, *everything* is life,
new wine is swirling.

Yet in the deserted arbor,
Ah, I think, if only *she* were here!
I would bring her these grapes,
and *she* – what would *she* give to me?

The mood of this poem is much gloomier than in "May Festival", even though it was written soon afterwards, not more than three months later. Once again, nature mirrors the inner condition of the poetical self. "A gray, gloomy morning" is not very promising, and the poetical self speaks of its bygone love. "Sunshine and happiness", which is what Friederike meant to him, are no longer accessible. Their companionship is fading and "every pleasure" is blown away. The poetical self becomes hopeless and "gloomy like my face". The period of maturation has arrived, and "all around, everything is life". Yet the poetical self feels lonely and no longer believes that meeting with Friederike could cause a change. "And she – what would she give to me?" sounds hopeless rather than shameless. What has happened? The tempo and vigor of "May Festival" are missing; consequently the poem moves slowly. The colors are muted and the rhythm halting. The poetical self faces life as if an observer and feels cut off from the autumnal activity associated with the harvest.

In reality, Goethe turned away from Friederike as if fleeing from her, yet the reasons for his sudden rejection remained inscrutable, even to himself. He mentioned inexplicable mood swings. Emotional instability – "heavenly jubilating" to "deadly despaired" – was a recurrent theme throughout Goethe's life (*Egmont*, Act 3, Scene 2). It is well-known that changes such as these can occur without an external cause, and while external events can trigger such changes, their causes must be sought elsewhere, such as in temperamental mood swings. Attempts are often erroneously made to explain these mood swings by attributing them to more or less meaningful events. For Goethe, this would imply that he sought romance while in a euphoric state, but that he would have to break it off again when he fell into a depression.

A second conjecture about Goethe's sudden withdrawal from Friederike has to do with his fear of commitment. This could have been due to his strong attachment to his family home and to his sister, or to his sexual immaturity. Goethe was audacious enough to fantasize about the mysteries of Eros, but recoiled from an encounter with a real woman. A third possibility is that Goethe's abrupt retreat from Friederike was motivated by his incipient vocation to become a famous poet and intellectual. He may have sensed that restlessness and solitude were the necessary conditions for his creativity at this time. It is possible that he had to experience, to suffer a deeper level of desperation in order to be truly productive. We can find important indications of this in "Welcome and Departure", another poem from his Strasbourg period.

Welcome and Departure

My heart pounded; quickly, to horse,
And away, wildly, like a hero into battle!

Evening already cradled the earth,
And on the mountains hung the night.
Already the oak stood in a misty cloak,
A towering giant there,
Where darkness out of the bushes
Peered with a hundred black eyes.

The moon from a cloudy hill
Peered sleepily out of the mist;
The winds lightly flapped their wings,
Soughed frightfully in my ears.
The night created a thousand monsters—
But my courage was thousandfold;
My spirit was a consuming fire;
My whole heart dissolved in a glow.

I saw you, and mild joy
Flowed from your sweet look to me.
My heart was wholly at your side,
And every breath for you.
Spring's rosy-colored light
Lay on your dear face,
As did tenderness for me, you gods!
And though hoped for, I didn't deserve it.

The departure, how pressed, how faded!
Out of your glances your heart spoke.
In your kisses, what love,
Oh what delight, what pain!
You went; I stood, and looked to the earth,
And gazed after you with moist regard;
And yet, what bliss! to be loved,
And to love, you gods! what bliss!
                                 (Wellbery, pp. 28–29)

This poem from the year 1771 begins with a description of the route to the beloved. It begins with physical arousal, symbolized by the pounding heart and violent departure: "And away, wildly, like a hero into battle!" In the 1789 version, Goethe replaced the second verse with the much milder "faster than thought, it was done". The heroic rallying cry seems not to have been to his taste after all. After the furious beginning, a quieter mood sets in, one where the earth is "cradled". Then the night becomes frightening, with menacing phantasms that follow the poetical self "with a hundred black eyes".

The moon is no longer the "sister of the first light"; instead, it appears sleepy, and the forces of nature are experienced as hostile. The winds are frightful, and the night creates "a thousand monsters". At the end of the second stanza, though, the poetical self responds to the threat posed by the thousand monsters with fresh courage, and its excitement – the fire in its veins and the glow in its heart – drowns out its fear. In the third stanza, the beloved greets it with "mild joy", and the terrors of the night give way to "spring's rosy-colored light" and the tenderness of the beloved. What was Goethe fleeing from? The poetical self provides an unequivocal answer, an answer that seems quite strange at first glance: "Out of your glances your heart spoke" and "In your kisses, what love", which indicate that the nascent love is felt to be a threat. This drives both the poetical self and the real Goethe to flee. This flight is also a triumph, though. Goethe took this love with him, and it made him feel inspired and invigorated: "And yet, what bliss! to be loved,/And to love, you gods! what bliss!"

The poem illustrates once again how Goethe had learned to deal with painful and humiliating experiences: by transforming them into a poetical triumph. This may seem to be an unappealing and egotistical life strategy, but it will become clear that Goethe's behavior, which appears despicable to us, was the only way he was able to overcome his profound fears. A dream he had after an evening of dancing with Friederike will make this clear:

> I saw Lucinda, after her impassioned kiss, drawing fiercely away from me, and, with glowing cheek and sparkling eyes, uttering that curse, by which she intended to menace her sister alone, but by which she also uncon- sciously threatened innocent persons, totally unknown to her. I saw Frederica[2] standing opposite to her, paralysed at the sight, and pale already from the consequences of the curse, of which she knew nothing. I found myself between them, as little able to ward off the mental effects of the incident as to avoid the evil-boding kiss. Frederica's delicate health seemed to hasten the threatened calamity, and now her love for me began to wear a most unhappy aspect, in my eyes, and I wished that lands and seas lay between us.
>
> (Smith, vol. 2, pp. 11–12)

The next morning, Goethe was tormented by an almost superstitious fear that he was capable of harming Friederike with his amorous advances. His fears, though, were mixed with a large dose of narcissistic self-aggrandizement:

> But I will not conceal something still more painful to me, which lay in the back of my mind. It was a kind of self-conceit which kept that superstition alive in me;—my lips, whether consecrated or accursed, assumed a new importance in my eyes, and I felt no little complacency in the conscious- ness of my self-denying conduct, in renouncing many an innocent pleasure, partly to preserve my magic privilege, partly to avoid injuring a harmless

being by giving it up. But now all was lost and irrevocable: I had returned to a mere commonplace position, and I thought that I had harmed, perhaps irretrievably, the being dearest to my heart. Thus, far from my being freed from the curse, it was flung back from my lips into my own heart ... The sight of Frederica, the feeling of her love, the cheerfulness of everything around me—all reproved me for being able in the midst of such days to harbour such dismal night-birds in my bosom.

(Smith, vol. 2, p. 12)

It seems true that Goethe had profoundly harmed the feelings of Friederike Brion. When he departed, she was left speechless and forlorn; soon afterwards, she became physically ill. In a letter to Frau von Stein eight years later, Goethe confessed, "I had to leave her at a moment that almost cost her her life ...". Höfer (2002) has pointed out that Friederike led a very retired life for a very long time after this separation, and she never married. She is purported to have confessed to one of her sisters that anyone who had been loved by Goethe could not love anyone else.

While it is true that Goethe needed this separation from Friederike in order to overcome his fears and in service of his creative development, this does not excuse him. It is clear from the poems we have explored that he experienced tender feelings for his beloved, but more in her absence than in her presence. He was then able to use poetry to recreate her image within the confines of his mind, where he could give free rein to his amorous longings. But it is possible that this is an aspect of all art: the presence of something is created in its absence. This explains why the partners of creative people are so likely to suffer, yet they would not exchange their relationships for a life of stable equanimity. Even so, Goethe was conscious of his guilt:

My heart was torn by Frederica's answer to my written farewell. It was the same hand, the same thought, the same feeling, which had developed in her for me and through me. Now, for the first time, I felt the loss which she suffered, and saw no means of compensating her for it, or even of alleviating the pain. She was ever present with me; I always felt the lack of her, and, what was worst of all, I could not forgive myself for my own unhappiness. Gretchen had been taken from me; Annette had left me; now, for the first time, I was to blame, I had wounded the loveliest heart to its very depths; and this period of gloomy repentance, in the absence of that refreshing love which I had been wont to enjoy, was agonizing, nay, unbearable.

(Smith, vol. 2, p. 67)

Returning to the question of what caused this reversal during Goethe's time in Strasbourg, everything indicates that Goethe suffered from mood swings and attributed them to external events. Research has shown that poets are three times more likely to experience such mood swings than the general populace (Ludwig 1997). As we will see on further occasions, Goethe orchestrated ambivalent relationships that provided him with material and energy for his poetical creativity. Relational conflicts with women were part of his "creative bipolarity" (Holm-Hadulla 2017).

Notes

1 Now spelled "Sessenheim". *Trans.*
2 The translator of *Poetry and Truth* Anglicized many names, including that of Friederike Brion. I have left them as translated. *Trans.*

Chapter 5

Refuge at home again

Frankfurt, 1771–1772

You have poured/Into the early-wilting heart
A double life . . .

On his return from Strasbourg, Goethe was in better health than he had been at the end of his studies in Leipzig. Yet he was still in a state of unstable equilibrium, and "there was still about him something over-strained, which did not point to perfect health of mind" (Smith, vol. 2, p. 51). On his twenty-second birthday, he applied for permission to practice law at the court in Frankfurt. Legal disputes were not of much interest to him, though, and he was thankful that he was able to limit his work as a lawyer because his father was willing to shoulder much of the load. He continued to read a great deal, and he was especially enthusiastic about Shakespeare. He continued to dedicate himself to his poetic work. This helped him to deal with feelings of guilt over his treatment of Friederike:

> At the time when I was troubled by my grief at Friederika's sad position, I again, as had ever been my wont, sought the aid of poetry. I continued that confession in verse which I had already begun, so that by this self-tormenting penance I might be worthy of inner absolution. The two Marys in *Goetz von Berlichingen* and *Clavigo*, and the two bad characters who play the part of lovers to them, may have been the results of such penitent reflections.
>
> (Smith, vol. 2, p. 68)

Supported by the constant urging of his sister, Goethe completed the historical drama *Goetz von Berlichingen* in only six weeks, although it did not appear in public until 1773, after extensive revisions. The play was enthusiastically received and it was a literary breakthrough for Goethe. The play is set in the year 1517, shortly after Luther had set the Protestant Reformation in motion. Goetz von Berlichingen is a historically attested person, whom Goethe turned into a character of the same name who fights for freedom and justice. He champions the cause of those who are downtrodden and defends himself against the annexation of his tiny territory by the Diocese of Bamberg. His freedom is also his doom, though; he is unable to correctly read the signs of the time. He joins a peasants' revolt in good faith in order to prevent violence, but he has underestimated the anarchical force of the mob, a force he is unable to control. Now found guilty, he is deprived of his titles and banished to his castle.

The play contains a wealth of historical, political, social, and legal subjects (see Boyle 1991), but it is also interesting from a psychological point of view. From this perspective, we notice there is a second protagonist, Adelbert von Weislingen, an imperial knight, like Goetz, with whom he has been friends since childhood. When Weislingen enters service at the court of the Bishop of Bamberg, though, it results in a rupture between them. While this step does lead to a loss of independence, it also leads to an increase in political influence; in his new position, Weislingen is charged by the emperor to call Goetz to order. The instigator of this betrayal is Adelheid, a femme fatale at the court in Bamberg. Goetz succeeds in leading Weislingen back to the independence of a knight, at least at first, and to celebrate, he betroths Weislingen to his sister, Marie. Adelheid, though, turns Weislingen's head and induces him to marry herself instead. But she quickly tires of him and seduces both a knight who is a friend of Goetz's and one of Weislingen's squires, the latter of whom she finally persuades to poison Weislingen.

In giving Weislingen this form and fate, Goethe was also working through his own faithlessness to Friederike Brion. When he asked Salzmann to send a copy of the published play to Sesenheim, he commented that "poor Friederike" would be somewhat comforted by the poisoning of "faithless Weislingen". Goetz represents steadfastness in the face of opportunistic faithlessness, whereas Weislingen gives in to it. Goethe struggled with these alternatives in many different situations. In *Poetry and Truth*, he admits that Weislingen's story ended up being so extensive because he himself had fallen in love with Adelheid while writing, even though she represented the embodiment of the female intriguer. Boyle (1991) is of the opinion that Goethe, unlike Goetz or Weislingen, was able to maintain his identity while writing the play because he was able to escape the clutches of Adelheid, who was written as a caricature of Friederike. For Boyle, *Goetz von Berlichingen* contains two dramas with two heroes and two possible roles Goethe was confronted with: a knight in the best tradition, or an inconstant, emotionally ambivalent person who is unable to fulfill his tasks.

In December 1771, Goethe met Johann Heinrich Merck, a court official who was eight years his elder and who would come to have an even greater influence on Goethe's life than Behrisch and Herder. For instance, Merck was the driving force behind the publication of *Goetz von Berlichingen*. Moreover, Merck firmly supported Goethe's decision to embark on a literary rather than a legal career. He himself published a periodical in which contemporary work in philosophy and literature was discussed. The *Frankfurter gelehrte Anzeigen* (*Frankfurt scholarly announcements*) developed into the main forum for the *"Sturm und Drang"* (Storm and Stress) movement,

> that extolled and decried, yet far-famed epoch of literature, in which a number of young and gifted men, with all the audacity and presumption peculiar to their own youthful age, produced, by the exercise of their powers, much pleasure and much good, and by the abuse of them, much suffering and harm.
>
> (Smith, vol. 2, p. 66)

Goethe frequently traveled to Darmstadt to visit Merck; there, a circle of "Sentimentalists" had formed. They took walks in the woods together and circulated sentimental letters, and Goethe composed poems for the ladies. He shied away from entering into another relationship, though:

> My heart was untouched and empty; I conscientiously avoided all intimacy with ladies, and so remained unconscious of the fact, that, heedless and unconscious as I was, a good and friendly genius was in secret hovering around me. A gentle loveable woman cherished a secret affection for me, of which I was ignorant, and was therefore all the more cheerful and animated in her kindly presence. Many years afterwards, when she was dead, I heard of her secret and devoted love, in a manner that could not fail to shock me. But I was innocent, and could truly and honestly pity an innocent being; and that all the more sincerely, as the discovery occurred at a time when, free from all passion, I was fortunate enough to be living for myself and my intellectual tastes.
>
> (Smith, vol. 2, p. 68)

We can see how much space for himself Goethe still needed during this time and how important his moratorium on love – a period of waiting – was to him. In his familial home, he felt protected, and in the woods on his long walks, he found himself. He turned his lingering feelings of guilt into a practical interest in his fellow man:

> But man must live; hence I took a genuine interest in others; I sought to unravel their difficulties, and to keep together those who were about to part, that they might not have to suffer the same lot as myself. I was known, in consequence, as the "confidant".
>
> (Smith, vol. 2, p. 67)

Although he was occupied with his artistic work and his lively interest in human contact, Goethe did not forget his other strategies for maintaining his health, especially that of physical activity. Early in 1772, he traveled long distances on foot, from Frankfurt to Darmstadt and Bad Homburg. Although he felt physically healthy and full of energy, he continued to avoid close relationships and was happy to play the role of the lonely wanderer:

Pilgrim's Morning Song

Morning clouds, Lila,
Cover your tower;
Will I not see it
This last time!
But there hover
A thousand images
Of blissful memory
Holy, warm about my heart.
How it stood so,
Witness of my delight,
When the first time
You encountered,
Frightened, loving,
The stranger,
And all at once
Cast eternal flames
Into his soul! -
Hiss, North Wind,
Thousand snake tongued,
Around my head!
You shall not bow it!
You may bow
The heads of childish branches,
Separated from the sun's
Maternal presence.

All-present Love,
You glow through me!
You turn my brow against the weather,
My breast against dangers!
You have poured
Into the early-wilting heart
A double life,
Joy to live,
And courage!

(Wellbery, pp. 108–109)

The "Pilgrim's Morning Song" is yet another poem of leave-taking. It was composed on the way from Frankfurt to Wetzlar, passing through Bad

Homburg. The "tower" is the tower of the castle where Lila, one of Goethe's friends from the circle of Sentimentalists, lived. The poetical self comforts itself with "images / Of blissful memory" to ameliorate the pain of leaving. These images, which cause him to feel "holy, warm about my heart", are his treasure and are no longer dependent on his lady friend, even though she had "encountered [him], / ... loving". This friend had a more important function, that of unleashing a new confidence in him, "eternal flames" that endow him with steadfastness in rough times, when the "north wind hisses" around him. The poetical self feels strengthened to continue living, even when it is "Separated from the sun's / Maternal presence".

In the second stanza, the poetical self is euphoric when it speaks of "All-present Love". It appears that it is claiming its independence from its parents, sister, and the previously mentioned lady friend and is finding stability and coherence as part of a larger whole. On the other hand, the effusive tone seems to drown out the "dangers" directed at the "breast" and the despondency of the "early-wilting heart". The poetical self brings itself into being. "And courage" sounds like a magic spell uttered against the suffering Goethe was about to experience.

Chapter 6

Passion and renunciation

Wetzlar, 1772

> Once the toil and pain of life has been withstood,
> And happiness gives you rest and delight,
> Don't forget him, who – alas! With his whole heart,
> Loved you, and loved with you.

From May to September 1772, Goethe resided in the free imperial city of Wetzlar. Following a recommendation of his father's, he planned to continue his legal training at the Imperial High Court. But he found the High Court in a ruinous state of affairs. It was said there was a backlog of almost 20,000 court cases, and some of the judges were accused of taking bribes. Goethe felt no urge to get further involved with such dead-end work:

> Since I had done my best to realize all these circumstances, both old and new, it was impossible for me to hope for much pleasure from my stay in Wetzlar ... All this made the most dismal picture, and could not lure me to plunge more deeply into a pursuit, which, already involved in itself, seemed to be still further complicated by wrong-doing.
>
> (Smith, vol. 2, p. 77)

Goethe preferred to seek more interesting society; he was accepted into the "Order of Transition", but he could not take it seriously. Nevertheless, the personal friendships he soon made there were important to him, and he maintained them for some time:

> In this ever-increasing circle of German poets there developed, together with many and various poetical gifts, another mental attitude, to which I can give no satisfactory name. It might be called the need of independence, which always arises in times of peace, and at a time when, properly speaking, there is least dependence ... One will tolerate no authority over oneself; we will not be restrained, no one shall be restrained; and this tender, indeed morbid feeling, appears in noble souls under the form of justice.
>
> (Smith, vol. 2, p. 80)

Goethe preferred to indulge in Homer, Socrates, and Plato rather than to work on juridical cases, and he liked to make the acquaintance of literary writers. Two weeks after his inscription at the court in Wetzlar, he met 18-year-old Charlotte Buff at a ball. He felt an immediate attraction to her and visited her the next day at her own home, where she had assumed the role of mother to her 11 siblings after the death of their mother the year before. The fact that Lotte was already betrothed did not stop Goethe from falling violently in love; it is not difficult to believe that her unattainability only stoked the flames of his passion. He was also able to befriend Charlotte's fiancé, Johann Georg Kestner, a legation secretary. This configuration allowed Goethe to indulge in his infatuation without having to worry that he would succeed:

The new comer, perfectly free from all ties, was without care in the presence of a girl who, already engaged to another, would never interpret even the most obliging services as acts of courtship, and therefore found all the more pleasure in them. At first he went quietly his own way, but was soon so attracted and enthralled, and at the same time treated by the young couple with such intimate friendliness, that he no longer knew himself ... So through the splendid summer months they lived a true German idyll to what the fertile land and pure affection lend its poetry.

(Smith, vol. 2, pp. 88–89)

Goethe's affection for Lotte and her fiancé was mutual. But despite his esteem for Goethe, Kestner soon became annoyed by him. He wrote in his journal at the end of June 1772:

When I've done with my work and go to see my girl, I find Dr. Goethe there. He's in love with her, and though he's a philosopher and a good friend of mine, he's not pleased when he sees me coming to have a pleasant time with my girl. And although I'm a good friend of his, I don't like it that he should be alone with my girl and entertain her.

(qtd. in Maugham, p. 7)

The situation became increasingly uncomfortable, and Goethe realized that what had started as a dalliance had become a passion with no hope of return. During this period, he received the news that his friend Schlosser was planning to marry his sister Cornelia:

And I now realized for the first time that I was really jealous about my sister; a feeling which I was the less able to conceal from myself, as, since my return from Strasburg [sic], our relationship had become even more intimate ... I was now forced to resign myself, and try not to grudge my friend his happiness, though my self-confidence did not fail to assure me in secret, that if the brother had not been absent, the friend would never have so prospered in his suit.

(Smith, vol. 2, pp. 96–97)

Goethe was shaken by the upcoming separation from his sister and the hopelessness of his love for Lotte. He was tormented by his exclusion from real love affairs. Kestner wrote in his journal that Goethe was full of resentment and was developing strange fantasies. After Goethe "got a good talking-to" from Lotte, emphasizing that he could hope for nothing more than friendship, he was "very depressed" (qtd. in Maugham, p. 7). Kestner documented a conversation that took a dark turn, touching on leave-taking and death:

> He, Lottchen, and I, had a remarkable conversation about the future state; about going away and returning ... We agreed that the one who dies first should, if he could, give information to the living, about the conditions of the other life. Goethe was quite cast down.
>
> (*Works* 13, p. 177)

By the morning following this conversation, Goethe had fled Wetzlar, leaving behind a message for Kestner dated 10 September 1772:

> He is gone, Kestner; when you get this letter, he is gone. Give Lottchen the enclosed note. I was very composed, but your conversation has torn me to pieces. At present I can say nothing to you but farewell. Had I remained with you a moment longer, I could not have kept myself together. Now I am alone, and to-morrow I go. Oh, my poor head!
>
> (Bell, p. 95)

On the same day, he wrote a similarly abrupt note to Lotte: "I am now alone, and may weep. I leave you happy, and shall remain in your hearts. And if I shall see you again, but not to-morrow is never. Tell my boys he is gone. I cannot go on" (Bell, p. 95: HH).

Lotte read the note with tears in her eyes; she claimed that she could only speak of him and could do nothing but think of him after his departure. As in the incident with Friederike in Sesenheim, Goethe left Lotte quite suddenly, leaving behind perplexity and sadness as well. Kestner sensed Goethe's inner strife and was amazed at

> how love can transform even the strongest and most independent people into the strangest creatures. For the most part I felt sorry for him and was a prey to inner conflicts: on the one hand I thought I might not be able to make Lotte as happy as he could, while on the other I could not bear the thought of losing her.
>
> (qtd. in Friedenthal, p. 116)

It is possible that Goethe found himself able to conceive of a relationship with Lotte and therefore had to flee so abruptly. He believed that Lotte was in good hands with Kestner, and so he felt no qualms in leaving so suddenly. He dedicated himself completely to his own suffering and took to his feet again:

The Wanderer's Storm Song

He whom thou ne'er leavest, Genius,
Feels no dread within his heart
At the tempest or the rain. . . .

. . .

Poor heart!
There, on the hill,–
Heavenly might!
But enough glow
Thither to wend,
Where is my cot!
                    (Bowring, pp. 175–178)

Deeply distressed, the poetical self calls on its genius to save it from loneliness and desperation. Once again, Goethe is inwardly torn and can only find his way back to himself via his artistic work. He will only be able to find a degree of inner calmness much later. The cottage ("cot") yearned for was still far away. Looking back, he wrote to his friend Zelter, "When I look closely into the matter, it is only the talent implanted in me, that helps me through all the unsuitable conditions, in which I find myself entangled, by false tendencies, accident, and the adoption of foreign elements" (Coleridge, p. 126). On the one hand, Goethe yearned for a close relationship and a home. On the other hand, an internal drive forced him onward on life's journey. He was faced with a long period of wandering and could only dream of a happy ending, much like in "The Wanderer", which he wrote early in 1772.

The Wanderer

Young woman, may God bless thee,
Thee, and the sucking infant
Upon thy breast!
Let me, against this rocky wall,
Neath the elm-tree's shadow,
Lay aside my burden,
Near thee take my rest.

. . .

Farewell!
O Nature, guide me on my way!

The wandering stranger guide,
Who o'er the tombs
Of holy bygone times
Is passing.
...
And when I come home to my cot
At evening,
illumined by the setting sun,
Let me embrace a wife like this,
Her infant in her arms!
(Bowring, pp. 259–264)

Remarkably, Goethe, a lonely seeker, did not become bitter or jealous. He did not complain about his disappointments, nor did they cause him to become sullen or frustrated. He remained sincerely attached to Kestner, as we can see from the dedication quoted at the beginning of this chapter, where he declared that Kestner should never forget the person who "with his whole heart,/Loved you, and loved with you". Despite their rivalry, Kestner remained connected to Goethe by the bonds of friendship. In addition, he praised Goethe in his letters to others for his lively imagination, his good character, and his love of children. Kestner's connection to the poet remained almost tender. The letters they exchanged show a high degree of intimacy, and Goethe did not shy away from rhapsodizing about Kestner's fiancée. Thus we find in a letter to Kestner from late September 1772:

Lotte has not dreamt of me. I take that very much amiss, and it is my will that she shall dream of me this night ... And – have I not been with her, body and soul! And dreamt of her day and night ... Good night. I have just said that to Lotte's silhouette.

(Bell, pp. 98–99: HH)

On his return to Frankfurt from Wetzlar, Goethe visited a married couple, the La Roches, in Ehrenbreitstein, where he also met up with Merck. Sophie von La Roche was close to the circle of Sentimentalists in Darmstadt and had just completed an epistolary novel. Her 16-year-old daughter, Maximiliane, immediately became a new object of desire to Goethe, and his alarming emotional state became more settled. Later, he magnanimously commented on the situation: "It is a very pleasant sensation to feel a new passion stirring in us, before the old one is quite extinct" (Smith, vol. 2, p. 105). Like Charlotte, Maximiliane was also already betrothed. Her fiancé had less patience for Goethe than Kestner, though, and firmly banned him from the house. Goethe was devastated and wrote to Kestner that the roller coaster of hopes and disappointments had led him to consider suicide. Years later, he was to describe his depression and weariness of life thusly:

This loathing of life has both physical and moral causes; the former we will leave to the investigation of the physician, the latter to that of the moralist ... Nothing occasions this weariness more than the recurrence of the passion of love.

(Smith, vol. 2, pp. 120–121)

Goethe returned to Frankfurt in the fall of 1772, in pain from his recently dashed hopes.

Chapter 7

Period of genius
Frankfurt, 1772–1775

> Here sit I, forming mortals
> After my image;
> A race resembling me,
> To suffer, to weep . . .

Goethe returned home after only four months in Wetzlar. This period of disappointed love and poor career prospects was the start of the most productive time in his life. Goethe took up themes and subjects that would come to characterize his entire literary oeuvre, from the epistolary novel *The Sufferings of Young Werther* to the tragedy *Faust*. The routine work associated with his career as a lawyer seemed to be more stabilizing than disruptive for him:

> Even while working in this way to cultivate, foster, and maintain any talent, taste, or other inclination of the kind that might be in me, I devoted a good part of the day, according to my father's wish, to my profession of advocate ... I delighted in this occupation all the more as it brought me nearer to my father, who, being perfectly satisfied with my conduct in this respect, was prepared to look with an eye of indulgence on my other pursuits.
>
> (Smith, vol. 2, p. 108)

Once again, he was able to improve his despairing moods by successfully employing, in addition to his artistic work, another remedy: dependable emotional bonds. Although his relationship with his father was not perfect, each was nevertheless able to be of use to the other one and to accept his help. His mother was also able to remain cheerful and calm in the face of her "little pet's" turbulent moods. He and Cornelia held each other in confidence, and she was persistent in encouraging him to continue his work, for instance on *Goetz von Berlichingen*:

> In the course of my work on this subject I had discussed it thoroughly with my sister, who was interested, heart and soul, in such matters. I reverted to the topic so often, without, however, setting definitely to work, that at last,

in her impatient desire for my success, she urgently entreated me not to be always casting my words into space, but, once for all, to set down on paper the thoughts which were so vividly in my mind. Determined by this instigation, I began to write one morning, without having made any previous sketch or plan. I wrote the first scenes, and in the evening read them aloud to Cornelia. She highly approved of them, but only conditionally, since she doubted if I should ever continue them; and even openly expressed her want of faith in my perseverance. This was only a further incitement; I wrote the next day, and again the third. Our daily discussions increased my hopes, step by step the whole conception gained in vividness.

(Smith, vol. 2, p. 113)

Goethe's need to communicate with other people was beneficial to his work. He was inspired by agreement, but criticism did not discourage him. He was pleased by Merck's approval of the manuscript of *Goetz von Berlichingen* and overlooked, with humor, the sarcasm of Herder, who wrote poems besmirching *Goetz*. He was able to accept positive feedback, and negative feedback had hardly any effect on his creative energy. Interesting was also the way Goethe dealt with solitude during his creative periods, something that is often a source of misery for authors:

Having always spent his most pleasant hours in society, he devised the following plan for changing even solitary thought into social conversation: When he was alone, he would call up before his mind any person of his acquaintance; then entreat him to sit down, walk up and down beside him, or remain standing before him, and discourse with him on the subject he had in his mind.

(Smith, vol. 2, p. 119)

During this creative period, his connection to Lotte and her fiancé continued unabated. Goethe wrote to Kestner from Frankfurt, sometimes multiple times a week, and he did not conceal his emotional reactions from him. He continued to discuss his feelings for Lotte in great detail:

I take care to talk a great deal about her, for then people smile and suspect she might be my sweetheart ... Yesterday evening, dear Kestner, I entertained myself for an hour with Lotte and you in the twilight; then it became dark, I was trying to grope my way to the door, and went a step too far to the right, fumbled against the paper – it was Lotte's silhouette, it was a pleasant sensation. I wished her a very good night.

(Bell, pp. 108–111)

In April of 1773, Goethe wrote,

The night flows away now in the evening, and poor Goethe puts up with it as usual ... So Herr Kestner, and Madame Kestner, good-night. I would

have ended here if something better awaited me in bed than my dear
brother [sleep]. But just look at my bed, it stands as sterile as a desert ...
but I do know our Lord God must be a very cold-blooded person if he
leaves to you Lotte.

(Bell, pp. 131–132)

On the one hand, Goethe is playing a coy game with the triangle relationship
between him, Charlotte, and Kestner. On the other hand, he was completely
serious; his loneliness and the changes around him were sources of suffering to
him. Not only his sister's approaching wedding, but also the marriage of
Caroline Flachsland to Herder, his friend and mentor, were especially difficult
for him. He confessed his despair to Kestner:

My poor existence is freezing into a barren rock. This summer, all are
departing. Merck to Berlin with the court, his wife to Switzerland, my
sister, Fräulein Flachsland, you, all. And I am alone. If I take no wife, or
hang myself, then say that I like life quite well, or something which does
me more honour, if you will.

(Bell, p. 136)

The lonelier he became, the tighter he clung to his relationship with Lotte
and Kestner. Nor did this change after the pair moved farther away to Hannover
in June of 1773. His letters continued to be intimate, imploring, and enthusiastically amorous:

Last night I dreamt whimsically of Lotte. I led her arm-in-arm through the
avenue and all the people stood still and looked at her ... And she looked
at me with her eyes (you know very well how one feels when she looks at
one) ... "Oh, Lotte," I said to her, "Lotte, may they only not hear that you
are the wife of another".

(Bell, p. 140)

Once again, we get the distinct impression that Goethe was able to surrender
himself to his erotic desires in dreams and infatuations more than he was
capable of in reality. More importantly, though, the "distant love" represented
prerequisites for his creative motivation. The letter to Kestner quoted above
accompanied a copy of the first edition of *Goetz von Berlichingen*; it continued
as follows:

And so I dream and wander through life, carry on dirty law-suits, write
plays and novels, and such like, drag, push and drive it as quickly as it will
go. And you are blessed like the man who fears the Lord. People say of me,
that the curse of Cain lies upon me. I have slain no brother! And I think the

people are fools. Here you have a piece of work [the play], dear Kestner; read it aloud to your little wife.

(Bell, p. 141)

Goethe's writings became his preferred method of maintaining connections with his loved ones. The most productive period of his life had begun, as he shared with Kestner in July of 1773:

I am very diligent, and if fortune is good you will soon receive something in a different style. I wish Lotte were not indifferent about my drama ... A year ago to-day it was quite different, I could swear at this hour a year ago I was sitting with Lotte. I am working up my situation into a drama in defiance of God and men.

(Bell, p. 143)

The play he refers to is *Prometheus*, in which he grappled with his own creative power. He found in the mythological Prometheus an allegory for human beings, who revolt against fate and the gods to create their own world. In the unfinished piece, written in 1774, the title character accuses the gods of being unable to alleviate human suffering and substitutes himself for God as the creator:

Prometheus

. . .

I honour thee! and why?
Hast thou e'er lighten'd the sorrows
Of the heavy laden?
Hast thous e'er dried up the tears
Of the anguish-stricken?
Was I not fashion'd to be a man
By omnipotent Time,
And by eternal Fate,
Masters of me and thee?

Didst thou e'er fancy
That life I should learn to hate,
And fly to deserts,
Because not all
My blossoming dreams grew ripe?

Here sit I, forming mortals
After my image;
A race resembling me,
To suffer, to weep,

To enjoy, to be glad,
And thee to scorn,
As I!

(Bowring, p. 182)

The poetical self is unmistakably describing Goethe's own experiences. It recognizes the "sorrows/Of the heavy laden" and the "tears/Of the anguish-stricken", and has gone through the frightening experiences that "forged [him] into manhood". It has distanced itself from the "blossoming dreams" of the boy and has worked up the courage to create both humans and itself, "to suffer, to weep,/To enjoy, to be glad", and to take life into its own hands. In this way, active humans become true creators who no longer need God.

When we think back on Goethe's fearfulness and despondency, we see that this is a major step for him. It sounds like a poetical protest, for he was in a state of change in his real life. Cornelia's marriage would soon divide them, and he faced their ultimate separation in the fall of 1773 with dark foreboding. Yet his creative powers were on the rise during this period, and the success of *Goetz von Berlichingen* drove him to increase his efforts. This in turn allowed him to observe the developments taking place in the lives of the women he loved, without envy. Lotte became pregnant in October 1773, and Cornelia's marriage seemed to be a happy one:

My sister is brave, she is learning to live! And only in complicated critical cases do men find out what is within them. She is well, and Schlosser is the best husband, as he was the tenderest and most constant of lovers.

(Bell, p. 166)

During this period, Goethe was extremely productive. He continued to address himself to questions of religion, and he became interested in the teachings of Mohammed. He wrote the wide-ranging poem "Mahomet's Song" that was to be included in the fragmentary dramatic piece "Mahomet". At the same time, he was studying the teachings of Pelagianism, which rejects the idea of original sin. He expanded his political, cultural, and scientific horizons by conversing with well-educated men and accompanying them on short trips. Goethe's acquaintance with the theologian, philosopher, and writer Johann Kaspar Lavater proved to be of great importance; Goethe accompanied him during his travels and visited him in Zurich. Yet despite all this activity, something was brewing inside him. Early in November 1772, Goethe had received news that Jerusalem, a 25-year-old legation secretary in Wetzlar, had committed suicide. Goethe was very busy when he received the news, or perhaps it took his subconscious a long time to process the idea of suicide, but it was not until February of 1774 that he was able to consciously perceive the full extent of his own shock. The long-festering wounds finally opened, and he became more and more hopeless about his loneliness. He saw similarities between himself and Jerusalem, whose unrequited love for the wife of a friend led him to shoot himself.

After a long incubation period, Goethe finally wrote *The Sufferings of Young Werther* in February of 1774. He committed the epistolary novel to paper in just four-and-a-half weeks, "externally completely isolated ... almost unconsciously, like a somnambulist" (Smith, vol. 2, p. 129). In this way, he was able to cope not only with his moods and suicidal ideas, but also with his separation from Cornelia, with his fruitless love for Lotte, and with his rejection by Maximiliane. He became more independent and found stability in a world that had been previously been full of chaotic emotions:

> For by this composition, more than by any other, I had freed myself from that stormy element ... I felt as if I had made a general confession, and was once more free and happy, and justified in beginning a new life.
>
> (Smith, vol. 2, p. 129)

Goethe felt as if he had escaped death and was new born. He would also experience his later work as a series of births under the threat of death. Boyle (1991) has hypothesized that the character Werther is not simply a reflection of Goethe, but that it also includes the outlines of the brother who died young, Hermann Jakob. There might also be undertones of Goethe's unconscious preoccupation with Cornelia's pregnancy and the associated fear of death. Going even further back, we are reminded that there are echoes of Goethe's birth experience in his conception. In any case, *Werther* allowed him to part with Lotte while also binding himself to her forever through his art. He wrote to Lotte in June of 1774, "Adieu, dear Lotte, I shall send you soon a friend who much resembles me, and hope you will receive him well, he is called Werther" (Bell, p. 187).

Lotte and Kestner were of the opinion that the figure of Werther was an accurate portrait of Goethe's character and way of thinking. They thought that the way they themselves had been portrayed, though, made them too easily recognizable, and they were incensed by some distortions. Nevertheless, the epistolary novel was received by the general public with enthusiasm. A French translation appeared only one year later, and an English translation in 1779. Other reactions were negative, even appalled: "The heart of every Christian ... must inevitably bleed when he reads 'The Sufferings of Young Werther' ... For the love of God, think of our youth, and how many of them could find themselves in the same situation". Many considered the book dangerous and thought it could drive its readers to suicide, and indeed, several cases of suicide were attributed to reading *Werther*. For this reason, Goethe felt compelled to add the following verses to the beginning of the second edition:

> Every youth for love's sweet portion sighs,
> Every maiden sighs to win man's love;

> Why, alas! should bitter pain arise
> From the noblest passion that we prove?
>
> Thou, kind soul, bewailest, lovest him well,
> From disgrace his memory's saved by thee;
> Lo, his spirit sighs from out its cell:
> Be a man, nor seek to follow me.
>
> (*Works* 9, p. 246)

Goethe, who put his suffering self at the forefront in *Werther*, felt compelled to warn others of the danger of focusing on thoughts of suicide. He himself found that *Werther* had allowed him to "escape from the waves of death". Years later, after the stepson of one of his nearest friends Zelter had committed suicide, Goethe wrote to him:

> When the *taedium vitae* seizes a man, he is only to be pitied, not blamed. That all the symptoms of this strange disease, as natural as it is unnatural, at one time raged furiously through my own innermost being, no one who reads *Werther* will probably doubt. I know full well what resolutions and efforts it cost me in those days, to escape from the waves of death; just as with difficulty I saved myself, to recover painfully, from many a later shipwreck.
>
> (qtd. in Coleridge, p. 92)

Goethe considered depression and suicide from many different perspectives. In his autobiography, *Poetry and Truth*, he considered depressive moods to be a symptom of an illness resulting from social isolation and loneliness,

> for all gloom is the child and pupil of solitude—whoever resigns himself to it flies all opposition, and what can be more opposed to his state of mind than the cheerfulness of society? The enjoyment of life felt by others is to him a painful reproach.
>
> (Smith, vol. 2, p. 120)

A few lines later, he described additional reasons for suicidal tendencies: "This loathing of life has both physical and moral causes; the former we will leave to the investigation of the physician, the latter to that of the moralist" (Smith, vol. 2, p. 120). After this skeptical introduction, he emphasizes his belief that the best means of forestalling depression is to maintain a rhythm of life that is regulated by nature and includes an abundance of human contact:

> All comfort in life is based upon a regular recurrence of external phenomena. The change of day and night, of the seasons, of flowers and fruits, and all other recurring pleasures that come to us, that we may and should enjoy

them—these are the main springs of our earthly life. The more open we are to these enjoyments, the happier we are; but if these changing phenomena unfold themselves before us and we take no interest in them, if we are insensible to such fair solicitations, then comes on the sorest evil, the heaviest disease—we regard life as a loathsome burden.

(Smith, vol. 2, p. 120)

These lines, probably written to educate, downplay his own artistic conflicts, for his fate was the same as that of many poets who are only able to experience the "heavenly powers" of creativity once they find themselves in solitude.

Goethe describes two more causes of depression, beyond withdrawing from nature and from society: passivity and high expectations. "We are here concerned with those whose life is embittered in the most peaceful circumstances by lack of actions and by the exaggerated demands they make upon themselves" (Smith, vol. 2, p. 125). A close reading of *Werther* allows us to infer the following important strategies for the treatment of suicidal tendencies and depression: those afflicted should dedicate themselves to their joys as well as to their sufferings, which they should then actively shape and communicate to others. Ultimately, this means that there are salutary effects associated with accepting the challenge of a creative life. Writing *Werther* was an act of self-therapy for Goethe, one that was arguably successful because, afterwards, he was free of depressive moods.

For by this composition, more than by any other, I had freed myself from that stormy element, in which, by my own fault and that of others, by a mode of life at once designed and accidental, of set purpose and by heedless precipitation, by obstinacy and pliability, I had been violently tossed to and fro. I felt as if I had made a general confession, and was once more free and happy, and justified in beginning a new life. The old recipe had this time done me excellent service.

(Smith, vol. 2, p. 129)

The *Sufferings of Young Werther* also brought more general questions to light, such as how to deal with the spread of the "sentimentalist affliction" that Goethe found to be a melancholy trend. And so *Werther* came upon a young generation "tortured by unsatisfied passions, with no outward inducements to important activities ... persisting in a dull, spiritless, commonplace life" (Smith, vol. 2, p. 125). Many young men identified with Werther, and a cult arose around the novel, which only served to add to its international renown. But Goethe himself also remained connected to the figure of Werther for a long time. He revised the novel again and again, and wrote the following eight years after its initial publication: "I have gone through my Werther and will write it out again in manuscript, he is returning to his mother's womb and you shall see him after his rebirth" (qtd. in Unseld, p. 66). Six years later, in June of 1786, he wrote in a letter to Frau Von Stein, "I am revising my Werther and find that the writer was wrong in not shooting himself when he had finished writing it" (qtd. in Ghibellino, p. 166). Fifty years after putting *Werther* to paper, Goethe recounted to Eckermann the following about his alter ego:

> That is a creation which I, like the pelican, fed with the blood of my own heart ... It is a mass of congreve-rockets. I am uncomfortable when I look at it; and I dread lest I should once more experience the peculiar mental state from which it was produced.
>
> (Oxenford, vol. 1, p. 117)

Goethe still felt remarkably close to *Werther* even as an old man, resulting in his memorialization of both the novel and himself in his *Trilogy of Passion.*

The *Sufferings of Young Werther* would not have attained this epoch-making significance if it were merely an outlet for the unrequited love of a young man for an unattainable young woman. As indicated above, *Werther* included a variety of themes. First, there is the issue of religion. Goethe grappled with his own religious desperation: "Is not this the voice of a creature oppressed beyond all resource, self-deficient, about to plunge into inevitable destruction, and groaning deeply at its inadequate strength, 'My God! my God! why hast thou forsaken me?'" (*Works* 6, p. 92). During his *Werther* period, Goethe had not sought revelation in organized religion in quite some time; instead, he looked for it in nature and in human creativity. To him, both spheres were holy; the divine revealed itself to him in nature and in art, and he drew the sustenance he needed from both spheres. Immersing himself in nature and art, he was able to conceive of himself as part of a larger cosmic movement. Religion alone could not sustain him. Like Goethe, Werther received religious instruction in his youth. He frequently employs images and expressions from the Bible in his speech, even after leaving the church. Even if he could, he does not wish to pray, and for this reason he finds himself alone with his desperation: "I revere religion — you know I do. I feel that it can impart strength to the feeble and comfort to the afflicted, but does it affect all men equally?" (*Works* 6, p. 91).

Despite his many references to the Bible, Werther has renounced his ties to the church. Goethe had also left the world view of orthodox Protestantism far behind and could now recognize something holy in nature and in human activity. In *Werther*, the ecstasy of boundary-expanding erotic surrender is depicted as a transcendent way to experience religious dimensions:

> A dim vastness is spread before our souls: the perceptions of our mind are as obscure as those of our vision; and we desire earnestly to surrender up our whole being, that it may be filled with the complete and perfect bliss of one glorious emotion.
>
> (*Works* 6, p. 27)

In his old age, Goethe would no longer experience this immersion as ecstatic and urgent, but would view it with cheerful composure. In the poem "The One and the All", it says:

To find himself in the limitless,
the individual will gladly disappear;
there all satiety is overcome;
instead of ardent wishes, violent desires,
instead of burdensome demands, strict obligations,
self-surrender is a pleasure.

(Appelbaum, p. 195)

For Goethe and for Werther, it is impossible to transcend the boundaries of the self within a religion formed within the confines of the church. Religious yearning can only materialize in a loving relationship with another person: "I cannot pray except to her" (*Works* 6, p. 56).

But Lotte belongs to another; hence, the path to boundless, absolute love is closed to him. Death appears to be the only way he can meld with the "All-Loving". The mysterious connection between love and religion is one of the basic themes of the novel, and now, the connection between love and death is added. In both love and death, the Self is unbounded. Later, Goethe will identify a successful path to the dissolution of boundaries in his poem "Blissful Yearning": Here, physical union turns into a vision of melding lovingly with natural and cultural life that is characterized by an interplay of dying and becoming. From a psychological point of view, Goethe expresses a narcissistic delusion of grandeur in both *Werther* and *Prometheus*. He views himself as a self-created subject, one who proudly has command over his own existence and whose unbounded freedom also gives him the right to take his own life. He is something special and is allowed to narcissistically reject all vocational work and common ties: "This heart that is my only pride, that is the sole source of everything, — of all strength, all bliss and all misery. All that I know everybody can know, but my heart is exclusively my own" (HA 6, p. 74: HH). The self has thus triumphed over commitments, guilt, and shame. As most therapists are aware from their own experience, young people who commit suicide do not actually want to die; rather, they want to free their own magnificence from feelings of shame and guilt. This is referred to as narcissistic suicide, which is not quite as self-referential as it may initially appear. In most cases, any reproaches against others – the terrible world, unsympathetic parents, and disappointing loved ones – are hidden. Finally, the young person absolutizes his own sensations, deeming them to be the only true ones, thereby devaluing mortal life with all its troubles and cares.

The unhealthiness of Werther's ecstasy becomes more and more apparent over the course of the novel, which is why his friends – Wilhelm, Albert, and Lotte – do not feel devalued and annoyed, but are instead concerned about him

and feel pity for him. The reader reacts similarly, viewing Werther's development toward suicide with understanding and concern from the very beginning.
The theme of suicide is already discernible at the start of the novel, before
Werther even knew Lotte or anything about her; it is a consequence of the
limitations of human nature and religious revelation. Only later is it connected
to desperate love. The theme of suicide finally leads to the idea of a sublime,
all-encompassing freedom. This idea is fatal, though: It rescues the narcissistic
ego, but the price is death. In the end, this narcissistic suicide is a capitulation to
man's limited possibilities:

> And what is man – that boasted demigod? Do not his powers fail when he
> most requires their use? And whether he soar in joy, or sink in sorrow, is
> not his career in both inevitably arrested? And, whilst he fondly dreams that
> he is grasping at infinity, does he not feel compelled to return to a
> consciousness of his cold, monotonous existence?
>
> (*Works* 6, p. 98)

Goethe used *The Sufferings of Young Werther* to deal with his conflicts with
normal limitations, disappointed love affairs, and his own personal narcissism,
at least temporarily. He created a novel that ended tragically, but which dazzled
the public with its rhythm, sound, and its rich imagery. Shortly after *Werther*
was published, Auguste zu Stolberg wrote to him:

> I will soon know my copy of "Werther" by heart. Oh, it is indeed an almost
> too divine book! And yet it often happens to me, as it does to you: I wish it
> were not printed; I always think that it is too good for this world.
>
> (HA 6, p. 530: DS)

But, as has already been mentioned, there were also critical voices, especially
among the clergy. The clerics Homius, Balle, and Jansen demanded that the
novel be censored and wrote

> that this novel must be labeled as a piece of writing that mocks religion,
> downplays vice, and can corrupt the heart and public morals, and indeed
> this novel is even more dangerous for the innocent and for those who are
> not sufficiently firm, because the author made enough effort to present
> everything in a beautiful style and with a vivid delivery.
>
> (source: typewritten brochure at the Lotte House in Wetzlar: DS)

The emphatic glorification of suicide, in particular, was seen as sacrilegious,
but the romanticization of adultery, even if not actually committed in the novel,
was also considered offensive. The critics were not able to impede the success
of *Werther*, though. Goethe enjoyed his sudden celebrity and felt encouraged to
continue writing. A large public was now rewarding him for his laborious

internal work on overcoming his psychological wounds and disappointments, rather than suppressing them. Goethe had matured as a person and grown from a youthful dreamer to an adult man. The song "The King of Thule", which Gretchen sings in the *Urfaust* and which was also composed in 1774, nicely expresses this maturity:

> There was a king in Thule,
> Was faithful till the grave,
> To whom his mistress, dying,
> A golden goblet gave.
>
> Nought was to him more precious;
> He drained it at every bout;
> His eyes with tears ran over,
> As oft as he drank thereout.
>
> When came his time of dying,
> The towns in his land he told,
> Nought else to his heir denying
> Except the goblet of gold.
>
> He sat at the royal banquet
> With his knights of high degree,
> In the lofty hall of his father
> In the castle by the sea.
>
> There stood the old carouser,
> And drank the last life-glow;
> And hurled the hallowed goblet
> Into the tide below.
>
> He saw it plunging and filling,
> And sinking deep in the sea:
> Then fell his eyelids for ever,
> And never more drank he!
> (*Works* 9, p. 130)

This is not the voice of an exalted, narcissistic young poet with the world at his feet. In entrancing minor chords, the faithfulness and longing of a lonely old man are described. Goethe selected Thule, a legendary kingdom in the north, to paint a vivid portrait of leave-taking and dying. The king has retained the goblet given to him by his dying beloved as a symbol of love and faithfulness. "He drained it at every bout" and thus is repeatedly, painfully reunited in his heart with his beloved. "Nought else to his heir denying", he bequeathed the heir all of his other earthly possessions, but the remembrance of his beloved is preserved within himself and the goblet. He "drank the last life-glow" with her, and then both "sank deep in the sea". Hermann Hefele characterized the poem as

> one of the greatest and deepest poems ever written by man, and within the series of Goethean creations it is also a model for the perfected maturation of artistic intention and poetic technique, which he, then only twenty-four years old, brought himself to do. How vividly is it portrayed here, the Goethe-esque ur-experience of faithfulness, or more precisely, of permanence, as witnessed by the symbols of wife and wine, the two potential means for the individual to enhance his life, melded together with the profoundness of the thought of death, a profoundness both untragic and like that of classical antiquity, in this simple depiction of concrete clarity.
>
> (HA 1, p. 511: DS)

Goethe's poetic work was important to him not only when he was feeling melancholy, but also when he was feeling elated; it helped him to stay centered and on firm ground. At times, he was so exuberant that he alarmed himself. Like the beautiful prince Ganymede, he was able to have an experience of being "embraced and embracing" by the bliss of life:

Ganymede

How, in the light of morning,
Round me thou glowest,
Spring, thou beloved one!
With thousand-varying loving bliss
The sacred emotions
Born of thy warmth eternal
Press 'gainst my heart,
Thou endlessly fair one!

Could I but hold thee clasp'd
Within mine arms!

Ah! upon thy bosom
Lay I, pining,
And then thy flowers, thy grass,
Were pressing against my heart.
Thou coolest the burning
Thirst of my bosom,
Beauteous morning breeze!
The nightingale then calls me
Sweetly from out of the misty vale.

I come, I come!
Whither? Ah, whither?

Up, up, lies my course.
While downward the clouds
Are hovering, the clouds
Are bending to meet yearning love.
For me,
Within thine arms
Upwards!
Embraced and embracing!
Upwards
into thy bosom,
Oh Father all-loving!
                    (Bowring, p. 183)

In this poem, probably composed in early 1774, the lyrical I, in a sublime mood, addresses Spring as "beloved one", who presses against its heart with "loving bliss". The poetical self wishes to embrace "sacred emotions" and endless beauty. It is initially able to do so by simulating nature and pining on its bosom. The nightingale's joy in the flowers, grass, morning wind, and singing "cools the burning thirst" and assuages its yearning. But the poetical self questions where the path of the ecstatic experience of nature leads: "Whither? Ah, whither?" The path climbs higher and higher, and the poetical self experiences its ecstasy as reaching the bosom of divine nature. It dissolves into a universal Eros, "embraced and embracing", and feels united with an "all-loving" father. This unification in the bosom of divine nature means that the poetical self is no longer completely its own creation, as in *Prometheus*. It receives its inspiration as a gift of a quasi-religious nature. What is interesting here is that love does not require a human partner. Rapture is a universally erotic sensation that the poetical self severs from the reality of human relationships in this poem.

But, Goethe himself remained close to Lotte and Kestner, even after the publication of *Werther*, the composition of which was a form of catharsis for Goethe. He even pressed the couple to name their son after him:

But now – I hope that Lotte – for the boy is baptised whilst I am writing on the 11th May – that Lotte may have vehemently broken through all deliberation, and said: *His* name is Wolfgang, and the boy shall be called so too! You seem to incline to it, and I wish that he should bear that name because it is mine.

                                                                    (Bell, p. 182)

He continued to feel a passionate closeness to Lotte, even in his dreams. In August of 1774, he wrote breathlessly:

Lotte, and Lotte, and Lotte, and Lotte and Lotte, and without Lotte, naught and want, and sorrow and death ... But in the night I dreamt of you; how I had come again to you, and you had given me a hearty kiss. Ever since I have been away from you, neither waking nor dreaming have I seen you so distinctly before me.

(Bell, p. 199)

Goethe had created an image of Lotte and himself that outlasted their separation. In the end, *Werther* made them and their love immortal.

Despite this catharsis, Goethe continued to be at the mercy of his varying moods, but he transformed these using his creative activities. His friend Knebel described it thusly:

Goethe lives in a constant state of internal war and upheaval, because everything has an effect on him ... I have a pile of fragments from him, including fragments of a work "Doctor Faust", that have exceptionally superb scenes. He pulls manuscripts from every nook and cranny of his room.

(FA 28, p. 418: DS)

During this period, Goethe received many invitations from Frankfurt society and was celebrated as a young genius. He was introduced to Lili Schönemann, the sixteen-year-old daughter of a banker, at the turn of the year from 1774 to 1775. Her grace and beauty immediately awakened in him a marked inclination. He sensed "a sweet and gentle attraction" (Smith, vol. 2, p. 213). But then something quite unusual happened. At the same time Goethe was falling in love with Lili, paying her visits, accompanying her to balls, and visiting her relatives, he was becoming devoted to someone else: Auguste, Countess zu Stolberg. The countess, who lived in a convent, was deeply impressed by *Werther* and had written to the poet to share her enthusiasm. Goethe was so pleased with her letter that he immediately replied,

My dear ——, I will give you no name, for what are the names Friend, Sister, Beloved, Bride, Wife, or a word which comprises a complex of all those names, beside the direct feelings — to the —— I cannot write further, your letter has caught me at a wonderful time. Adieu, though at the first moment! —— Yet I return —— I feel you can endure it, this disjointed stammering expression, when the image of the Eternal stirs in us. And what is that but Love? —— If He was forced to make man after His own image, a race that should be like Himself, what must we feel when we find brothers, our likeness, ourselves doubled?

(Bell, p. 222)

Goethe initiated what would come to be a profound connection to Auguste zu Stolberg with this letter, composed over several days, from 18 to 30 January

1775. The connection itself is marked by its psychotherapeutic character. Goethe took this complete stranger and turned her into his most important confidant, assigning her a variety of roles – friend, sister, beloved, bride, wife – and confiding all of his chaotic emotions and feelings to her. Interestingly, this self-therapy-by-letter began *after* his relationship with Lili Schönemann had started to become more serious. It would seem that Goethe needed this distant correspondent in order to cope with his fear of a real romantic attachment. "New Love, New Life", a poem that was composed during this period, reveals his anxious expectations and conflicting feelings.

New Love, New Life

Heart, my heart, what will come of this?
What oppresses you so greatly?
What an unfamiliar, new life!
I no longer recognize you.
Gone is everything you loved,
gone the cause of your sorrows,
gone your diligence and your peace —
Ah, how did you get this way?

Are you enchained by the youthful blossom,
by this lovely form,
do these eyes full of fidelity and kindness
enchain you with infinite power?
If I want to withdraw from her swiftly,
to pull myself together, to escape her,
at the very same moment,
alas, my path leads me back to her.

And by this magic thread,
which cannot be torn,
the dear, wanton girl
holds me fast this way against my will;
I must now live as she sees fit
within her magic circle.
Ah, what a great change!
Love, love, let me go!
(Appelbaum, pp. 37–39)

Love bestows an "unfamiliar, new life" on him, while also vexing and bewildering him. Love appears strange because it dismantles familiar structures: "Gone is everything you loved". Goethe's creative powers were his main source of fulfillment during this period, and he feared their loss. But why should love steal "your diligence and your peace" from the poetical self? Is it the erotic attraction of the "youthful blossom" or is it the attachment, "eyes full of fidelity and kindness", that would rob Goethe of his freedom? He has no answers to these questions, nor any solutions. The only option is to flee: "I want to withdraw from her swiftly". On the other hand, the poetical self longs for a sweetheart and clings "by this magic thread" to the "dear, wanton girl". It feels weak-willed and trapped in a "magic circle"; moreover, it cannot bear the "great change" and must run away: "Love, love, let me go!"

In this state of turmoil, a manifestation of Goethe's fear of a romantic attachment, his correspondence with Auguste zu Stolberg allowed him to collect himself and to impose a certain degree of order on the chaos of his emotions. In February of 1775, he wrote to Auguste:

> If you can picture to yourself, my dear, a Goethe in a laced coat, otherwise from head to foot in tolerably consistent finery, illuminated by the unmeaning splendour of sconces and chandeliers, amidst all kinds of people, kept at the card-table by a pair of beautiful eyes, and, in varying dissipation, driven from company to concert, and from thence to a ball, and with all the interest of frivolity paying court to a pretty Blondine; you have the present Carnival-Goethe, who lately stammered forth to you a few gloomy, deep feelings, who cannot write to you, who sometimes too forgets you, because in your presence he feels himself quite unbearable.
>
> (Bell, pp. 223–224)

A close reading of this letter shows that Goethe was not comfortable in Lili's mundane world. While participating in her social activities, he found himself acting puffed up and feeling adrift. Feeling as though his identity were destabilized, Goethe sought reassurance in the letters he exchanged with the countess. His love for a lady who lived far away and behind convent walls seemed much more reliable and secure than the various activities undertaken with a lively young woman. He confessed to Auguste that he was more comfortable as the Goethe

> in grey beaver coat ... who, ever living, striving, and working in himself ... asking neither on the right nor left ... He it is, from whose mind you are never absent, who suddenly in early morning feels a summons to write to you.
>
> (Bell, pp. 223–224)

Goethe turned Auguste into his own personal psychotherapist, one who sympathetically supported him, understood him, and provided him with the space to sort through confusing experiences. He discussed his conflicts with her and re-enacted them by assigning her different roles and working through the conflicts with each of the roles. As in psychoanalysis, the distance of the friend, i.e. the abstinence of the psychoanalyst, was a necessary condition for Goethe to unreservedly open up and to reflect on his problems:

> Moreover, if it were disclosed to me who and where you are, it would make no difference; when I think of you I feel nothing but equality, love, nearness! And so remain to me, as I surely remain, through all whirl and hurly-burly, unalterable.
>
> (Bell, p. 225)

Goethe was under the impression that Lili was a serious threat to his creativity and to his sense of coherence. He wrote to Bürger in February that he felt muddled and unproductive, and he characterized himself to both Sophie von Laroche and Auguste zu Stolberg as "Carnival-Goethe", useless. He told Johanna Fahlmer that he was "quite unbearable" and had been "very stupid and mad" when he had run across Lili and her mother while on an outing. A few days after the Carnival ball with Lili and her relations, he poured his heart out to Auguste once again: "God knows I am a poor youth ... I wish I could rest on your hand, repose in your eyes ... In vain, my head is overstrained ... Oh, if I did not write dramas now, I should perish!" (Bell, pp. 228–229)

As evidence of this claim, Goethe wrote a new drama, *Stella*, during this period. This play, like *Clavigo*, which was written a short time later, features a fickle man who cannot commit to anyone. The protagonists of *Stella* and *Clavigo* are unable to love the women who respond with loving abandon. In these dramas, Goethe gives expression to his own conflicts and works through his relationship problems. However, his own life appeared quite complicated and confused, and in March, he wrote to Auguste zu Stolberg:

> It is time again for prosperity and adversity for me, so that I am not sure whether I am in the world, and then it seems to me that, indeed, I am in Heaven ... Go after me, I beg of you, go after me then with your letters and save me from myself.
>
> (FA 28, p. 441: DS)

Goethe became engaged to Lili Schönemann in April 1775. But there were impediments to the union, both Goethe's internal and external circumstances. Lili's mother did not approve of the young man's uncertain career prospects, and Goethe's parents were opposed to the young lady, as well. Goethe himself was seeking social advancement at that time, but he felt uncomfortable in the aristocratic circles Lili moved in. Three weeks after becoming engaged, Goethe began to avoid contact with Lili and struck out on a trip to Switzerland with some friends. He wanted to be independent and free again. At the end of May, he wrote the following to Johanna Fahlmer:

> Dear Aunt — In the open air! ... Louise[1] is an angel, the brilliant star could not withhold me from picking up a few flowers which fell from her bosom, and which I keep in the breast-pocket near my heart. Weimar also came and is kind to me ... Everything is better than I thought. Perhaps because I love I find everything lovable and good.
>
> (Bell, p. 243)

Goethe was able to breathe easily again and could go into raptures over Lili, now that he was far away from her. He stopped en route to Switzerland to visit his sister in Emmendingen, remaining ten days with the Schlossers. Continuing his journey, Goethe joined the Stolberg brothers and their friends, whose unfettered and carefree merriment he relished. On the one hand, he felt liberated, but on the other, his memories of Lili continued to have a stranglehold on him. On 15 June 1775, Goethe composed the poem "On the Lake" at Lake Zurich, revealing some of the psychological foundations for his fear of commitment, but also the coping strategies that had become typical for him:

> Now through my navel-string
> I suck nourishment from the world.
> And splendid all around is Nature,
> holding me to her bosom!
> The wave lifts and rocks our boat
> in the rhythm of the oars,
> and mountains, cloud-girt,
> counter our course.
>
> Eye, my eye, why do you fall?
> Golden dreams, can you return?
> Away, dream, gold though you be;
> Here too is love and life.
> On the wave there glitter
> a thousand drifting stars,
> dear mists all around drink up
> the towering distance,
> morning wind surrounds with wings
> the shadowed bay
> and in the lake is mirrored
> the ripening fruit.
>
> (Boyle 1991, p. 205)

The poetical self "sucks nourishment from the world" through its own umbilical cord. At first glance, this is a confusing image. Like Ovid's Narcissus, the poetical self is reflected in the nature around it, but unlike Narcissus, whose reflection vanishes when he approaches it, the poetical self is able to provide itself with vitally important psychological sustenance. Poetical creativity allows it to experience nature like a mother who "holds me to her bosom" and nourishes it. A womb-like sense of security is found in the poem when it describes how the "boat" of personal existence is gently rocked. But there is also an association with Moses and other royal children who were abandoned in boats. Yet the sense of being sustained and of oneness with nature dominates the poem. It is only in the second stanza that the poetical self is disturbed by a memory: "Eye, my eye, why do you fall?" It is reminded of "golden dreams", but also the golden cage, with Lili. However, the poetical self banishes troubling memories: "Here too is love and life." It revives the feeling of being sustained by nature, by the glittering and drifting stars, by the "dear mists" and by the winged "morning wind". There is even something intimate about the "sha-dowed" bay. Experiencing nature and experiencing culture coalesce into a sublime whole; here an intact sense of self and sense of the world are palpable. "And in the lake is mirrored the ripening fruit." This refers to the poet himself, his personality, and his artistic self, which, like someone enjoying art, has the experience of "finally releasing my soul entirely", as Goethe expresses it in his poem "To the Moon". At this time, though, he was not yet mature enough to experience this sense of fulfillment in a real romantic attachment.

In July, Goethe cut short his trip, which was supposed to take him as far as Italy, and returned home to Frankfurt. His inner turmoil was pushing him even further into a new crisis, and once again, he toyed with the idea of taking his own life. He complained that *Werther* was merely the babbling of children compared to his current state of suffering. In July 1775, he resumed his self-therapeutic exchange of letters with Auguste zu Stolberg:

> If I become too miserable, I will turn north, where she will be 200 miles behind me, dear sister [Auguste] ... I must be blown about even more, and then a moment against your heart! – That has always been my dream, my prospect as a result of a great deal of suffering ... Do not cease to be on my side as well.
>
> (FA 28, pp. 460f.: DS)

Three days later, Goethe appeared even more desperate when visiting with Lili's relations once again. In a room away from the others, but next to the room in which Lili was changing for a ball, he wrote the following letter to Auguste:

> and yet these tears and this oppression! What discord. O that I could tell you all! Here in the room of the girl who makes me unhappy, by no fault of hers, with the soul of an angel, whose bright days I trouble — I! ... In vain for three months have I wandered about in the open air, absorbing a thousand new objects in all my senses. Angel, and I am sitting again in Offenbach, become as simple as a child, confined as a parrot on the perch ... At night, on the terrace by the Maine [*sic*], I look across and think of you! ... and I

find no atmosphere for writing ... And yet, Angel, betimes when the need in my heart the greatest is, I call out, I call to you: Comfort! Comfort! Endured and it will happen ... It is this passion that will set us ablaze, in this moment of need we will gain ground and be dutiful, and act, and be good, and be driven, to where tranquility does not reach the mind ... It changes with me a hundred times a day! ... Often, even to me, the outlines of dearest friendship are dead letters [of the alphabet], when my heart is blind and deaf — Angel, it is a horrible state of futility. In the night, the heavens totter against darkness — Forgive me for this muddledness and everything — it is a good thing for me that I can speak so with you, a good thing when I think that you will hold this page in your hand! ... I will not be able to stand it here for long, I must leave again ... The Restless One. For God's sake let no one see my letters!

(Bell, pp. 247–248)[2]

This moving letter documents Goethe's struggle with his inner turmoil, illustrating painful and conflicting emotions. In Auguste, he had found a counterpart whom he hopesd would understand him. His letters to Auguste zu Stolberg resemble confessions, something very familiar to psychotherapists. The texts are not always so elaborate, but they are frequently just as moving. During periods of crisis, many people look for someone with whom they can share their inner turmoil. Relief and personal development often result from the effort of putting emotional conflicts into words and from finding support in a relatively neutral person, one who becomes a sounding board for chaotic feelings, as was the case here for Goethe. These confessions only become art, though, once they have been given a form that is poetic and universally valid.

The letter cited above is so psychologically revealing because it portrays what its author is experiencing: Goethe is in a separate room while his fiancée is dressing and elsewhere in the house, a party is going on. But he feels alone, excluded, and adrift. His passion is like a fire that he cannot contain or control. He must rein himself in, "be good", and suppress his chaotic drives. With Auguste's brothers, he felt happy and free; with Lili, depressed and bewildered. From a psychoanalytical point of view, we can determine that he was not yet able to integrate sexual arousal, emotional commitment, and a shared way of life at this time. It was logical that he would seek a respectful, understanding, but sufficiently distanced partner in the early stages of his identity diffusion, and he found one in Auguste. Between 14 and 19 September 1775, he wrote to her every night. In these letters, he seems restless and driven; even his new project, *Faust*, cannot set him at ease. After a sociable evening in company with Lili's circle of friends and relations, he confessed to Auguste:

Through all this, I was like a rat who has eaten poison, it runs into every hole, gulps down everything moist, swallows everything eatable that comes in its way, whilst its inside burns with inextinguishable destroying fire. A week-ago today Lili was here. And at that time I was in the fearfullest, gayest, sweetest state in all my life.

(Bell, p. 257)

This excerpt highlights Goethe's perturbation in the face of his sexual desire and his conflicted feelings in connection to it. He had no other option but to flee. After separating from Lili in mid-September 1775, he felt liberated and regained his equanimity; in October, the engagement was broken off. Through a stroke of luck, he was also able to distance himself physically from Lili and her circle of friends; the newlyweds Louise and Carl August von Weimar invited the poet to stay with them. He accepted the invitation with a thrill of pleasure, but also with wistful feelings. The poem "Bliss in Melancholy", which is said to have been written during this period, transformed Goethe's conflicting emotions into a work of art of unparalleled beauty:

Bliss in Melancholy

Don't dry, don't dry,
tears of eternal love!
Ah, to eyes that are only half dried
how dreary, how dead the world appears!
Don't dry, don't dry,
Tears of unhappy love!

(Appelbaum, p. 43)

Once again, Goethe portrays the importance in "eternal love" of enduring pain and sadness. Without tears, the world is lackluster and empty. In reality, he was not yet willing to acquiesce to a relationship that might have also had sad or unhappy aspects. While he was able to face this conflict in his poems, he could not do it in daily life. Thus, the poem does not evoke a concrete love, but rather "eternal love". Nevertheless, the reader is immediately moved by these six lines, surrounded in an enchantment that leaves a feeling of gratitude for life. Fifty years later, Goethe would look back on his complicated love for Lili while working on his memoirs. While thinking of her, and knowing that she had already passed away, he composed the poem "The Bridegroom" in 1824. The poem ends with the following words:

At midnight! — the bright stars, in vision blest,
Guide to the threshold where she slumbers calm:
Oh be it mine, there too at length to rest, —
Yet howsoe'er this prove, life's full of charm!

(Bowring, p. 65)

Here we see an example of Goethe's lifelong preoccupation with his relationships, something that appears to have been essential for him in order to develop his personal identity. In his paper of the same name, Sigmund Freud (1914) showed that *remembering, repeating*, and *working-through* are essential therapeutic principles that give coherence and structure to people and to their relationships. Goethe *remembered*, he *repeated* his conflicts over and over again, always in a new form, and he *worked through* them, especially in his work. This not only gave him a certain degree of mental stability, but it also made it possible for him to have at his disposal a unique abundance of emotions and insights.

Notes

1 Carl August von Weimar's bride, whom Goethe met in Karlsruhe.
2 Perhaps honoring the request in the last line, Bell did not include the full text of this letter, so I have translated parts of it myself. *Trans.*

Chapter 8

Early dramas

Reflection of Goethe's emotional conflicts

Oh, if I did not write dramas now, I should perish!

Goethe's dramas are important evidence of his path to self-realization, a journey which took the form of literary remembering, repeating, and working-through. During the years 1773 and 1775, it became evident just how essential it was to him to write dramas, allowing him to achieve emotional stability, coherence, and self-efficacy.

Prometheus

In the fragmentary drama *Prometheus*, Goethe addresses his growing conviction that his own experience and not God's design had made him the man he was. At the same time he was writing the play, he was asserting his independence from his parents. The protagonist of *Prometheus*, with whom Goethe identified, rebels against his mother and father at the beginning of the play. He is admonished, though, by Mercury, the messenger of the gods, and reminded that his parents gave him the gift of life and cared for him. He responds that they have already received in return his obedience as a child, as well as having the opportunity to form him according to their will.

The psychological dimensions of the dramatic fragment reveal Goethe's efforts toward autonomy. He attempts to dissociate himself not only from his parents, but also from any divine powers. This is reminiscent of the hubris of many adolescents who, in their narcissistic exuberance, wish to rid themselves of any ties they feel are holding them back. Goethe's Prometheus is defiant in his desire to be the creator of his own self. He employs the sarcastic coldness used so frequently by adolescents to make their parents' lives miserable. Goethe articulates the elevated feelings of the young person delighted by his first independent creations.

> *Prometheus.* Here's my world, my universe!
> Here I feel who I am!
> Here are all my wishes
> Embodied in physical forms,

>My spirit is divided thousandfold
>And whole in my precious children.
>   (Vs. 90–95)

Prometheus wants productive humans to reify themselves in their creations, an act that does not require ties to either parents or gods, and he triumphantly celebrates his independent artistry.

>*Prometheus.* Look down, oh Zeus,
>On my flourishing world.
>I have formed it in my likeness,
>Humans who are the same as me,
>To suffer, to weep, to enjoy, and be pleased by themselves,
>And without respect for you,
>Like I am!
>   (Vs. 241–247)

After uttering these words, which we recognize from the poem *Prometheus*, the poetical self dedicates himself to earthly things and encourages humans to take control of their own lives. Ultimately, Prometheus glorifies death as the final outcome of independent striving. As in *Werther*, desire, joy, and suffering dissipate in the sublime experience of the dissolution of boundaries that is death. This is not meant literally, though; rather, death leads to rebirth in an eternal cycle.

From a psychological point of view, the dominant theme in the fragmentary drama *Prometheus* is detachment from parents and religious authorities in order to poetically create one's own self. Goethe himself went through this transitional narcissistic stage, after which he overcame his adolescent self-referentiality and dedicated himself to his social relationships. His interpersonal conflicts and his strategies for solving them are expressed in his works with general validity, especially in *Clavigo, Stella, Brother and Sister*, and in the *Urfaust*. The self-reflection found in these dramas represents the pandemonium unique to human emotional development. These plays employ distinctly aesthetic forms to express general truths about mankind, hence their continued vitality. Although we are focusing on the psychological aspects of the plays, I would like to remind you that Goethe's dramas also include a wealth of religious, political, social, and artistic themes. I do not want to give the impression that psychological studies of the plays can completely explain them. What these studies can do, though, is shed light on important motifs that appear and are further developed in a particular work.

Clavigo

One of the primary themes of the tragedy *Clavigo*, written in 1774, is social advancement. Clavigo, the king's archivist, sees his writings as a means of enchanting women, but also securing and improving his position at court. The author wanting to establish himself in the world of the nobility and seeking social advancement was also one of Goethe's personal issues. Another theme found in the play is Clavigo's problems with commitment, a theme that reflects Goethe's own conflicts. Despite his desire for social recognition and advancement, Clavigo falls in love with Marie Beaumarchais, whose humble life makes her think she is not worthy of him, even though he himself is not someone of distinction. Clavigo is supported in his social ambitions by his friend Carlos, who warns Clavigo that he will not be able to perfect his talents with Marie at his side. Clavigo allows himself be convinced.

> *Clavigo*. Forward! forward! There it costs toil and art! One needs all his wits;
> and the women! the women! one loses far too much time with them.
> (*Works* 8, p. 160)

Clavigo is wracked with guilt over choosing to pursue his courtly ambitions over continuing his engagement with Marie and betraying her. He finds himself at odds with himself and his faithlessness, even as Carlos dangles the prospect of more eminent and more wealthy matches before him. Being jilted throws Marie into a state of despair. Her sister, Sophie, trying to comfort her, describes Clavigo's behavior as contemptible, but Marie is unable to hate him. Marie's brother, Beaumarchais, is the one to seek revenge; he demands that Clavigo confess to being a horrible person and to humiliating Marie for no reason. Moreover, he wants Clavigo to sign a statement so his misconduct will become common knowledge at court. Clavigo, feeling that he is in a hopeless situation, admits that he was led astray by his own vanity and appears remorseful. He wants to redeem himself and to marry Marie. Beaumarchais does not accede to this wish at first and insists on the declaration of guilt, but is led to make one concession: he will allow Clavigo to try to convince Marie of his contriteness and to propose to her before making the declaration public. Clavigo's effusive declaiming is successful, and he is able to reclaim Marie's hand.

Marie forgives Clavigo, and her brother (and avenger) also reconciles with him. Clavigo, though, remains weak-minded and proves to be easily swayed by Carlos's blandishments, such as his prediction of a future position as a minister of state for Clavigo, and once again, he talks him out of marrying Marie. Weak-willed, Clavigo agrees to take part in a scheme, but leaves the details to his friend Carlos. In the meanwhile, Marie finds herself in a whirlwind of emotions. Her doubts prove to be well-founded: Clavigo jilts her again. She dies of a broken heart, and Clavigo, despairing, slumps onto her coffin. While he is giving himself over to his pain, he is stabbed by Marie's brother. Collapsing, Clavigo whispers:

> *Clavigo (falling)*. I thank thee, brother; thou marriest us.
> (*Works* 8, p. 208)

Here, love has again become an experience of boundaries dissolving, an experience beyond the behavioral norms of the bourgeoisie or nobility; it can only be consummated in death. Goethe had not yet succeeded in entering into a romantic relationship in his own life, and Clavigo, uncertain and ambivalent, was a reflection of this. In *Poetry and Truth* he wrote,

> At the time when I was troubled by my grief at Frederica's sad position, I again, as had ever been my wont, sought the aid of poetry. I continued that confession in verse which I had already begun, so that by this self-tormenting penance I might be worthy of inner absolution. The two Marys in *Götz von Berlichingen* and *Clavigo*, and the two bad characters who play the part of lovers to them, may have been the results of such penitent reflections.
>
> (Smith, vol. 2, p. 68)

As a matter of fact, many of the conflicts having an impact on Goethe's life in 1774 were compressed into *Clavigo*. The tone of the piece is also reminiscent of many passages found in his letters to Charlotte Buff and Auguste zu Stolberg, including a desire for social advancement into the highest circles, a fear of endangering his career by entering into a serious relationship, and unconscious anxieties about committing himself to one woman. Also notable are his feelings of guilt toward Friederike Brion, feelings he was unable to shake for many years, and his sensitivity to the sufferings of jilted women. What is astounding is his admitting his own lack of determination and weakness.

Stella

Like *Clavigo*, the central theme of *Stella, A Play for Lovers*, is the problem of an indecisive man. Fernando, a young nobleman, is imaginative and affectionate, but unable to make a commitment. This leads him to abandon Cecilia and their daughter, Lucy, to seek happiness with Stella. But it is not long before he deserts her, too. The play opens at an inn, where Cecilia and Lucy have stopped for the night before presenting themselves the next day to the baroness Stella, whose companion Lucy will be. Cecilia is practical and has come to terms with the loss of Fernando, but she has also lost all of her zest for life and every hope of finding love in the future. On his way back to Stella, Fernando encounters Lucy, quite by accident, but they do not realize that they are father and daughter. Lucy, lively and chatty, tells him about her mother's unhappy situation; nevertheless, she says she is grateful to her unknown father for siring her. They discuss love and disappointment, and Fernando, when taking his leave, exclaims, "He who lives may lose" (Boyesen, vol. 3, p. 190).

In the second act, in which Stella meets Lucy, her future lady's companion, and Lucy's mother, Cecilia, we are able to see the baroness's burning longing for love.

Stella. . . . And yet why should I not love? I need much, very much to satisfy this heart of mine! Much? Poor Stella! Much? – . . . *For a moment she is lost in thought, then quickly starts up, and presses her hands to her heart.* No! Fernando, no! I did not mean to reproach thee!

(Boyesen, vol. 3, p. 191)

Goethe's empathetic, psychologically differentiated portrayal of Stella and the other female characters in the play is impressive. Fernando, though, remains a flat character, one unable to win much sympathy from an audience. This portrayal is an expression of Goethe's self-criticism and feelings of guilt about his faithlessness and coldness.

In the play, Stella and Fernando are reunited in the third act. Overjoyed, they embrace each other and promise to be eternally faithful. Shortly after this lovers' oath, Fernando encounters his wife, Cecilia, who has brought her daughter Lucy to meet Stella prior to becoming her lady's companion; he does not recognize her at first. When he becomes aware that his wife is standing before him, he quickly leaves the room, but he soon returns to hear her life story. In the end, both are so moved that they fall into an embrace and Fernando swears eternal devotion to her. He concocts a plan to flee with Cecilia and their daughter. But once alone, he is immediately beset by doubts. The tone of his soliloquy is strikingly similar to that of one of Goethe's letters to Auguste zu Stolberg.

Fernando. (Alone.) Away? – Whither? whither? –A dagger stroke would clear the way for all these pains and hurl me into that dull insensibility for which now I would give everything . . . Oh, my sin, my sin weighs heavy upon me at this moment! Both these dear ones deserted! And I, at the moment when I find them again, deserted by myself! Oh, my heart!

(Boyesen, vol. 3, p. 200)

Fernando remains weak-willed, and his feelings of guilt seem self-referential and superficial. We get no sense that he is interested in these women or even loves them; rather, he is only concerned with his own pleasures and sufferings. Both readers and theater-goers are exasperated by his narcissistic behavior. We are reminded of Goethe's lack of determination and equivocation, which certainly tormented his lady friends but also stabilized his narcissistic equilibrium. His feelings of guilt were of no use to Käthchen, Friederike, Charlotte, or Lili, but he was able to employ his effusive, self-referential feelings to pull himself out of the morass of his fear of commitment. Fernando acts in a similar way.

In the fourth act, Fernando meets with Stella again. She is full of happiness, but Fernando is full of doubt and lies to Stella. He is completely absorbed by his own sensations and has no sense of his beloved's feelings. A servant interrupts Stella's eulogizing of love and Fernando's tactical maneuvering to remind him that it was time to leave, because Cecilia and Lucy were waiting for him, as they had all agreed on. At first, Stella cannot believe this betrayal, but she is forced to the realization that she has been deceived. Fernando continues to be self-referential, though, and dwells on self-recrimination.

> *Fernando.* Stella, I am a scoundrel and a coward and can hide nothing from thee! Flee! I have not the heart to thrust the dagger into thy breast and would secretly poison thee, murder thee! Stella!
>
> (Boyesen, vol. 3, p. 203)

At this point, he explains that Cecilia is his wife and Lucy his daughter, and Stella faints. Fernando is completely helpless; Lucy must revive Stella. When Fernando takes to his heels, the three women affirm their mutual affection and esteem.

In the fifth act, we find Stella immersed in her pain. She is unable to part with Fernando; her love for him is too strong. Meanwhile, Fernando is immersed in a soliloquy, full of complicated feelings of guilt. He thinks about Stella's despair, but he himself feels cold, and he considers suicide. This is reminiscent of so-called narcissistic suicide, which was covered during our discussion of *Werther*: someone immature, who does not actually want to die, will resort to suicide to preserve their self-image when faced with a humiliating reality.

Cecilia is much more clear-headed and finds that the best solution would be for her to leave. Fernando does not want to accept this sacrifice, but Cecilia convinces him with a story: A count left his wife behind to travel to the Holy Land. He was captured there, but the daughter of his master freed him. They survived the hardships of war together, and the count brought her with him when he returned home. His wife accepted this rival, the three rejoiced in their love, and God's representative on earth gave them his blessing. At the end of the earliest version of this play, after narrating the story, Cecilia calls Stella to her; everyone seems to be reconciled to each other, and they embrace.

> *Stella, on his neck.* I may? -
> *Cecilia.* Will you thank me, that I called you back, fugitive?
> *Stella, on her neck.* Oh, you! – –
> *Fernando, embracing both.* Mine! Mine!
> *Stella, holding his hand, hanging on him.* I am yours!
> *Cecilia, holding his hand, on his neck.* We are yours!

Later, Goethe found this ending implausible, so he made significant changes for the 1806 stage version. The *ménage à trois* was exposed as not being a real solution.

For Goethe, both *Stella* and *Clavigo* were a confession and an attempt at self-healing, rolled into one. His bewildering relationship with Lili, as well as his memory of the abandoned Friederike, had a variety of effects on *A Play for Lovers*. As in *Clavigo*, the protagonist, here Fernando, is portrayed as untruthful, unconcerned, and weak, but the author shows a great deal of respect toward the female characters, writing them as differentiated figures and with empathy. In a set of notes for the performance, Goethe specified the following: "Cecilia will soon leave behind her initial appearance of being weak and oppressed and will appear before us in splendor, free, as a heroine of the spirit and the mind". Psychologically, Goethe's delineation of Stella's character is even more trenchant and multilayered: "She must not only display an indestructible affection, her ardent love, her glowing enthusiasm, she must convey her feelings to us, must sweep us along with her" (HA 4, p. 574: DS).

Stella is completely in love, authentically and passionately, and both women reveal a deep benevolence, but Fernando remains fickle, weak, and banal – a buffoon. We can surmise that Goethe was staging his own negative sides here – buffoon or popinjay – in order to work them through. The next tragedy he would write would portray a mature man who overcomes the fickleness and narcissism of adolescence with deeper feelings and more significant, but also more dangerous, deeds: Faust.

Urfaust

Goethe began his literary treatment of the Faust legend in 1773, and in October of 1774, his friend Boie wrote in his journal,

> Spent a whole day alone, uninterrupted, with Goethe; with Goethe, whose heart is as great and noble as his spirit! … He had to read much to me, completed and fragmentary, and in everything – the original voice, his power, and in the case of everything peculiar or irregular – all of it bears the stamp of his genius. His "Doctor Faust" is almost complete and appears to me to be the greatest and most idiosyncratic of them all.
>
> (HA 3, p. 423: DS)

And in fact, the *Urfaust* is an authentic expression of Goethe's hopes and fears, his striving and seeking, "original and idiosyncratic". As such, it is appropriate for summing up our reflections on Goethe's psychological development over his lifetime.

Faust accompanied Goethe through almost 60 years of his life. In July 1831, he recorded the following in a letter:

> It is wondrous, how egotism – particularly isolating, partially revolutionary, partially reclusive egotism – pervades lively activities of every kind. Mine, I just want to confess, I have withdrawn into the core of production, and I have arranged the second part of "Faust", which I took up again in earnest a full 4 years ago, in itself … I have known for a long time what, even how,

> I wanted it, and I have carried it around with me for so many years like an inner fairytale ... Even if it contains problems enough, because solving the last problem always presents – the same as in world and human history – a new problem to solve, it will certainly please those who are experts at expressions, hints, and quiet suggestions. They will even find more than I was able to give.
>
> (HA 3, p. 459: DS)

The "inner fairytale" Goethe carried around with him fulfilled a vital function. The "transitional object" is familiar to us from psychoanalysis (Winnicott, 1971). This is an object such as a pacifier or a blanket, later a doll or a teddy bear, that a small child lays claim to and that gives the child a feeling of familiarity, stability, and continuity. The transitional object mediates between external and internal reality: on the one hand, it is a real object, but on the other hand, the child has used its imagination to turn the object into something particular to the child. In adulthood, the continual challenge of creating a coherent bond between internal and external reality leads to the motivation to work and to be creative. These activities arise not only from "reclusive egotism", but also from the need to be seen and responded to. This is why the reader, listener, and viewer are so important; they have the right to "find more" than the author was "able to give". Communication with the author develops within this "more", an idea that was definitely in accordance with Goethe's views.

Much remained hidden even to the author himself, though, which Goethe described in December of 1831 thusly:

> About my "Faust" there's a lot and little to be said ... Through a mysterious psychological development (which perhaps deserves closer study) I think I lifted myself to a level of production which created in a condition of complete consciousness material which still meets with my approval, without perhaps ever being able to swim in this river again, indeed what Aristotle and other writers would ascribe to a kind of madness.
>
> (qtd. in Parry)

He is clearly referring to unconscious processes that take a conscious shape during artistic production and are then surrendered back to unconscious and intuitive thinking. It is left to the reader, who can also be the author, to understand the unconscious content. This is one of Goethe's most important health strategies, one which psychoanalysts, for instance, also consider to be a decisive factor in effective psychotherapeutic treatment. During therapy, the patient's narrative imposes a coherent structure on chaotic emotions and diffuse mental processes, which has a salubrious effect. Therapists act as midwives – practitioners of maieutics – to help birth the fruit of psychological organization. Another strand of psychology, cognitive behavioral therapy, also considers the creation of a coherent narrative to be an essential factor in order for therapy to be effective. These views are supported by findings from neuroscience, which show that both conscious and unconscious intellectual activity lead to vitally important coherent networks (Holm-Hadulla 2013). Freud (1923) probably had biopsychosocial coherence in mind when he penned his famous dictum "Where id is, there shall ego be".

The *Urfaust* seems to be just such a narrative, one that synthesizes physical, mental, and social experiences into a coherent whole. Goethe had committed most of the play to paper before departing for Weimar in the fall of 1775; the extant version was copied during the winter of 1775/1776. This early work wonderfully compresses together the previously discussed aspects of Goethe's psychological development. It also serves as a useful summary of this psychobiography so far.

First, the *Urfaust* documents the importance of remembering, experiencing followed by reflecting, and literary working-through. Starting in childhood, the poet found a "transitional space" in the acts of re-experiencing, imaginative staging, and poetical creation, a space where he developed his internal and external reality. In the process, he, like every other child, also had to learn to deal with horrors. In Goethe's case, his early intellectual processing was an important factor. There is documented evidence from at least since the time of his brother Heinrich's death that Goethe attempted to cope with painful experiences using his powers of thought and imagination. But not everything can be overcome by means of mental effort, which is why "intellectualization" is often used as a pejorative in psychological circles. This term refers to ostensible attempts to work through feelings and experiences using reasoning, but actually, the feelings and experiences are merely repressed. This is the psychological punch-line to the "Scholar's Tragedy" in the *Urfaust*, which the later versions of *Faust* hewed closely to. The frequently quoted beginning of the *Urfaust* – "Now I've studied, oh . . ." – shows the limitations of human intellect. Faust not only recognizes that "there's nothing we can ever know", but he also feels that his "search for truth ends in confusion". For this reason, he abandons himself to unconscious powers in order to understand life.

> *Faust* . . .
> I'll know what makes the world revolve,
> Its inner mysteries resolve,
> No more in empty words I'll deal –
> Creation's wellsprings I'll reveal!
> (Vs. 29–32)

Faust seeks life and joy and creates a magical relationship between heavenly bodies, classical deities, and the spirit world.

> *Faust*. . . .
> How all into a wholeness weaves,

Each in the other moves and lives!
The powers of heaven ascending and descending,
And to each other golden vessels sending,
With fragrant blessings winging,
From heaven to earth their bounty bringing –
In harmony the universe is ringing!

(Vs. 94–100)

But his excitement is short-lived, and even observing the ordered cosmos cannot still his yearning.

Faust. . . .
Ah, what a spectacle! But a spectacle, and no more.
Where can I grab you, infinite nature?
Your breasts, where? The springs of all life,
On which heaven and earth hangs on,
To which the wilting breast is urged -
You pour, you saturate and I languish in vain?

(Vs. 101–106)

Carnal desire makes itself felt here, but Faust, submerged in the chaos of his thoughts and feelings, wishes to be free of it. But first he continues to search through his own ideas and discovers the Earth Spirit. This figure is Goethe's own mythical creation. He sees in it the origin and the actuating principle of life.

Spirit. In all life's storms and surging tides
I ebb and flow
From birth to grave,
Weave to and fro,
An endless wave
In all life's changes.
On time's humming loom, as I toil at the treads,
For God's living garment I fashion the threads.

(Vs. 149–156)

From a psychological point of view, the Earth Spirit represents unconscious, biological powers. It can only approximate an understanding of conscious thought.

Faust. Industrious spirit, to the world's furthest end
You rove; how close you seem to me!
Spirit. You match the spirit that you comprehend,
Not me! *(Vanishes.)*
Faust (shattered). Not you?

Who then?
I, made in God's image,
No match for you?

(Vs. 157–164)

The limitedness, even laughableness, of every effort to cope intellectually with life is demonstrated in a dialogue between Faust and his assistant Wagner. In contrast, Mephistopheles teaches that gross sensuality can lead to knowledge.

Mephistopheles. . . .
We all learn only what we can.
But who seizes the chance,
He is the right man . . .
Especially learn to guide the women!
Their everlasting woe and ache
So thousandfold
Is to be cured from one point.

(Vs. 410–420)

While searching for "what makes the world revolve", Faust encounters Gretchen[1] and is immediately enchanted.

Faust. That girl is just so lovely, she
Has really captivated me.
Demure and virtuous, you can tell –
But with an impish look as well.
And such red lips and cheeks so bright,
How could you ever forget that sight!

(Vs. 461–466)

He seeks to break through the dark boundaries of thought by means of sensual pleasure and to allow love to cast a spell on him.

Faust. . . .
Is there some magic spell around me?
I lusted for her, and I find
A dream of love comes to confound me.
Are we the playthings of a breath of wind?

And what if she should come while you are here?
You'd answer for your recklessness, and all
Your bold bravado would just disappear –
Abject and sighing at her feet you'd fall.

(Vs. 573–580)

Faust, however, must avail himself of Mephistopheles' help, which leads to him becoming ensnared in a web of lies. During this process, certain themes become obvious, themes that Goethe himself was occupied with. He continued to experience feelings of guilt over Friederike and his faithlessness, yet a more mature longing for a real partner had taken hold of him. As we have already seen, there is evidence for this in Gretchen's song, "The King of Thule". But Faust had gotten himself entangled in murderous deeds. If the ostensible accidents in *Faust* are taken as an expression of an unconscious tendency, then the following interpretation would be the logical result: Faust has Gretchen drug her mother with a sleeping potion, which leads to the mother's death. This could be an indication that sexual union signifies a parting or separation from the mother. Nevertheless, Faust fears he is not man enough to permanently endure the closeness resulting from this union, or to be a father. Like many of the protagonists in Goethe's plays, to say nothing of Goethe himself, Faust remains an indecisive man fearing to lose his freedom and productivity to romantic attachment and fatherhood. He seeks the experience of dissolving boundaries, but impersonally; he is unable to view Gretchen as either a person or a partner. In the end, Gretchen, the incarnation of the loving wife, is destroyed.

> *Gretchen. . . .*
> Wherever I may be,
> I feel such misery
> Within my bosom aching.
> When I am on my own
> I weep, I weep alone,
> My fearful heart is breaking.
>   (Vs. 1293–1298)

The fruit of their love, the child, must also die. Although Faust is tormented by guilt, he is incapable of saving Gretchen or his child. Goethe describes Gretchen's tragedy with astonishing empathy. Her blinding love for Faust – psychologically speaking, the idealization of the love interest – allows her to become guilty without guilt. Faust pushes her pregnancy to the back of his mind, nor can it be a coincidence that, in the hectic activity of both the *Urfaust* and its later version, Gretchen's pregnancy is almost completely omitted. This could be a hint that Goethe also had problems with the outward signs of female fertility. It is well known that he reacted fearfully to physical changes and that he found it difficult to see both his wife Christiana and his closest friends during their illnesses. Faust is just as weak, fickle, and unfaithful after he has ruined Gretchen. While he does feel sorry for her, using tender words, he is unable to help her in any way.

> *Faust.* In misery and despair! Pitifully wandering the country all this time! That sweet, hapless creature shut up in a dungeon as a criminal, exposed to appalling suffering. For so long! And you kept this from

me, you treacherous, despicable demon! Yes, stand there rolling your malevolent devil's eyes at me, stand and defy me with your insufferable company. In prison! At the mercy of evil spirits and the pitiless judgement of humanity, in irredeemable misery. And meanwhile you lull me with vulgar pleasures, you conceal her growing misery from me and let her perish helplessly.

(Williams, p. 438)

The above dialogue with Mephistopheles rather resembles a soliloquy. Faust makes vague attempts to free Gretchen that are ultimately unsuccessful. He must listen to her hallucinations and helplessly watch her downfall.

> *Gretchen.*
> My mother, the whore, she's
> Murdered me.
> My father, the villain, he's
> Eaten me.
> My little sister found
> The bones that lay around.
> In a cool place she laid them down.
> I turned into a little bird that day.
> Fly away! Fly away!
> (Williams, p. 440)

In this gruesome song of Gretchen's, the parents' relationship to the child is portrayed as violent, even cannibalistic, in opposition to the ideal of parental love firmly established in her culture. The child psychoanalyst Melanie Klein (1957) has argued quite plausibly that an unconscious wish for annihilation could also play a role in normal parent–child relationships. Marie Langer (1987), in her book *Das gebratene Kind und andere Mythen* (*The Roasted Child and Other Myths*), describes how ancient communities would eat their children in times of famine. This cultural inheritance is frequently portrayed in fairytales such as "Hansel and Gretel" and "The Juniper Tree", the source of Gretchen's song. Here we get a glimpse into Goethe's lifelong preoccupation with infanticide. We might ask whether he was processing and giving form to the hazy, unconscious fears and proto-mental impressions of a small child who had wordlessly witnessed his siblings' deaths, in the womb and in the cradle, and the ensuing atmosphere in his home. A causal link cannot be directly drawn between this point and Goethe's interest in women who killed their children, yet all of these elements visibly play an important role in many of his works. If Goethe's poetical work were a form of atonement for the archaic destructiveness mentioned above, this would be relevant for our understanding of his tireless artistic activity.

We know from developmental psychology that very young children in Goethe's situation feel responsible for their siblings' deaths and for their parents' distress. Viewed from this perspective, art serves the same function as the pages the eight-year-old Goethe composed for his dead brother Heinrich: it resurrects the dead and makes amends for something terrible. Faust is unable to do this. He remains helpless and unable to free Gretchen. Neither his love nor his art are able to make amends for what has happened.

> *Margarete*. Kiss me! Can't you kiss any more? What? Why? You're my Heinrich, and you've forgotten how to kiss? Once I felt all heaven overwhelm me in your arms. You used to kiss as if you would stifle me and kill me with passion. Heinrich, kiss me – or else I'll kiss you! *(She seizes him.)* Oh, no! Your lips are cold! Dead! They don't respond!
>
> (Williams, p. 441)

In the end, Margarete begs Faust to live so he can arrange for the graves of all those who have died. One of the most important functions of art is symbolized here: It should act as a witness to events and should remember, repeat, and work-through the sufferings and joys we have experienced. Remembering, repeating, and working-through are lifelong tasks people repeatedly fail at. Thus, when Goethe became a member of the highest advisory body in Weimar, he lost all sensitivity toward and empathy for a desperate woman who had killed her illegitimate infant; he was jointly responsible for the decision to execute the 24-year-old maidservant.

Note

1   Short form of Margarete, which is used more in the *Urfaust*.

Chapter 9

Period of maturity
Weimar, 1775–1786

Tell me, what will fate have in store for us?
Tell me, how did it bind us together so perfectly tight?
Ah, in ages long past you were
my sister or my wife.

The Duke of Saxony-Weimar, 18-year-old Carl August, sought an encounter with Goethe at the instigation of his mother, Anna Amalia. During a trip to visit his future bride, he stopped in Frankfurt, where he held long conversations with Goethe about public policy. The two men got on together so well that Carl August soon offered him a position as a civil servant in Weimar. During his mother's 17-year regency there, she had fostered the arts and sciences. Anna Amalia was highly educated, composed music, and was widely read, which is how Goethe had come to her attention. For instance, she was so taken with his ballad *Erwin und Elmire* that she composed music to accompany it.

For Goethe, the invitation from Carl August was a welcome opportunity to withdraw from the awkward situation in Frankfurt. Even though his engagement to Lili Schönemann had been broken off, he continued to feel uncomfortable and tried to completely avoid Lili and the circles she moved in Frankfurt. He arrived in Weimar on 7 November 1775, and immediately found himself a member of a circle of important men that included Wieland, Carl August's tutor, and von Knebel, the tutor of the duke's younger brother, Prince Constantin. Not two months after his arrival, Goethe wrote to Johanna Fahlmer at the new year:

> I ought to write to my mother, therefore I write to you, that you may together enjoy and digest my letter. I am still in the most desirable position in the world. I am hovering over all the most secret and important matters, have a happy influence, enjoy myself, learn and so on.

(Bell, p. 274)

Goethe had escaped from the embarrassing emotional and social situation in Frankfurt, but he quickly filled the void left by Cornelia, Friederike, Charlotte, and Lili with Charlotte von Stein, a lady-in-waiting at the court in Weimar.

Within a very short time after his arrival in Weimar, he had made her acquaintance and had immediately become entangled with her in an infatuation. Höfer (2002) has described her as delicate and sickly. She also resembled Goethe's sister Cornelia in that she was cool and stern. She was unhappily married to the duke's stable master, and her seven pregnancies had taken a heavy toll on her health. Moreover, only three of her children survived childhood. It stands to reason that Goethe had sensed something of this when he made her his new unattainable beloved. Charlotte von Stein may have resembled Cornelia, Goethe's sister, but she had also suffered a fate similar to that of Catharina Elisabeth, Goethe's mother, which may have contributed to his effusive love for her. When he writes to Charlotte von Stein that, "in ages long past", she would have been his "sister or his wife", he seems to be adding her to the constellation of relationships that connected him to his mother, to his sister, to Auguste zu Stolberg, and to other women. He projected onto Charlotte his ideals of female companionship in order to cope with his own wounds and the wounds of the women in his life.

His infatuation with Charlotte was urgent, sometimes even unbridled. Goethe visited her almost daily after making her acquaintance. He assailed her with letters like the following, which he sent her at the end of January 1776: "dear Lady, suffer because I love you so. If I can love someone more, I want to tell it to you. Want to leave you unvexed. Adieu, Gold. You don't comprehend, *how much* I love you" (FA 29, p. 20: DS).

During this period, he ceased corresponding with Auguste zu Stolberg, and his relationship with Cornelia also began to fade. He allowed himself to become utterly captivated by Charlotte von Stein, or rather, he captivated her in order to stage his own personal drama with her anew. He not only made her his platonic ideal of a beloved, he also brought his emotional conflicts up to date in the relationship. Some of the time, this relationship resembled the therapeutic relationship found in psychoanalysis, much like his earlier relationship with Auguste zu Stolberg. In February, Goethe (under the alias "Gustel") wrote to Charlotte von Stein,

> I must leave, but you should still have a good night anyway. You, the only one I can love so much without it vexing me – And yet I live half in fear – Now it may be. All my trust belongs to you, and God willing, you should also gradually have all my intimacy. Oh, if only my sister had a brother like I have a sister in you. Think of me, and press your hand to your lips, because you will not break Gustel of his bad habits; they will only end along with his agitation and love in the grave. Good night. Once again, I only saw your eyes during the whole of the masked ball.
>
> (FA 29, p. 25: DS)

A short time later, after meeting the singer and actress Corona Schröter, Goethe took up his pen during the night to write, "Adieu. I am dulled with sleep. – Schröter is an angel – If God wanted to give me such a wife that I could leave you two together in peace – but she does not look enough like you. Adieu. —" (FA 29, p. 30: DS). In April 1776, he characterized his mysterious spiritual kinship with Charlotte thusly:

> I cannot explain the significance, the power, that this woman has over me in any other way than by the transmigration of souls. Yes, we once were man and wife! Now we know each other – but veiled, in an ethereal aura. I have no name for us – the past – the future – the universe.
>
> (Boerner, p. 44: DS)

This letter forcibly illustrates that Goethe's infatuation, which appears extravagant to the modern reader, represents the concentration of various emotional tendencies. On the one side, we find the erotic longing for human completeness achieved by the union of man and woman, as portrayed by Plato in his mythological *Symposium*. Moreover, his advances toward Charlotte fulfilled his wish of understanding the inner life of women. Here, as in his relationship with Cornelia, Goethe showed a special ability to dissociate himself from his male role and to perceive and affirm the female side of himself and others. It is possible that this ability to transcend a fixed psychosexual role schema, which could be described as bisexual openness, was an important impetus to or factor in his creativity. He played out various relationship conflicts, fantasies, and moods in his work, compressing together diverse experiences. In the poem "To Charlotte von Stein", he describes the fanciful projections that led to him idealizing Charlotte.

> Why did you give us the deep insight
> enabling us to see hints of our future,
> so that we can no longer, in a blissful delusion,
> trust our love, our earthly happiness?
> Why, fate, did you give us feelings
> enabling us to read each other's hearts
> in order to spy out our true situation
> amid all the strange turmoils?
> [...]
> loving each other without understanding each other,
> seeing in each other something we never were,
> setting out to find a dreamer's happiness again and again,
> and also wavering in the danger of dreams.
> [...]
> Tell me, what will fate have in store for us?
> Tell me, how did it bind us together so perfectly tight?
> Ah, in ages long past you were
> my sister or my wife.
> ...
>
> (Appelbaum, pp. 45–47)

In the poem, the poetical self is faced with the very human fate of having a presentiment of its future. It knows that love and happiness will not ever be complete and wonders why it does not venture to trust to fortune. Only through "feelings" can it become close to and to understand the other person, i.e. "to read each other's hearts". The poetical self loves without understanding, seeing in the other person something it never was, which describes the previously mentioned fanciful projections that always end with the "dreamer's happiness". In real life, the two were not able to surrender to each other as if in a dream. The poetical self, however, is able to express its dreams and longings in the poem and to experience anew the fantasies and fears of "ages long past". As a result, echoes of earlier relationships are found in the relationship with Frau von Stein, and they are remembered, enacted, and transformed again.

Goethe was bound to Charlotte von Stein by more than the feelings and longings he had encountered with his mother and sister. Needless to say, his conscious and unconscious erotic fantasies originated also in his other relationships and also in his narcissistic relationship with himself. Nevertheless, it is possible that, in his relationship with Charlotte, he was unconsciously seeking to rediscover his relationships with his mother, his dead siblings, and his sister, and to come to terms with them by enacting them anew.

In the real world, Goethe cared devotedly for Charlotte's son Fritz. His motivation for educating this boy, on a deep, unconscious level, may have been resurrecting his dead siblings. Perhaps he was driven by his infatuation with Charlotte to give new life to her mortally wounded inner child and her lost hopes. Perhaps he was using projection to combat his own fear of death. This concentration of hopes and fears meant that their relationship had to remain unfulfilled; otherwise, Goethe would have once again come too close to the "untrodden, not be trodden" realm of the Mothers. As in the creative process described in the "Dark Gallery" scene, he successfully drew creative energy from the interaction between his amorous inclinations and renunciation.

Goethe and Charlotte shared many ideas and suggestions with each other, and they repeatedly bolstered each other in the face of a life potentially filled with boredom and ossification. Charlotte, though, withheld any kind of erotic intimacy from Goethe and moderated his agitation and exuberance. She had a cathartic influence on his restlessness. In the poem "Huntsman's Evening Song", it says:

> Whenever I think of you, I feel
> as if I were looking at the moon;
> a quiet peace comes over me,
> I don't know how it has happened.
> (Appelbaum, p. 43)

The following lines from "To the Moon" have a similarly soothing effect:

Blessed is the man who shuts himself off
from the world without hatred,
clasps a friend to his breast,
and, together with him, enjoys

that which, not known to people
or not considered,
walks through the labyrinth of the heart
in the night.

(Appelbaum, p. 51)

Even after the initial turbulence had subsided, the first ten years of their relationship were not always as serene and harmonious as the poems quoted above would suggest. While it is true that Goethe saw Charlotte as a muse, someone congenial to his political, social, and pedagogical work, he was nevertheless rankled by her complete rejection of physical closeness. He wrote to her in October of 1776, "You have appeared to me for some time like Madonna rising to Heaven, and he who was left behind stretches out his arms to her in vain" (HA Letters 1, p. 229: DS). But the sweet misery of being unable to find sexual fulfillment with her only drew him more tightly to her. Hope and painful renunciation continued to be essential elements of Goethe's creative energy.

During his first few months in Weimar, Goethe developed a close friendship with Duke Carl August, only 18 years old at the time. In December 1775, Goethe penned a letter to Carl August late in the evening, before going to bed, and added the following verses:

Be happy midst the hundred lights aglow
That brightness round thee spend,
And faces all arow
That round about thee bend,
And at the board attend.
Yet wilt though find true joy and peace alone
Midst souls as true and simple as thine own.

(Bell, p. 269)

Goethe moderated the duke's unruly, impetuous behavior at that time in a sustainable way. He entered into Carl August's excesses, at least in part; rumors floated around about their wild, boisterous doings. Johann Heinrich Voss wrote to his bride during the summer of 1776, full of indignation about the state of affairs there: "Alarming things are happening in Weimar. The Duke chases round the villages with Goethe like a wild lad; he gets drunk and enjoys his girls with him like a brother" (FA 29, p. 737). Clearly, Goethe shared many an adventure with Carl August, but more importantly, he was able to gain Carl August's trust and hence to have a lasting influence on the duke in his role as a teacher and advisor. He was very successful in nurturing Carl August's personal development, which the court at Weimar observed with appreciation. Later, Goethe remarked to Eckermann that "in the beginning he caused me much trouble and anxiety. Yet his noble nature soon cleared itself, and formed itself to the highest degree of perfection, so that it was a pleasure to live and act with him" (Oxenford, pp. 102–103). The Duchess Anna Amalia was especially pleased with his cultivating effect on her son, while Goethe himself seemed to find emotional stability in dealing with Carl August. He was able to experience the turmoil of being 18 again, without being caught up in the powerful mood swings of late adolescence.

During this period, his emotional equilibrium was influenced both by his relationships with Charlotte and Carl August and his focused, objective professional activity. He was involved in a great deal of work in the administration of the government, and he carried out his tasks conscientiously and discreetly. In June 1776, he was made a member of the duke's privy council, which was composed of three highly influential men, for which he received a handsome salary. His elevated professional and social position increased his sense of self-worth considerably. He wrote the following to his friend Merck in January 1776: "My position is advantageous enough, and the Duchies of Weimar and Eisenach are at all events a stage on which to try how one's rôle in life suits one" (Bell, p. 276). Goethe's friend Wieland, in turn, wrote in June 1776,

> I have not *been able* to see our Goethe for eight days. He is now Privy Councillor and has a seat in the ministry of our Duke – he is favourite minister, factotum, and bears the sins of the world. He will do a lot of good, hinder a lot of evil, and that will have to console us, if it is possible, for the fact that as poet he is lost to the world for many years.
>
> (Ghibellino, p. 37)

Goethe himself commented on "the pervading vileness of this temporal splendour" (Bell, p. 276).

His salary, as stated in many legal documents, was large, especially after 1777, when he took over the leadership of the mining commission in addition to his duties as one of the duke's councilors. The level of industry in the duchy was very low, causing much suffering among the populace; Goethe was quite affected by both of these problems. For 30 years, he tried to improve the duchy's mining capabilities, with little success. Nevertheless, he found his economic, social, and political activities fulfilling. They gave him the opportunity to be effective and useful. His interest in mines and mining continued unabated into old age; at the age of 81, he took his two grandchildren on a trip to familiarize them with mining. Despite this, he did not completely throw himself into his work with the government during his first period of living in Weimar; he was frequently involved in arranging parties, readings, and theater performances. Then, in the midst of these happy times, he received a message on 16 June 1777, announcing the death of his sister.

Cornelia's life had taken an unhappy turn. After her marriage to Schlosser, a jurist 11 years her senior, in 1773, she moved with him to Emmendingen, where he took a respectable civil servant position. Goethe had reacted to her marriage with jealousy; her husband was of the opinion that her love for her brother was the reason why she was unable to feel a deeper affection for himself. Her letters show her rejection of herself and her own femininity. Her first pregnancy was very difficult, and she spent a lot of time on bed rest; it was a long time before she recovered after the birth. She felt apathetic and depressed and was demoralized by her "continual ailments of the body". In her letters, Cornelia described a "sort of melancholy" that persisted for two years. She felt lonely and was unable to be creative on her own terms without the motivation of her brother. While still in Frankfurt, she wrote in her journal that her days were very monotonous and that the retirement she found herself in held no attractions for her. Unlike her brother, who reacted to the blues with creative work, Cornelia was unable to be active during her depressive periods. She wrote plaintively from Emmendingen, "It is quite bad, that I cannot employ myself with anything, not with sewing, or with reading, or with playing the piano".

Cornelia recuperated slowly during the spring and summer of 1775, and by the beginning of the year 1776, she felt new made, thanks to the physician and philosophical writer Johann Georg Zimmermann. Zimmermann was respected as a good psychologist, and Goethe commented that he had enchanted the whole world, "especially the ladies". After visiting with Cornelia's parents, Zimmermann spent several weeks in Emmendingen, where Cornelia underwent what appears to have been successful psychological treatment. Afterwards, she was able to experience the beauty of nature again and became more sociable. She was finally able to become attached to her child, and she came to esteem her respectable, devoted husband. Her enjoyment of their lovely home and her life of relative ease also increased. In January of 1776, she wrote the following about her successful treatment: "Zimmermann, my good genius, came to rescue me, body and soul. He gave me hope and heartened me so much that I have had hardly a completely dark hour since."

In the fall of 1776, though, she experienced physical weakness and melancholy moods in conjunction with her second pregnancy. In December, she wrote, "and I creep rather slowly through the world, with a body that is useless for anything but carrying me to the grave". Cornelia gave birth to her second daughter after a difficult pregnancy and died four weeks later. Goethe received the news eight days afterwards and was heart-stricken. He noted in his journal, "Dark, lacerated day ... Sorrows and dreams." He sent his mother the following lines: "I can say nothing to you, but that fortune always behaves alike to me, and that the death of my sister is all the more painful to me because it has overtaken me in such happy times" (Bell, p. 287).

Goethe really was happy during this stage of his life in Weimar. He gave word to his pain over Cornelia's fate in a letter to Auguste zu Stolberg, the very words that I have chosen as the motto for this book:

> *The gods, the infinite ones, give everything*
> *to their favorites, entirely,*
> *all joys, the infinite ones,*
> *all pains, the infinite ones, entirely.*

These verses illustrate not only his acceptance of fate, but also his closeness to Cornelia. In his one-act play *Brother and Sister*, we find another indication of his strong rapport with her. He wrote the piece in only two days in October 1776. The focus of the play is the love between two siblings who are allowed to marry at the end because they discover they are not related after all. We also come across Goethe's sibling theme in *Clavigo*, and it finds its highest manifestation in *Iphigenia in Tauris*. In *Iphigenia*, which we will return to later, other themes dominate, such as purging guilt and passion, and healing from mistrust, fear, and hate. Goethe's relationship with Charlotte von Stein also left its mark on the drama. Nevertheless, the sibling theme recurs throughout the play. Echoes of sibling love are also found later in *Wilhelm Meister's Apprenticeship* but then retreat into the background.

Other strokes of fate affected Goethe at this time and reactivated his own emotional turbulence. In his ode "Journey to the Harz in Winter", written in December 1777, he processes the highs and lows of his life in Weimar up to that point and reflects the crises and hazards he and others have to face:

Journey to the Harz in Winter

Like a great bird of prey,
which, resting with gentle pinions
on heavy morning clouds,
looks around for its quarry:
thus let my song soar!

For a god has
predestined
everyone's course,
which the happy man
swiftly races
to its joyous goal:
but the man whose heart
has been constricted by misfortune

beats in vain
against the barriers
of the bronze thread of fate
that only the shears, bitter though they be,
will cut one day.

Into the shelter of the thicket
the rough wild animals are pushing,
and, along with the reed warblers,
the rich folk have long since
submerged into their swamps.

It is easy to follow the chariot
that Fortuna leads,
just as the easy-paced pack train
follows after the prince's entry
on improved roads.

But, off the path there, who is that?
His trail is lost in the shrubbery;
behind him the bushes
close up,
the grass springs up again,
the wilderness swallows him up.

In the first stanza, the poetical self soars over the world's hazards and seeks sustenance for his creative drive. In the second stanza, we find a resignation to fate: the "happy man/swiftly races to his joyous goal" while the unhappy man, "whose heart has been constricted by misfortune", struggles against his fate. Goethe had found himself in each of these roles at different times, but we can discern his sister in the role of the unhappy person because she was unable to resist her fate, and the "shears, bitter though they be", cut through the "bronze thread of fate" too early for her. But there are also those among the living who fall into despair in the "thicket". During the dark winter, the "rich folk" have "submerged into their swamps", i.e. they have retreated to their city apartments – symbols of comfort and safety – while others suffer. The poetical self could easily take this path as well and follow Fortuna, but instead, it is interested in the person standing off to the side who is swallowed up by the wilderness.

In this poem, Goethe is remembering his trip to visit the desperate philosopher Plessing, who was in a state of psychological distress. The unsuccessful young man had applied by letter to the author of *Werther* to seek his support. In Plessing, Goethe saw an alter ego, a side of himself that could have failed, like any other person. He paid Plessing a visit during his trip to the Harz Mountains in the winter of 1777 while the duke and the court were hunting. In the next stanza of the poem, he devotes himself to Plessing:

> Ah, who will heal the pains
> of a man for whom balm has become poison,
> a man who imbibed misanthropy
> from the abundance of love?
> Formerly despised, now a despiser,
> he secretly consumes
> his own worth
> in unsatisfying egotism.

Goethe is describing the loneliness of someone, "who imbibed misanthropy/ from the abundance of love". The poetical self reflects on the way in which grievances give rise to a contemptuous attitude toward the whole world, the consequence of which is the further destruction of one's own sense of self-worth. It asks God for mercy, healing, and relief.

> If your psaltery,
> Father of love, possesses a tone
> perceptible to his ears,
> then refresh his heart!
> Open his clouded eyes
> to the thousand fountains
> alongside the parched man
> in the desert!

After appealing to God to save "the parched man/in the desert", the poetical self also asks for divine blessings for the happy man.

> You who provide many joys,
> an overflowing measure for everyone,
> bless the brothers of the chase
> on their track of game
> with the youthful exuberance
> of merry blood lust:
> belated avengers of the damage
> that for years now, in vain,
> the peasant has warded off with cudgels!

In this stanza, the poetical self muses on the exuberance of the hunting party, on which is bestowed an "overflowing measure" of joys. The members of the party are able to abandon themselves to their aggressive impulses with "youthful exuberance" and a clear conscience. Again, though, the poetical self asks about "the solitary wayfarer" and hopes that the poet will shed light on him and can put him on the right path.

> But envelop the solitary wayfarer
> in your golden clouds!
> Encircle with wintergreen,
> until the rose is again ready to blossom,
> the damp hair
> of your poet, O Love!
>
> With your twilight torch
> you light his way
> through fords at night,
> over bottomless precipices
> on barren stretches of ground;
> with the thousand-colored morning
> you smile into his heart;
> with the corrosive storm
> you bear him high aloft;
> wintry streams plunge from the cliffs
> into his psalms,
> and he finds an altar for dearest thanksgiving
> in the snow-hung summit
> of the dreaded peak
> that, in the visions of people of old,
> was garlanded by ghostly round dances.

Like Goethe, the poetical self finds in poetry a light to accompany it across emotional "fords at night". It is thankful that it is carried "high aloft" by poetry, something Goethe also wishes for Plessing. The poetical self, though, must also humbly bow to the unexplorable riddles of the world.

> You, peak, with your unexplored bosom, stand
> mysteriously apparent
> above the astonished world
> and look down from the clouds
> upon its kingdoms and magnificence,
> which you irrigate from the veins
> of your brothers alongside you.
>   (Appelbaum, pp. 53–57)

Like the poetical self, Goethe is astonished by his ability to observe and to give form to his own life "with his unexplored bosom" and aesthetic pleasure. He seems to sense that things could have gone differently for him. In this poem, a deep unease about failure is expressed, but the poetical triumph over existential threats we have so often seen also finds expression.

Goethe's insights into the dangers to himself fed into his sense of responsibility, which contributed to both his astonishing capacity for work and his broad political scope of action. In January of 1779, he noted,

> The pressures of business are very pleasant to the soul; once it has been discharged, the soul plays more freely and enjoys life. There is nothing more miserable than the comfortable person without work; the most wonderful of gifts becomes loathsome to him.
>
> (FA 29, p. 156: DS)

On the other hand, he was entrusted with such a large variety of tasks that his powers of poetic creation dried up. In 1779, he assumed the role of president of the war council, where he was in charge of overseeing conscripts into Weimar's army, all of this on top of his other duties. He bore a huge responsibility because the political situation was so volatile. The War of the Bavarian Succession (1778–1779) threatened to pull the Duchy of Saxe-Weimar into the conflicts between Prussia and Austria over hegemony within the territory of the German Reich. Goethe convinced the duke that it would be better to voluntarily supply the Prussians with troops than to risk forcible conscription of recruits from Saxe-Weimar. In addition, he was head of the Roads and Waterways Commission, where he was in charge of repairs to infrastructure such as roads and bridges. In 1782, after being named president of the chamber of finance, he assumed the additional, time-consuming office of finance minister. He dedicated himself to all of these tasks with an astonishing energy and commitment. He seems to have appreciated the practical occupation and the accompanying feeling of emotional stability.

During this period, his relationships with women continued to be dominated by unfulfilled erotic longings, yet he was successful in using poetry to make his peace with his loneliness. In the poem "Wayfarer's Night Song [Another]", which Goethe wrote in 1780 on the walls of a simple wooden hut near Ilmenau during a night spent alone there, we find this sad but beautiful reconciliation.

Wayfarer's Night Song [Another][1]

Over all mountain peaks
there is rest;
in all treetops
you perceive
barely a breath;
the songbirds are silent in the forest.
Just wait, soon
you will rest too.

(Appelbaum, p. 67)

Goethe ensnares the reader with simple words. In the German, the long vowel found in the second line conveys a sense of perfect tranquility that suffuses both nature and ourselves in the twilight. Life comes to a standstill, but there is no fear to cause us to catch our breath; rather, we are carried away on a breath. Death is not horrible; instead, it is a liberating image of peaceful transfiguration. Goethe's poetical effort at coming to term with loneliness, unfulfilled love, and thoughts of death were given profound expression in this poem; it is no coincidence that Franz Schubert, who also loved in vain, chose to set it to music, culminating in a piece that still moves and fascinates listeners two hundred years later.

Goethe's first few years in Weimar were a period of maturity for him. Taking on duties and responsibilities freed him from the turmoil of adolescence. In August 1779, he noted programmatically in his diary,

> Let us do the right things from morning till evening, and give us clear conceptions of the effects of things; that you are not like those who spend the day in complaining of headache, and drink too much wine every night against the headache.

> (FA 29, p. 184: HH)

Boyle (1991), like many other Germanists, is of the opinion that Goethe's political and social engagement had a negative impact on his powers of poetic creation. His play *Iphigenia in Tauris*, which he worked on for almost ten years, is said to be evidence of this. His poems and other plays, though, show that he continued to be poetically active and hereby found expression for his emotional problems. It is likely that *Iphigenia* occupied him for so long because the play was so tightly interwoven with his own conflicts, much like *Tasso* and *Faust*, which is a good reason to take a closer look at the psychological aspects of the play.

Iphigenia in Tauris and Torquato Tasso

Iphigenia in Tauris

Iphigenia, the daughter of Agamemnon, is supposed to be sacrificed in order to propitiate the gods before the upcoming war in Troy. The goddess Diana, the sister of Apollo, saves her from death and brings her to Tauris, where she is to serve as Diana's high priestess. Iphigenia longs to return to her home in Greece, but Thoas, the king of Tauris, wants to make her his wife and will not agree to allow her to leave. Thoas had even discontinued the ritual of human sacrifice for her sake, but Iphigenia continued to rebuff him. Finally, he agrees to allow Iphigenia to leave, but only on the condition that she perform a final human sacrifice of two strangers who have just arrived in Tauris. Iphigenia recognizes one of the two strangers: her brother Orestes. After he had murdered their mother in revenge for her betrayal and murder of their father, Agamemnon, the oracle of Apollo had pointed him toward Tauris: if he brings one sister home, he will have atoned for the murder. Orestes understands this to mean he is supposed to steal a statue of Diana from Tauris. To his amazement, the sister he finds is his own, who had been believed dead.

Orestes and Pylades, the other prisoner and their cousin, plan an escape, but Iphigenia's sense of morality will not allow her to betray the king. She tells him about the plot, but she also makes it clear that he has no right to detain her or her companions. Glowering, he gives them permission to leave, but Iphigenia wishes to part from Thoas on good terms, because she venerates him as a second father. She vanquishes his truculence with her morality, and they part as friends.

The play depicts Iphigenia's attempts to introduce moral action to a world determined by power and mythical constraint. In the end, Iphigenia's humanity is able to overcome barbaric violence. On a psychological level, the protagonists' development is portrayed as a cure, which is one of the main themes of the dramas produced during Goethe's first few years in Weimar (Borchmeyer 1999a). Accordingly, Orestes is cured, in the sense of a psychological cure, of his fear of persecution by his sister's charisma.

Goethe wrestled with this play for a long time, from 1779 to 1789, even though the first version, in prose, was completed quickly in February and March of 1779. He found himself pulled between his practical and political activity and his creative urge. He tried to bring both fields of aspiration into harmony, noting the following in his diary while dictating *Iphigenia* to his amanuensis:

> My soul is gradually being released by the dulcet tones coming from the volumes of minutes and legislative acts. Four steps into the next room, the green room, I sit and softly call the distant figures over to me. Today, I will produce one scene, I think; it will be difficult to avoid it. Good night. I got a good letter from my mother.
>
> (FA 29, p. 27: DS)

Once again, poetry became his means of remaining in contact with himself, with his fantasies and feelings, and of securing the continuity of his personal history and the coherence of his personality. This was quite necessary, as his real cares were considerable. Finding recruits for the army was a demanding task, and he was shaken by the populace's distressed situation. It is clear from his diary that he was intent on remedying the misfortunes of the local indigent working-class families by improving the productivity of the local manufacturers in the village of Apolda. His work on *Iphigenia* was only half-hearted at this time, as he set down in March of 1779: "The drama will not advance a step: it is cursed; the King of Tauris must speak as if no stocking-weaver in Apolda felt the pangs of hunger!" (*Works* 13, p. 350).

Looking at Iphigenia from a psychological perspective, we once again note how empathetically Goethe depicts the female protagonist, while the male characters remain flat. Iphigenia is typical of Goethe's female characters. They are "the only vase into which we moderns can pour our identity; nothing can be done with the men" (Oxenford, vol. 1, p. 424). At the end of Orestes' last speech, he says in respect to the prototypical Iphigenia:

> Cunning and force, the proudest boast of man,
> Fade in the lustre of her perfect truth ...
> *(Works* 11, p. 89, Vs. 2142–2144)

Goethe created a psychological drama from a classical tragedy, one that is influenced by an interiority with roots in Christianity. Erich Trunz (1981) has surmised that another psychological impetus for *Iphigenia* was Goethe's feelings of guilt about Lili Schönemann. Goethe wrote in August of 1775, while fleeing from Lili, "Perhaps the invisible scourge of the Eumenides will drive me again from my Fatherland" (Bell, p. 250).

Time and again, he attempted to heal his inner turmoil by means of platonic love. His glorified love for Charlotte von Stein, "my sister or my wife", would therefore also have had a psychological effect on *Iphigenia*. Another indication that he identified with the play is his decision to play Orestes in the play's debut performance. What is psychologically interesting is that Orestes, a young man pursued by the Furies and filled with a longing for death, is given new life in the presence of Iphigenia. Like Goethe himself, he is cured of disorienting feelings of guilt and fear by a woman who has renounced the erotic but is loved like a sister.

Goethe transfers this liberation from emotional turmoil to a mythical world that conforms to human psychological needs, much as Mozart did in *The Magic Flute*, composed around this same time; both found the voice of truth and humanity to be more audible in art than in reality. Goethe, as does Mozart in *The Magic Flute*, senses the unsoundness of the idealized reconciliation between irreconcilable forces in his work. But some ambivalence remained. Soon after the play's premiere, while writing about the war with France, he noted that "its tender strain was foreign to me now", criticizing the "lofty sanctity" (Farie, p. 210) of his own idealizing plays and characterizing *Iphigenia* as "most devilishly human" (Schmitz 1845, p. 393).

Torquato Tasso

The biographical outlines are even clearer in Goethe's play *Torquato Tasso*. In May of 1827, he confessed to Eckermann,

> I had the life of Tasso, I had my own life; and whilst I brought together two odd figures with their peculiarities, the image of Tasso arose in my mind, to which I opposed, as a prosaic contrast, that of Antonio, for whom also I did not lack models. The further particulars of court life and love affairs were at Weimar as they were in Ferrera; and I can truly say of my production, *it is bone of my bone, and flesh of my flesh.*
>
> (Oxenford, vol. 1, p. 415)

He had begun *Tasso* in the fall of 1780, and there are unmistakable signs that his own psychological conflicts at the court in Weimar had found their way into it. His emotional entanglement with the figure of Tasso was so pronounced that he was not able to make much headway with the play for a long time. It was only during his Italian journey (1786–1788) that he was finally able to further develop it. While in Rome, he explained,

> so also I could compare myself with *Tasso* in respect of fate. The painful character of a passionate soul, which is irresistibly drawn away to an irrevocable banishment, pervades the whole piece. This temper of mind did not leave me throughout the whole journey, in spite of all distractions and diversions.
>
> (Morrison and Nisbet, p. 547)

Apparently, Goethe required distance from the court at Weimar in order to be able to deal with his own set of problems. But he also found it difficult to put into words his relationship with his protagonist, as tightly woven as it was, during his sojourn in Italy.

> Should I not, perhaps, do better were I to write the "Iphigenia at Delphi", instead of amusing myself with my fanciful sketches of "Tasso"? However, I have bestowed upon the latter too much of my thoughts to give it up, and let it fall to the ground.
>
> (*Works* 12, p. 279)

The translator of the above quote rendered the German "Eigne" as "my thoughts", but it should be translated literally as "my own" meaning Goethe's self with all the emotions, reflections, and experiences that he had "bestowed . . . too much of" on *Tasso*.

We see that Goethe worked through essential aspects of his own psychological conflicts by writing the play *Torquato Tasso*. Historically, the Italian poet Torquato Tasso (1544–1595) had been described as melancholic even as a young man and had become increasingly unhappy with age. He grew lonely and poor and finally became mentally ill. The fate of this "talented, sensitive, and refined but reserved character" had a magnetic attraction for Goethe (Morrison and Nisbet, p. 163). It most likely made him think of the mentally ill Clauer, Lenz, and Plessing, but also the dangers he himself faced.

The play is set at Belriguardo, the Duke of Ferrera's summer residence, where the historical Torquato Tasso is known to have stayed. Princess Leonora d'Este, the sister of Duke Alphonso of Ferrera, and her companion Countess Leonora Sanvitale are weaving laurel wreaths for the busts of the classical poets in the garden and discussing the Golden Age of poetry. The conversation of the two women soon turns to Tasso, a young poet who is in love with the princess but is constrained by court protocol and may only address his poems to the countess of the same name. Duke Alphonso, Tasso's noble patron, is concerned about Tasso's lack of progress on his poetry. He comments on the negative effects of withdrawing into solitude and seeking undue independence and is therefore relieved when Tasso presents him with the mostly completed manuscript of *Gerusalemme liberata*. The duke crowns his court poet with the laurel wreath he has taken from the bust of Virgil in the garden. The poet, though, rejects the honor with effusive agitation and withdraws into his own lonely musings.

Tasso's ecstatic, melancholic self-accusations are interrupted by the arrival of the duke's secretary, Antonio. He has just returned from a successful diplomatic mission and finds the court's enthusiasm for the poet, who has become the ladies' plaything, excessive. A jealous quarrel arises between Antonio and Tasso. Antonio is motivated by more than jealousy, though; he is afraid he will not measure up to the poet's artistic experience.

> *Antonio* ...
> While from a well-tuned lute
> Madness wildly seems to gnaw ...
> For all these poets, all these laurel wreathes
> All these fair ladies festive attire moves me
> Out of myself into a foreign land.
> (*Works* 11, p. 127, Vs. 731–741: HH)

Antonio, a practical sort, finds the arts frightening, because they challenge customary boundaries and destabilize established structures. He embodies everyday reality and is unsettled by the reverberations caused by both the artistic and the erotic transgression of limits.

In the second act, we find a Tasso beset by doubts; he cannot decide whether he should withdraw into solitude or offer his love to the princess. She tactfully evades his advances, but he does not relent in his pursuit of her. Finally, she is forced to reject him more emphatically. Tasso reacts rhapsodically.

> *Tasso.* Stunned by the tumult, dazzled by the glare,
> Impetuous passions stirring in my breast,
> I by thy sister's side pursued my way
> In silence through the stately corridors,
> Then in the chamber entered, where ere long
> Thou didst appear supported by thy women.
> Oh, what a moment!
> Princess, pardon me! As in the presence of a deity
> The victim of enchantment feels with joy
> His frenzied spirit from delusion freed;
> So was my soul from every fantasy,
> From every passion, every false desire
> Restored at once by one calm glance of thin.
> (*Works* 11, pp. 131–132, Vs. 868–880)

The princess's prior severe illness has made her diffident and modest, and she attempts to chasten Tasso while at the same time consoling him. She advises him to give himself over to solitude – something Goethe did time and again, such as in his "Journey to the Harz" and later in *Wilhelm Meister*. Tasso's narcissistic idealization of erotic ecstasy is doomed to failure.

> *Princess*. Upon this pathway, Tasso, nevermore
> Will glad companionship be ours! This track
> Leadeth us on through solitary groves
> And silent vales to wander; more and more
> The spirit is untuned; and fondly strives
> The golden age, that from the outer world
> For aye hath vanished, to restore within,
> How vain so ever the attempt may prove.
> (*Works* 11, p. 135, Vs. 970–978)

She indicates to him that happiness can only be rediscovered in the intellectual or spiritual companionship shared by those who love respectfully, and in the recognition of the actual conditions of human life. Tasso is unable to accept the princess's friendly advice. He reacts with distrust and jealousy, and he surmises that the princess has a relationship with someone else, hence the rejection. When she denies this, he assails her again until she gives him a firm "no".

> *Princess*. No further, Tasso! many things there are
> That we may hope to win with violence;
> While others only can become our own
> Through moderation and wise self-restraint.
> (*Works* 11, p. 140, Vs. 1119–1122)

These verses are reminiscent not only of Charlotte von Stein's rebuffing of Goethe, but also his recurring theme of renunciation as a condition for artistic self-realization. The monologue by Tasso that follows reverses this insight. He falls prey to an illusion and believes, despite the princess's unequivocal rejection, he will be able to win her love.

Under the delusion that he does not have to forgo the princess's company and that he will be able to win her over with the proper courtly behavior, Tasso impetuously tries to gain Antonio's friendship. Antonio responds rather reservedly, depreciates Tasso's poetry, and is finally so dismissive of him that Tasso feels provoked to pull his dagger on the older and higher-ranking man. This is a serious breach of the rules of the court, and Antonio urges Duke Alphonso to punish Tasso appropriately. The duke is inclined to be lenient, though, and asks Tasso to remain in his room until given permission to rejoin the courtly society. Once again, Tasso's reaction is excessive; he feels he has been deprived of his honor and lays down both his sword and the laurel wreath.

> *Tasso.* Thine earnest word, O prince, delivers me,
> A freeman to captivity! ...
> *Alphonso.* Thou takest it, Tasso, more to heart than I.
> *Tasso.* ...
> I only hear my sentence, and submit ...
> Weak mortal! To forget where thou didst stand!
> Thou didst forget how high the abode of gods.
> And now art staggered by the sudden fall.
> (Works 11, pp. 156–157, Vs. 1536–1554)

Tasso is so narcissistic that he unrealistically increases his own suffering, finally developing negative megalomania. Psychologically, the logic goes as follows: If I am not already spectacularly successful, I want to at least fail spectacularly. In psychoanalysis, this type of conflict resolution is referred to as a masochistic triumph. The duke cannot get through to Tasso to soothe him, nor is Tasso, blinded by his narcissistic rage, able to accept the duke's propositions, which are meant to placate him.

In the third act, Princess Leonora and the countess discuss potential ways to rehabilitate Tasso. We learn from their private conversation that the princess has been cut off from social life in the city by her illness, and it is Tasso who brought light and joy back into her life. The two try to think up ways to keep the lonely poet from falling into pathological melancholy and madness.

In the fourth act, we find the poet severely distraught and vulnerable. Tasso has become more deeply entangled in his distrust and has developed the early stages of paranoia. He is unable to see Countess Leonora's well-meaning suggestion to leave the court at Este for a while as anything but a veiled attempt to get rid of him once and for all. Alone again, he indulges in accusations and suspicions; his narcissistic injury is so excruciating that he considers breaking off all ties to his friends and patrons and committing suicide.

> *Tasso (alone).* I must believe, forsooth, that no one hates me, –
> That no one persecutes, that all the guile,
> The subtle malice, that environs me,
> Is but the coinage of my own sick brain!
>
> ...
>
> Leonora's self, Leonora Santivale.
> Considerate friend! Ha, ha, I know thee now!
> Oh, wherefore did I ever trust her words?
>
> ...
>
> Yes, I will go, but not as ye desire:
> I will away, and farther than ye think.
> (Works 11, pp. 191–193, Vs. 2468–2531)

Tasso's pathological oversensitivity and feelings of inferiority led him to misinterpret Countess Leonora's intentions. He feels he has been handed such a crushing defeat that the only way he can preserve his grandiose self-image is by committing suicide. At the pinnacle of his despair, Tasso severs ties with his surroundings in the same manner as Werther.

In the fifth act, the duke acts disgruntled about Tasso's plans to leave. Antonio declares he did everything possible to reconcile with Tasso; he claims Tasso's perturbation is the result of his lack of moderation and his neglect of himself and others.

> *Antonio*. It is most certain, an intemperate life,
> As it engenders wild, distempered dreams,
> At length doth make us dream in open day.
> What's his suspicion but a troubled dream?
> (*Works* 11, p. 207, Vs. 2918–2921)

Despite his displeasure, the duke continues to treat Tasso with clemency and understanding. He agrees to Tasso's wish to leave the court and promises to provide him with a letter of recommendation to friends of his in Rome, but he is unwilling to return the manuscript Tasso had given him just hours before. He wants to prevent Tasso from destroying his own work under the sway of negative feelings. Tasso's sense of aggrievement prevents him from perceiving that the duke is actually acting benevolently towards him. Furthermore, he feels he is being disregarded, maliciously persecuted even. He feels his poetic abilities are no longer sufficient to help him cope with his despair.

> *Tasso*. ....
> I feel, yea, deeply feel, the noble art
> That quickens others, and does strength infuse
> Into the healthy soul, will drive me forth,
> And bring me to destruction.
> (*Works* 11, p. 214, Vs. 3133–3135)

Tasso wishes to leave without being reconciled to either the duke, his patron, or his beloved princess. His plan is to seclude himself at the home of his sister, who shares Goethe's sister's name, Cornelia. The princess attempts to tell Tasso a few home truths about his overblown mistrust, but she fails as well.

> *Princess*. .... and reveal
> Some healing plant, or potion, to restore
> Peace to thy bewildered senses, peace to us!
> The truest word that floweth from the lip,
> The surest remedy, hath lost its power.
> (*Works* 11, pp. 216–217, Vs. 3215–3219)

The princess's placating words and gestures, though, have the opposite effect on Tasso; rather than calming him, they increase his agitation until he transgresses by throwing himself into her arms and embracing her. The princess tears herself from his embrace and flees his scandalous behavior. The duke then orders Antonio to take Tasso into custody. Tasso, continuing to believe he is the victim of intrigue, pours forth his paranoid suspicions, multiplying his unhappiness. Antonio attempts, with little success, to dispel Tasso's paranoid mistrust, but it is Tasso himself who is finally able to free himself from the ecstasy of his private world. He is able to give expression to his conflicts, thereby returning to the shared world of communication. Saved from himself, he summarizes his situation thusly:

> *Tasso.*   ... but one thing still remains, –
> Tears, balmy tears, kind nature has bestowed.
> The cry of anguish, when the man at length
> Can bear no more – yea, and to me beside,
> She leaves in sorrow melody and speech,
> To utter forth the fulness of my woe:
> Though in their mortal anguish men are dumb,
> To me a God hath given to tell how I suffer.
> (*Works* 11, p. 224, Vs. 3426–3433)

Unlike Werther, Tasso ends his tale not by suicide, but by overcoming the affliction of his desperation; poetical creation has saved Tasso from self-consuming misery. And, unlike the real Torquato Tasso, whose early success was followed by a lack of further productivity and mental deterioration, Goethe was able to deal with his conflicts using his art. He processed not only his professional and artistic advancement but also his grievances and rejections in a productive manner. He formed and transformed his experiences of yearning for love and of receiving disappointments, but also the conflicts he felt between a strict sense of duty and artistic independence. In doing so, Goethe put himself in the precarious position of exploring the border experiences of melancholy and madness through art. He portrayed Tasso as a typical representative of the melancholy poet, who must come to terms with his own experiences of suffering as a necessary prerequisite to artistic productivity.

Here I would like to remind you that we cannot simply equate Goethe with Tasso. Some of his own personal sentiments and ideas are incorporated in other characters, such as in Antonio. As the holder of numerous public offices, Goethe's position was more like that of Antonio's than that of Tasso's. Goethe's protagonists, from Werther to Faust, are not merely replicas of one person, but rather aggregations of many people. Caroline von Herder outlined this idea in a letter to her husband:

> The poet depicts a *complete character*, as it appears in his mind; such a character, though, does not belong solely to a single person ... The fact

that he takes characteristics from his friends, from the living people around him, is both right and necessary. In this way, the people [in his works] become real, without being able or being allowed to be complete, living characters.

(qtd. in Borchmeyer 1999a, p. 159)

For Goethe, the act of condensing together characters and conflicts in this way always contains within itself an attempt at a solution. *Werther, Tasso*, and *Faust*, the works, triumph over Werther, Tasso, and Faust, the characters. During the period when Goethe was collecting material for *Torquato Tasso*, he himself was in a labile state between poetical rapture and coping with real life. In June of 1780, he wrote to Frau von Stein, "My soul is like an eternal firework without rest ... Yet wondrously, each person is ensnared in his individuality" (HA, p. 548: HH).

Unlike Tasso, but similar to Antonio, Goethe had found security and structure in his work at the court in Weimar. And yet his creative work on *Tasso* had also helped him to cope with social conflicts, such as the tension between noble and bourgeois lifestyles, more successfully than his protagonist. Borchmeyer had the following to say about this:

Goethe's *Tasso* is a multifaceted reflection of the artist's subsistence problem at the end of the *ancien régime*; on the one hand, the artist remains dependent on the court, but on the other hand, he develops a bourgeois self-awareness unaffected by the claims of the court.

(1999a, p. 152: DS)

Yet Goethe's solutions to this existential issue were not perfect either. In the end, the tension between the drive to create art and the performance of his duties became so unbearable that he practically fled court life to start his famous Italian journey.

Note

1 The word "Another" appended to the title refers to a second poem titled "Wayfarer's Night Song" ("You who are from heaven ...").

Rebirth in Italy, 1786–1788

To be sure, you're a world, Rome, but without love
the world wouldn't be the world, nor would Rome be Rome.

When Goethe stole away from Weimar in September of 1786, he had been secretly out of sorts for some time. The restless wanderer had become a sedate minister and respected educator. He was connected to Duke Carl August by the bonds of friendship, and he was held in esteem by the society of Weimar. He had become a mature, recognized man. But it was this stability that cut him off from his creative wellspring; he was unable to complete any of the drafts he had begun. His passionate but unconsummated love for Charlotte von Stein no longer provided a spark for his poetical work; rather, it caused his vital spirit to wither. He needed to make a break with everything around him, but this sent him into a state similar to the one he found himself in when separating from Käthchen Schönkopf, Charlotte Buff, and Lili Schönemann. He was more mature, but nonetheless, he was desperate. He knew that leaving in secret would probably cost him Charlotte and other stabilizing relationships; nevertheless, he was willing to accept the hardships of the journey – riding in uncomfortable coaches for days on end, staying in dirty, lice-ridden inns, eating poor food, and encountering fellow travelers of a dubious nature – in order to find his way back to himself the way he had been able to during his long peregrinations while living in Frankfurt. Behind the façade of calm control visible in Tischbein's famous painting *Goethe in the Roman Campagna*, his unease was substantial.

Once again, Goethe felt restless, and sometimes even as if the ground had shifted beneath his feet. Even so, by cutting himself off from Charlotte, he was able to become closer to her again. Fifteen days after leaving Weimar, he wrote,

On this small piece of paper I am sending a sign of life to my dear ones, without actually saying where I am. I am well and only wish I could share with you the good things I am enjoying, a wish that often waylays me with longing.

(HA Letters 2, p. 11: DS)

He promised to maintain a "faithful journal" for Charlotte in order to uphold their connection. When he realized that she was upset and was pulling away from him, his letters started to sound fearful. On 13 December 1786, he wrote from Rome,

> If only, my dearest beloved, I could put down in this short note every good, true, sweet word of love and friendship, could tell you and assure you that I am near you, quite near you, and that I am glad of my existence, only for your sake. Your note gave me pain but mostly because I had caused you pain. You wish to say nothing to me? You wish to take back the evidence of your love? ... But perhaps there is already a letter from you underway to give me heart and comfort me.
>
> (HA Letters 2, p. 28: DS)

On 23 December, Goethe seemed almost desperate:

> My love! My love! I throw myself at your feet, I beg of you, smooth my way back to you, so that I do not remain exiled in the world. Magnanimously forgive me for what I have done to offend against you and set me right ... Forgive me! I myself fought with life and death and no tongue can express what was going on inside myself.
>
> (HA Letters 2, p. 33: HH)

These letters show how important the interplay between closeness and distance were for Goethe's creativity. As before, new creative energies arose in him during this crisis period of separation. Bolstered by his new friendships, he believed he would be able to make himself "complete" and hoped he would "return as a new person and live for the greater pleasure of myself and my friends" (HA Letters 2, p 18: DS). Later, in a letter to Carl August in January 1788, he explained the motive for his trip:

> The chief reason for my journey was: to heal myself from the physical-moral illness from which I suffered in Germany and which made me useless; and, as well, so that I might still the burning thirst I had for true art. In the first point, I was somewhat successful, and in the latter, quite so.
>
> (Richards 2010, p. 383; HA Letters 2, p. 78: DS)

> Here I am gradually recovering from my 'salto mortale' and study rather than enjoy ... This journey will hopefully have a blessed influence on my entire being.
>
> (HA Letters 2, pp. 26f.: DS).

In December, he had already reported to Herder that his *Iphigenia*, which had been at a standstill for so long, was completed. He wrote to Charlotte, "Every day, I shed another skin and hope to return as a person" (HA Letters 2, p. 40: DS). He protested against Charlotte's reproaches:

I have only *one* existence, which I have played *completely* this time, and continue to play. If I escape with my mind and body intact, if my nature, my spirit, my fortune overcomes this crisis, then I will compensate thousandfold what must be compensated. – If I perish, I perish; I was of no more use anyway.

(HA Letters 2, p. 44: DS)

In his letters to Duke Carl August he shows another side:

Here, as everywhere, it is not possible to get involved with the fairer sex without a loss of time. The girls or rather the young women, who present themselves to the painters as models, are occasionally quite lovely and accommodatingly allow themselves to be viewed and appreciated. In this way, it would be a very comfortable pleasure if only the French influences [i.e. venereal disease] did not make this paradise uncertain as well.

(HA Letters 2, pp. 47f.: DS)

This letter is a sign that Goethe was becoming less dependent on his relationship with Charlotte von Stein, a relationship that had both a stabilizing and a debilitating effect on him. In Italy, he allowed himself to feel sexual desire again and rediscovered his creative energies.

In February of 1787, Goethe left Rome to travel around Italy. He was fascinated by Naples, climbed Vesuvius, and increased his knowledge of geology and botany. In Sicily, he believed he had found the key to the ancient world. On 7 June, he returned to Rome and began to work even more intensively. But he remains closely connected with Charlotte:

I am restored to my own self and am yet all the more yours. With life as it was in recent years I would have (rather) wished death on myself and even from a distance I am more to you than I was then.

(HA Letters 2, p. 59: DS)

As during the crisis periods after he separated from Friederike Brion and Charlotte Buff, he was very productive and found his way back to himself through his work:

The fact that I am completing my older things serves to astound me. It is a recapitulation of my life and my art ... and so I am becoming properly acquainted with myself and my limitations and my own capaciousness.

(HA Letters 2, p. 63: DS).

Later, in his notes for his *Italian Journey*, he wrote of "a true new birth" that was "changing [him] within and without" and "continues to work" (*Works* 12, pp. 249, 251). In September 1787, a year after basically fleeing from Karlsbad, he wrote from Rome, "'Tis a year to-day since I left Carlsbad. What a year, and what a remarkable epoch for me is this day–this day, the Duke's birthday, and the birthday to me also of a new life!" (Morrison and Nisbet, pp. 405–406). The rebirth Goethe experienced was anything but easy and serene; it was only made possible by intensive internal work:

> It is well, my dear ones, that I am a man who lives by his exertions. These past days I have again worked more than enjoyed ... It is now my wish to know nothing more, but to produce something and duly practice my faculty. To know and not to do–I have been ill with that illness from youth up, God grant I may at last get over it!
>
> (Morrison and Nisbet, pp. 408–410)

Goethe busied himself with his earlier writings, which had been forwarded to him in Rome, underscoring the autobiographical nature of their contents.

> It really affects me strangely that these four small volumes, the results of half a lifetime, should visit me at Rome. I can verily say there is not one letter in them which has not been lived, felt, enjoyed, suffered, thought; and for that reason they now all address me so much more vitally.
>
> (Morrison and Nisbet, p. 411)

His poetical work once again made it possible for him to validate himself and to process the events that were assailing him.

> Vigorously penetrating minds are not content with enjoyment, but press forward towards knowledge. They are therefore incited to self-activity, sensible that however it may fare with them there is no true road to knowledge but that of production, and that a man is incapable of judging rightly that which he cannot himself produce.
>
> (Morrison and Nisbet, p. 421)

His Italian journey proved to be quite productive. He completed his tragedy *Egmont*, rewrote *Iphigenia in Tauris* in verse, revised *Torquato Tasso*, and wrote several scenes of *Faust*, including the devil's pact, the witch's kitchen, and the forest and cavern:

> I live in wealth and abundance of all that is genuinely dear and beneficial to me, and these few months for the first time I have rightly enjoyed my existence here. For the world is now clearing up before me and art is growing to me a second nature, born out of the heads of the greatest men,

like Minerva out of the head of Jupiter. Out of this fulness poured into me, you should draw entertainment in the future for days, nay, for years long.

(Morrison and Nisbet, p. 396)

But it was not only in the sphere of art that he felt like a new man. His style of living also changed, and he became more satisfied with his situation and also erotically more broad-minded. Thirty years after this trip, he wrote discreetly in his *Italian Journey* that he had found himself in Rome and "for the first time come into harmony with myself, and grown happy and rational" (Morrison and Nisbet, p. 521). He is more explicit in his letter to Carl August dated 16 February 1788, implying that he had sexual encounters on a regular basis. But there seems to be no justification for drawing the conclusion from this that Goethe had not had sexual contact with a woman before arriving in Rome, which has been the common argument since Eissler (1963) proposed it. Eissler based his supposition on the following lines from the letter:

You write quite convincingly that one must have a *cervello tosto* if he is not enticed into the beautiful flower garden. It appears that your excellent thoughts of the 22nd of January had an immediate effect in Rome, for by that date I could have recounted several charming excursions. Thus much is certain, and you as a doctor of the widest experience ["doctor longe experientissimus"] are quite correct in saying that such a moderate exercise refreshes the mind and brings the body into a precious equilibrium. An effect which I have experienced more than once in my life, as I have on the other hand noted the discomfort which resulted when I tried to withdraw from the broad road into the straight path of self-restraint and security.

(Cornish, p. 2)

It is likely that he was referring to an erotic relationship with a young Roman widow whom he had made the acquaintance of during the last few months of his stay in Rome. He gave her the ambiguous name "Faustina" in the *Roman Elegies*, in which he openly sang the praises of the joys of sexual love. The psychoanalyst Eissler came to the conclusion that the letter must have been referring to Goethe's first sexual relationship. And in fact, this was the first letter in which Goethe explicitly dealt with sexual acts in which he himself was involved. In December 1787, he had written the following to his friend and patron, Carl August, the "doctor longe experientissimus", who was very experienced and successful in all things sexual:

The sweet small god has relegated me to a difficult corner of the world. The public girls of pleasure are unsafe, as everywhere. The zitellen [the unmarried women] are more chaste than anywhere – they won't let themselves be touched and ask immediately, if one does something of that sort with them: *e che concluderemo* [and where will it lead]? Then either one must marry them or have them married, and when they get a man, then the mass is sung. Indeed, one can almost say that all the married women stand available for the one who will take care of their families. These, then, are the lousy conditions, and one can sample only those who are as unsafe as the public creatures. What concerns the heart does not belong to the terminology of the present chancellery of love.

(Richards 2003, p. 140)

Considering his fear of sexually transmitted diseases and the reticence of the unmarried women, it was only right for him that he had found Faustina, with whom he apparently had a sexual relationship lasting several months. But to take the contents of the letter as proof that Goethe had never had sex before is questionable: First, he was open-minded about sexual activity. He spoke unashamedly about masturbation, wrote pornographic verses, and enjoyed looking at naked bodies. Second, from the perspective of sexual medicine, it is highly unlikely that a sexually abstinent person would suddenly discover sexual desire for the first time at the age of 37, and then be able to go on to engage in partnered sex with pleasure and endurance for many years. After returning from Rome, both he and his later wife Christiane Vulpius described a shared sexuality that seemed to be rather vivid. Third, there is evidence of fondling with women since puberty, and it is hard to believe that he merely looked on during his friend Carl August's sexual escapades while they were carousing together. It is also unlikely that the long evenings spent alone with easy-going actresses were merely platonic. In any case, the comment in the letter about "an effect which I have experienced more than once in my life" would suggest previous sexual experiences.

Goethe showed himself sincerely thankful to his duke, who had made his trip to Italy possible. In his next-to-last letter to Carl August from Italy, he expressed himself thusly:

I may well say: in this one-and-a-half years of solitude I have found myself again; but as what? – As an artist! What I am beyond that, you will judge and make use of ... Take me in as a guest, allow me to complete the full measure of my existence by your side and take pleasure in life.

(HA Letters 2, p. 85: DS)

Chapter 11

His great love and public influence
Weimar, 1788–1805

> Let it be no cause for regret, darling, that you yielded to me
> so quickly!
> Believe me, I have no insolent thoughts, no low thoughts,
> about you.

Goethe returned to Weimar in mid-June 1788, in a slightly melancholic mood and with longings to return to Italy. To the outside world, he gave the impression of being active and full of hope, but his emotions were mixed. He had rediscovered his creative powers in Italy, yet he continued to be at odds with himself. Once again, he sought emotional stability from Charlotte von Stein, having never given up hope that she might return his love. The reality, though, was that he could no longer expect her affections. She made perfectly clear her indignation about his sneaking away to Italy and resentment of his behavior. Begging, he tried to win back her affection:

> I will stop by for a moment early this morning. I would be happy to hear everything you have to say to me, I must only ask that you not be too particular about my currently absent-minded, I will not say disjointed, state of being. I may well tell you that my inside is not like my outside.
>
> (HA Letters 2, p. 95: DS)

He felt quite alone: Duke Carl August was spending most of the summer as a major general with his garrison, Herder had left on his own trip to Italy in August, and "the weather is always gloomy and deadens my spirit; when the barometer has sunken and the countryside is colorless, how can one live?" (HA Letters 2, p. 100: DS). In this situation, there was only one thing to do: he turned again to his old resource, delving into his regular work in the administration of the duchy and working on *Tasso* and *Faust* during the periods when he had no duties.

But, he had become more open while in Italy and now, beyond the restraint of courtly etiquette, was receptive to the charms of Christiane Vulpius.

Christiane, a 23-year-old seamstress from a poor family, tried to improve her brother's precarious situation as a writer by approaching Goethe on his behalf. She appears to have immediately won Goethe's sympathy, and he felt emboldened to enter into a spontaneous sexual relationship with this attractive, uncomplicated young woman. For the first time in his life, he was able to have a carefree sexual relationship. The *Erotica Romana*, which were later renamed the *Roman Elegies*, were written during this period. They are the source of the lines found at the beginning of this chapter: "Let it be no cause for regret, darling, that you yielded to me / so quickly! / Believe me, I have no insolent thoughts, no low thoughts, / about you" (Appelbaum, p. 93). And in fact, he did not think of Christiane that way; within just a few weeks of their meeting, he brought her to live with him in his cottage. Beyond his desire to leave behind the rituals and pressures of courtly life, there were also internal factors that at last made it possible for Goethe to experience long-term erotic enjoyment. He saw himself freed from his desire for social advancement and released from the intellectual idealization of his romantic relationships. This sense of freedom allowed him to access his natural-born sexuality. Christiane responded to him, as revealed in her later letters, with a pleasure-loving sensuality.

It was obvious that the courtly society would react negatively to the passionate pair; they were able to conceal their relationship for almost a year, but at that point, it came to open hostilities. Despite the duke's protection, the couple was forced to move outside the city walls. Frau von Stein dropped her acquaintance with Goethe completely, and the other members of Weimar society avoided him, as well. But he seems to have taken everything in stride. The *Roman Elegies* tell of his first uninhibited experiences with a woman:

> Honor whomever you please! But I at last am in safety!
> Beautiful ladies, and you, men of the elegant world,
> Ask about uncles and aunts and second cousins and great-aunts,
> Then, after talk that's prescribed, start the wearisome game.
> (Hamburger, p. 227)

In the *Roman Elegies*, Goethe rebels against the conventions he had already attacked in his poem "Prometheus". Now he is able to enjoy his sexual liberation as well. He is no longer willing to be paralyzed by the "creeping poison" of renouncing relationships with women; rather, he wants to enjoy himself with "freshly sharpened points":

> Cupid's arrows have varying effects: some of them scratch a person,
> and his heart is ill for years with the creeping poison.
> But others, strongly feathered, with freshly sharpened points,
> penetrate to the marrow and inflame the blood rapidly.
> (Appelbaum, p. 93)

Goethe's erotic sexual encounters lead him to a pervading sense of veneration for creation:

> We lovers are pious, we quietly revere all demons,
>> wishing every god and every goddess to be favorably inclined toward us.
>>> (Appelbaum, p. 93: HH)

Creation finds a perfection in sexual love that includes all deities, even demons, but even if not every god is "favorably inclined", the "secret feasts" of sexuality are holy.

> Yes, we gladly confess it to you all: our prayers,
>> our daily service, is always consecrated to one goddess in particular.
> Roguishly, briskly, and earnestly we celebrate secret feasts,
>> and silence befits all initiates perfectly.
>>> (Appelbaum, p. 93)

His insurrection against the gods in his hymn "Prometheus" seems to have a close counterpart here. He understood that the "secret feasts" of fulfilled sexuality were always characterized by something private, something that was not always congruent with the public individual he had long styled himself. In the *Roman Elegies*, his fears that sexuality would drain him and cause him to lose his creative potency were completely removed:

> Is it not bliss to exchange tender kisses containing no dangers,
>> Sucking into our lungs, carefree, our partner's own life?
>>> ("Elegy XXI")

For the first time, secure bonding, sexuality, and a zest for life were reconciled, and for this reason, Goethe had no problem getting over society's condemnation of his love. He also remained unperturbed by criticism of the sexual permissiveness of his *Roman Elegies*, some of whose more pornographic verses he chose to tone down himself. The director of a school (gymnasium) wrote the following in July of 1795:

> Respectable women are scandalized by the brothel-like nudity. Herder put it very nicely: "He stamped this impudence with the imperial insignia. *Die Horen*[1] should be spelled now with a 'u'[2]". Most of the *Elegies* were written on his return [to Weimar] in the initial intoxication of his relationship with Madame Vulpius.
>> (Bode, vol. 2, p. 41: DS)

Despite this animosity, Goethe felt perfectly at ease with "Madame Vulpius". Their first son, whom they named after Duke Carl August, was born in

December of 1789; four more children followed but died soon after birth. From the medical records available, it is likely that the children died due to a Rhesus incompatibility or a blood group incompatibility between the parents. The couple was able to withstand these blows of fate, though, at least for the first few years. They continued to be erotically devoted to one another and enjoyed each other's company, even referring to their lovemaking, though in code, in their letters. Goethe was indefatigable in his efforts to assist Christiane's brother, and he was finally able to secure him a position at the court library in Weimar.

Nevertheless, despite his close relationship with Christiane, Goethe continued to quietly yearn for Italy. In September 1788, he wrote, "I cannot and may not express how much I suffered on my departure from Rome, how painful it was for me to leave that beautiful country". In December, he confessed to Herder, "I feel only too much, what I have lost, since I have seen myself relocated from that element to here". He felt the waning of the creative energy he had rediscovered in Italy, and his work on *Tasso* came to a standstill. Outside of the *Roman Elegies*, he did not write any other significant poetical works during the first few years after returning from Italy.

Goethe sought to maintain contact with Charlotte von Stein, even during the early days of his relationship with Christiane. In June of 1789, he wrote to Charlotte that he had little else but her on his mind and begged for her understanding: "It was something of a miracle that I should have lost the deepest, most intimate relationship with you ... I do not entirely give up hope that you will once again know me properly" (Ghibellino, pp. 168–169). Charlotte continued to be important for Goethe's emotional equilibrium, and his letters to her during this period have a beseeching quality to them reminiscent of those from his early days in Weimar, which themselves are similar to the self-therapeutic letters he wrote to Auguste zu Stolberg. Seven days after the letter cited above, he wrote, "I have never known greater happiness than in confiding in you, as I have always done without reserve; prevented from doing so, I am a different person and must continue to change still more" (Herzfeld and Sym, p. 32).

Goethe successfully changed himself, became independent of Charlotte, and was able to enter fully into his relationship with Christiane. In his letters, he often spoke of his longing for her, and he found his trip to Venice, at the behest of the Duchess Anna Amalia, to be a nuisance.

> In addition, I must confess, in confidence, that my love of Italy has received a deadly blow from this trip ... Added to this is my affection for Erotico, who was left behind, and the little creature in diapers ... One of the laudable things I have learned on this trip is this: that I can no longer be alone, nor can I live outside our Fatherland.
>
> (HA Letters 2, p. 124: DS)

A short time later, he wrote, "I confess that I passionately love the girl" (Richards 2010, p. 419).

His development was astounding. The impressive man of the world depicted in Tischbein's painting *Goethe in the Roman Campagna* had become a loving man who could acknowledge his "small desires". He had to make a trip to Silesia in July of 1790, during which the illustrious prince of poets and distinguished statesman wrote a letter to Herder, the tone of which was also very unassuming:

> I yearn to be home; I have nothing more to seek in the world … There is nothing but trash and trumpery everywhere, and I shall certainly not pass a single pleasant hour until I have dined with you and slept at the side of my lass.
>
> (Friedenthal, p. 260)

During this period, Goethe became increasingly interested in the natural sciences, and his activities ceased to be driven by his need to come to an understanding about himself and his place in the world through his creative writing. "My inclinations drive me now more than ever to natural science, and I am only surprised that in this prosaic German land a small cloud of poetry still remains floating over my skull" (Richards 2010, p. 417). It seems, however, that it was not "this prosaic German land" that was causing his poetical élan to run dry, but rather his loving relationship; he experienced a long period of happiness and contentment, and there were no painful passions to be poetically transformed. His interests began to take a practical turn, and he became increasingly involved in improving the living conditions of the impoverished populace of the duchy, for instance by endeavoring to increase the output of the mine at Ilmenau. He was worried that his decades of effort would not have any permanent effect.

We cannot wonder that Goethe, in this situation, was skeptical of the French Revolution, which put him at odds with many of the leading German thinkers of the day; to take one example, he criticized it sharply in his *Venetian Epigrams*. Although he had recognized the necessity of altering the feudal conditions prevalent at the time, he found the events associated with the Revolution, with all their cruelties, to be abhorrent and terrifying. At the same time, he sympathized with the suffering populace, saying to Eckermann in January of 1824 about the earlier events,

> Indeed, I was perfectly convinced that a great revolution is never a fault of the people, but of the government. Revolutions are utterly impossible as long as governments are constantly just and constantly vigilant, so that they may anticipate them by improvements at the right time, and not hold out until they are forced to yield by the pressure from beneath.
>
> (Oxenford, vol. 1, p. 122)

During the years before and after the French Revolution, Goethe's work as a minister of state and his studies in the natural sciences took center stage, yet his gift for writing poetry had not completely abandoned him. Encouraged by Duchess Anna Amalia, he repeatedly reviewed *Wilhelm Meister*, and he also worked on his light operas and theater pieces.

A military campaign in France in the year 1792 represents a major turning point in Goethe's life. In August of that year, at the duke's specific request, he had to follow him into war; the duke had already entered Prussia and Austria's war against France at the head of a regiment of soldiers. At first, Goethe attempted to make the best of the trip, but just one day after departing Weimar, he wrote to Christiane, "It is not at all useful for someone to absent himself from those whom he loves, the time flies, and there is no replacement to be found" (HA Letters 2, p. 149: DS). He interrupted his journey with an eight-day visit to his mother in Frankfurt, writing, "I found my mother cheerful and well, and all of my friends received me in a friendly manner" (HA Letters 2, p. 149). But he goes on to complain about the military campaign; he yearns to be back in Weimar with Christiane and his young son:

> I think constantly of you and the little one and visit you in the house and in the garden and think to myself how lovely everything will be when I come again. You must be fond of only me, though, and not be too lavish with making eyes at others.
>
> (HA Letters 2, p. 152)

Goethe's tender jealously is completely understandable; he was probably remembering the hours they had spent playing erotic games in the garden.

The campaign in France, however, proceeded less smoothly than initial estimates had promised. First of all, it was completely uncomfortable, although Goethe did try, in his own way, to be "diligent in silence". He was shaken after observing the first battles, though, and toward the end of the campaign, he was distraught over the catastrophic consequences of the war, having seen so many killed or horribly maimed.

> Much could be said about all of that, much will be said, and yet a large portion of this strange history will remain a secret ... We have endured and seen more toil, adversity, care, hardship, danger in these six weeks than in our entire lives.
>
> (HA Letters 2, p. 158)

Words failed the normally eloquent Goethe in the face of such unfathomable misery and destructive violence. A fragment from a letter written to his mother in November of 1792 contains the following words: "No pen, no tongue can describe the misery of the combined armies" (HA Letters 2, p. 159). Goethe was faced with an extreme experience that would preoccupy him for a long time afterwards.

During the French campaign, Goethe remained in close contact with Christiane by letter. Twelve letters documenting his deep attachment to and love for

Christiane have survived. He was anything but egotistical as a lover, and he confessed to her his fears, uncertainties, and jealous thoughts:

> You know that I dearly love you. If only you were with me now! There are big, wide beds everywhere, and you would not complain like you sometimes do at home. Alas! My beloved! There is nothing better than being together ... Stay fond of me! Because sometimes I have jealous thoughts and imagine that you could prefer someone else, because I find many men more attractive and more pleasant than myself. You should not see that, though; rather, you must think me the best because I love you dreadfully much and like nothing but you. I often dream of you ... Stay fond of me, and be a faithful child, that other thing subsides.
>
> (FA 3, pp. 630f.: DS)

Christiane's letters from this time have not survived, though. Her letters from the summer of 1793, after Goethe was required to join Carl August in a second campaign, have been preserved, though. It was their fifth year together, and she was pregnant again. She writes, "Farewell, you sweet man. Your eternally loving Christel ... I love you above all else ... but since you have been gone, I am unable to be pleased by anything ... every joy is halved when you are not there" (HA Letters, p. 124: DS). Their correspondence reveals that Christiane was not only tenderly attached to Goethe, but that she had also become his most important confidant. She was a passionate lover, a devoted mother, and a prudent housewife, but more than that, she was a respected partner and equal in the things of life. He was profoundly happy that his mother – unlike the court at Weimar – immediately accepted Christiane upon learning of her son's liaison with her.

The couple had good times together, and in her letters, Christiane showed herself to be cheerfully active:

> I am so happy to have a letter from you ... Everything has been called together, and for joy, a bottle of sweet wine will be drunk to your health ... When you come again, if the days are still nice enough that we can sometimes "make love" in the garden next to the house, I would be so pleased.
>
> (HA Letters, p. 130: DS)

Beyond these pleasures, she treasured Goethe's true devotion and was happy that he was so tenderly attached to their small son. He awaited the additional births with joy, as well. Their third child was born in November 1793, but this child died within a few days; their fourth and fifth children experienced the same symptoms and the same outcome. Despite these strokes of fate, Christiane and Goethe were quite happy during the first six years of their life together. Weimar society's opposition to the relationship had waned, or rather, Duke Carl

August was able to accept their common-law marriage; he presented Goethe with a house in Weimar in the summer of 1794, providing the little family with a fit home. What is remarkable about this happy period in Goethe's life, though, is his small output as a poet. The events of August 1794 changed all that: He developed a friendship with Schiller, which brought Goethe's creative activity back to the forefront.

Johann Christoph Friedrich Schiller would come to join the ranks of those who were of the utmost importance in Goethe's personal and artistic development – a series of people starting with Behrisch during Goethe's days at university in Leipzig, to Merck in Frankfurt, and Herder in Strasbourg and Weimar. Goethe's connection to Schiller stands out because Goethe had found a partner who complemented him in questions of aesthetics and who followed and supported his poetical work with a special passion. All this, despite the two being intellectual polar opposites, between whom "there was a division greater than the diameter of the Earth" (HA Letters 2, p. 545: DS).

Their friendship was sparked by a conversation they had following a meeting of the Jena Natural Research Society in July of 1794. For his part, Goethe expected that collaborating with Schiller would reinvigorate his moribund projects. As early as August of 1794, he stamped their association with his seal of approval:

> For my birth-day, which falls in this week, no more agreeable present could have come to me than your letter, in which, with a friendly hand, you give the sum of my existence, and through your sympathy, encourage me to a more assiduous and active use of my powers.
>
> (Calvert, p. 7)

Höfer (2002) emphasizes that it was initially thanks to Schiller's diplomacy that the two men became closer, but it was this letter from Goethe that ultimately broke the ice between the two such different personalities. Seven days later, Goethe even invited Schiller to his home.

> Next week, the Court goes to Eisenach, and for a fortnight I shall be alone and independent, as I have not a prospect of being soon again. Will you not, during this period, visit me, and lodge with me? ... You should live entirely after your own fashion, and be as much as possible as if you were in your own house.
>
> (Calvert, p. 13)

Their collaboration on Schiller's literary journal, *The Hours*, developed into a unique artistic friendship, a friendship almost completely free of jealousy or destructive rivalry. And yet they were perfectly aware that their natures were in opposition to one another. Nevertheless, during the days before and after Goethe's forty-fifth birthday, they forged an alliance that has become an archetype of an artists' friendship and collective effort (Borchmeyer 1999b). In the years leading up to this, Goethe had lived in intellectual isolation; he was therefore grateful for Schiller's friendship. "You have taught me to look at the manysidedness of the inner man more fairly, you have given me a second youth and re-fashioned me into a poet, which I nearly have ceased to be" (Schmitz 1845, p. 6: HH).

Goethe and Schiller overcame their aesthetic and philosophical differences using sympathy and mutual fascination. Goethe later confessed that *Wilhelm Meister's Apprenticeship*, a novel that was very important to him, would never have been written without Schiller's support. He was able to accept Schiller's detailed comments, to bear his own imperfections, and to admit his dependence on Schiller for his own productivity. Goethe was full of self-doubt about his artistic creation, but he was also so emotionally entangled in *Wilhelm Meister* that he was unable to assess the quality of his own work. He showed himself deeply grateful for Schiller's support:

> Cordially I thank you for your invigorating letter and for communicating that which you felt and thought about the novel, especially in the eighth book. If this is what you would have wished, you will not underestimate your own influence on it, because it is beyond doubt that, without our friendly relations, I should not have been able to bring the work to conclusion, at least in the manner I did it ... And so much should be added in order to express the singular case in which I find myself with you.
>
> (HA Letters 2, pp. 227f.: DS: HH)

Wilhelm Meister's Apprenticeship turned out to be the means of Goethe's rapprochement with his mother. She was enthusiastic:

> Dear Son! Thank you a thousand times for your *Wilhelm*! And what a treat it was for me! I felt thirty years younger ... If I could only express my sentiments adequately, you would be happy indeed to know what a day of delight you have given your mother ... One more thing! The sequel to *Wilhelm* will surely appear before long ... Don't make us wait so long for the sequel, because I am eager for it. Farewell! Kiss little August and also your bedfellow from your devoted Mother Goethe.
>
> (HA Letters 1, pp. 182f.: DS)

As delighted as Catharina Elisabeth was with her son's work, she continued to push him, urging him to complete its sequel. This was also an essential element of his relationship with Schiller, who steadily drove Goethe on, even while providing him with support and validation. The legendary friendship between the two intellectual giants as well as their philosophical and artistic collaborations were multifaceted, of course. Goethe found the following words to describe their relationship:

Friendship can only be bred in practice and be maintained by practice. Affection, nay, love itself, is no help at all to friendship. True, active, productive friendship consists in keeping equal pace in life: in my friend approving my aims, while I approve his, and in thus moving forwards together steadfastly, however much our way of thought and life may vary.

(Saunders, p. 114)

Goethe was often Schiller's guest when he was working in Jena, and the artists also included Schiller's wife in their discussions in the evenings. Christiane, on the other hand, was not invited to participate, even when the Schillers were guests in her home. Schiller's wife, in particular, was condescending toward, even disdainful of, Christiane. Schiller, although from humble beginnings like Christiane herself, could not understand his friend's socially unequal relationship.

Goethe's productive friendship with Schiller was not the sole reason for his traveling to Jena to work. He found it increasingly difficult for him to work from home, as he required a certain amount of solitude for his creative work; this led to Christiane feeling increasingly alone. While Goethe was working in Jena, she expressed her disappointment at his delay in returning home:

That you would not come today or tomorrow, my love, I would not have believed. I had already got everything ready ... Time hangs very heavy on my hands. I wish I were still with you, everything is nothing without you.

(HA Letters, p. 212: DS)

In October of 1795, Christiane gave birth to her fourth child with Goethe at her side, yet only six days later, he returned to Jena to continue work on *Faust*. Four days after that, he wrote to Christiane,

I am quite happy here and working diligently; if only I knew that you and the little one were doing well. Send me word as soon as possible. I may stay here until the end of the week, as the quiet of the palace is just the thing for thinking and working. I visit the Schillers in the evening, and we converse deep into the night. I hope to learn that you are well and that the little one is drinking, eating, and growing like a good little boy.

(Beutler, p. 238: DS)

Christiane answered that the baby was weak and sickly, so Goethe cut short his trip and hurried home. Five days later, the baby died, leaving the couple deeply sad. Goethe later resumed two possibilities for dealing with pain:

to let grief have its natural way, or by the aid which culture offers us, to bear up against it. If one resolves upon the latter, as I always do, one is thereby bettered only for a moment, and I have remarked, that nature always at one time or another asserts her rights.

(Calvert, p. 109)

He remained very close to Christiane during this difficult time, but their relationship had lost its erotic spark. This transformation was reflected in Goethe's lyric poetry, as had happened so frequently before. Goethe had composed the poem *"Frech und Froh"* ["Saucy and Cheery"] in 1788 with Christiane in mind, as in his *Roman Elegies*:

Saucy and Cheery

My heart despises love's agony,
Meek misery, sweet sorrow;
I want only to know about bravery,
burning glances, earthy kisses.
Let poor dogs refresh themselves
With mixing pleasure and pain!
Maiden, give my fresh heart
Nothing of pain, but everything of pleasure!

(Ezust)

During the period in which this poem was composed, Goethe was celebrating sexual fulfillment in no uncertain terms. Seven years later, the tone of his work was more moderate, and it described a love that was less passionate, but still steadfast and true:

Nearness of the Loved One

I think of you when I see the sun's glimmer
    reflected from the sea;
I think of you when the moon's glitter
    is painted in the fountains.

I see you when on the distant road
    the dust rises;
late at night, when on the narrow footbridge
    the wayfarer trembles.

I hear you when, over there, with a muffled roar
    the wave surges.
I often walk in the silent grove to listen
    when all is still.

I am with you, no matter how far away you are;
    you are close to me!

> The sun is setting, soon the stars will shine for me.
>   If you were only here!
>   (Appelbaum, p. 103)

Goethe had been so impressed by a poem by Friederike Brun that had been set to music by his friend Zelter that he took it as his inspiration for his own poem, written in 1795. Unlike "Saucy and Cheery", it depended on the theme of the "distant lovers", like much of Goethe's early work. The poetical self perceives the "sun's glimmer" and the "moon's glitter" more intensely in the absence of the person being sung to. It senses a deep connection with the absent one, whether "on the distant road", "late at night", or "in the silent grove".

Goethe now felt closer to Christiane from afar than he did while sharing day-to-day life with her, repeating the pattern of his earlier love interests. He needed to spend time in seclusion at the palace in Jena, which he referred to as the "Canapé", to rediscover his poetical imagination. Christiane was understanding, but nevertheless could not help making a gentle remonstrance:

> I immediately thought that something would again be completed; my dearest one must always work hard. But I thought you were not starting something new, and that you would see that maybe the poem was finished, and would not do anything more for a while, because maybe it is actually a bit too much, and in the end, it could possibly be bad for you, too.
>   (qtd. in Damm 1998, pp. 232f.: DS)

Goethe felt increasingly constrained by both Christiane's desire to be near him and his diverse administrative duties, leading him to undertake all of the preparations necessary for another long journey. He dutifully got Christiane's financial affairs in order, but still his start was delayed. It was not until July of 1797 that he was able to start his third Swiss journey, accompanied on the first leg by Christiane and little August as far as Frankfurt to visit his mother. After he left his family behind in Frankfurt, Christiane was rather unhappy:

> Today I feel as if I could not endure being without you any longer. Today everything and everyone in the house complained of my foul humor ... Without you, there is nothing that makes me happy; since I left Frankfurt, I have not had a single pleasurable hour ... I have concealed it from you ever since, but I can no longer do so.
>   (HA Letters, p. 282: DS)

The rest of her letters show that she remained tenderly devoted to the man she "dreamed of every night"; Goethe himself wrote the following to his beloved in September:

I love you very much indeed, tenderly and you alone, and I wish for nothing more than that your love for me may remain forever the same … Think of me and don't make eyes too much, actually, it were best if you didn't do it at all, because it has not happened to me a single time on this whole journey.

(HA Letters 2, pp. 306f.: DS)

Nevertheless, Goethe felt pressured by Christiane. During this time, he composed the poem "Amyntas", in which a man is portrayed as a tree and a woman as the vines that are wrapped around it. This causes the man/tree to lose his vitality and threatens to strangle him:

And so she sucks out the marrow, sucks out my soul …
Nothing does reach to the crown. The supreme treetops
Dry out; the branch dries out stretching over the brook.
Yes, it is the traitress!, She flatteringly deprives me of life and fortunes,
Deprives me of striving strength, deprives me of hope flatteringly.

(HA 1, p. 197: HH)

Goethe suspended his trip, probably at Christiane's instigation, but in the future, he would be more resolute when he needed to withdraw to Jena. He also moved out of their shared bedroom, writing to Schiller in December of 1797,

I have again renewed the experience, that I can only work in an absolute loneliness, and that not merely conversation, but even the presence in the house of beloved and esteemed persons, draws off entirely my poetic springs. I should now be in a kind of despair, because every trace of a productive excitement in me has disappeared, if I were not certain of finding it again during the first eight days in Jena.

(Calvert, p. 372)

Ever after Schiller had relocated to Weimar, Goethe could not do without his workplace in Jena. Like Faust in the "Dark Gallery" scene, he had to go to the "tripod" of the "canapé" in Jena in order to carry out his creative activities. He withdrew from Christiane more and more, and he found her messages, especially those dealing with illness, to be annoying disturbances.

In the summer of 1802, Christiane realized she was pregnant again. She did not have a good pregnancy, and her fifth child died shortly after its birth on 16 December due to the previously mentioned blood group incompatibility. Christiane was sad about the loss, but she soon took up her household duties again. Goethe, though, became "daily more vexed", and in February 1803, Schiller wrote, "It is lamentable that Goethe allows his routine to prevail to such an extent … For a quarter of a year, he has not left home, not even left his room, without being ill" (FA 32, pp. 324f.: DS). Schiller was becoming increasingly irritated with Goethe's hypochondria and even flirted with the idea of seeking out a new place to live and a new sphere of activity. Christiane seemed more compassionate, writing to the physician Nikolaus Meyer,

> I am ... quite worried about the Privy Councilor,[3] he is sometimes quite hypochondriac and I must endure much, but because it is illness, I gladly do everything. But otherwise I have no one who I can trust and who I like.
>
> (FA 32, p. 341: DS)

Goethe recovered slowly; undeterred, though, he continued his work. That summer, he suggested to Christiane that she visit a spa town for her health. Her stay at Bad Lauchstädt lasted for some time, and the separation seems to have done the couple good. Christiane enjoyed herself dancing, and Goethe was able to write in peace. Both were very tolerant of each other's foibles, and he was able to rejoice in his wife's cheerfulness without being jealous; she sent him the following report of her enjoyments:

> from your letter of yesterday, I clearly see that you will not be coming. Nor do I want to torment you ... dancing is easy for me, I simply fly, and I always enjoy myself ... Herr von Nostiz, the grand officer, came to me in my box at the theater and invited me to a ball ... but my Lord, how beautifully he danced!
>
> (HA Letters, p. 383: DS)

The 54-year-old poet responded to the obvious enjoyment of his much younger wife with magnanimity: "How sincerely I love you, I feel it now more than ever, because I can delight in your happiness and contentment" (Gräf, vol. 1, p. 405: DS). The months after her return continue to be cheerful and companionable. Christiane wrote to a friend in January of 1804 that

> not one afternoon goes by that we do not have others to dine with us, then we go to the theater, where we always have many attractive men and girls ... I dance even more now than usual and feel quite well doing it.
>
> (Gräf, vol. 1, p. 405: DS)

During this period, Goethe was becoming increasingly involved in the theater in Weimar, on top of his normal duties. The next summer, Christiane returned to Bad Lauchstädt, drawn by the opportunities to dance and to take the waters. She was relatively carefree, and her son, August, was flourishing. In the winter of 1804, Goethe experienced a bout of renal colic so severe that his family feared for his life, as had happened three years previously. In April of 1805, Christiane wrote to a friend that her husband had had "scarcely one hour of health" in the last three months, and that his death was frequently on her mind. Höfer (2002) has described how Goethe's poor condition was exacerbated by another creative crisis and the unsuccessful premiere of his play *Götz von Berlichingen*. He became more discomfited by literary attacks, and he was no longer able to accept criticism as easily as when he was younger. Even Schiller was increasingly less inclined to put up with Goethe's peevishness and therefore played with the idea of leaving Weimar. He himself was already deathly ill, though, so it was too late to carry out his plans. The two men saw each other only infrequently that winter.

Schiller died on 9 May 1805. At first, no one dared to inform Goethe of the loss of his friend. Schiller's death was a deep wound for Goethe, and he initially cloaked himself in mournful silence. He was soon active again, however, and he wrote the following in response to an inquiry from Johann Cotta, his publisher, about a memorial for Schiller:

> My conviction is that art, when it unites with pain, should only stimulate the latter in order to alleviate it and resolve it into highly consolatory feelings, and it is in this sense that I shall try to represent less what we have lost than what remains to us.
>
> (Unseld, p. 168)

Nevertheless, a haunting emptiness took hold, and in a letter to Zelter three weeks after Schiller's death, he set down the following:

> Since the time I left off writing to you, I have had few good days. I thought to lose myself, and now I lose a friend, and in him the half of my existence. In truth, I ought to begin a new mode of life, but at my age there is no longer a way. Now therefore I only look straight before me at each day as it comes, and do what is nearest to me, without looking farther afield.
>
> (Coleridge, pp. 32–33)

He was distraught and felt beyond hope, and he experienced a relapse of his kidney disease. But soon he remembered his old self-treatment strategies: he carried out his normal tasks, set himself to work on further developing the first part of *Faust*, and intensified his personal relationships. His correspondence with the Berlin composer Carl Friedrich Zelter now became his main means of discussing with a friend what was happening in his life and in his work. He was able to share his personal and artistic concerns with Zelter, openly and unreservedly. The two men's friendly correspondence began in 1799, but after Schiller's death, it served as a space for Goethe to share and seek feedback about his thoughts and feelings. Zelter, for his part, saw in his relationship with Goethe the "actual center . . . of his existence" and the "richly bestowed compensation for all the rigors fate had presented him" (HA Letters 2, p. 630: DS).

Between the years 1788 and 1805, Goethe had become a mature man, which is clearly shown in his letters and his bildungsroman *Wilhelm Meister's Apprenticeship*. He was able to accept reality for what it was and was able to view his own conflicts as well as the problems around him with equanimity. He had also resigned himself to growing older and was able to recognize the possibilities available to a mature man. Now 50 years old, he wrote to his friend Knebel,

> Looking back on so many situations lived through, remembering so many moods felt, these make us as if young again, and if we feel that we have gained in taste and won an overall view, then we believe we have found a replacement if energy and abundance wane over time.
>
> (HA Letters 2, p. 397: DS)

This realization made him more sure of himself rather than causing him to become inactive, and it facilitated his political and scientific activities.

During this period, his relationship with his mother remained cordial and supportive. In December of 1797, she wrote to him regarding a short visit he had paid her: "Dear son! The first thing is to thank thee that thou hast given me a few weeks of this summer, during which I have so greatly rejoiced in thy society, and taken delight in thy remarkably good air and appearance" (Gibbs, p. 215). Catharina Elisabeth wrote to him regularly, took an active interest in life in Weimar, and was fondly attached to her grandson, August, and to Christiane, who was still living with Goethe without benefit of clergy. She wrote the following to Christiane at the beginning of 1801, after Goethe's severe illness:

> Dear daughter! Praise be – Thanks and worship to God! who can deliver from death, and who sent help ... But my dear, dear daughter! How can I thank you for all of the love and care you have shown my son.
>
> (HA Letters 2, p. 645: DS)

Catharina Elisabeth thanked her son for sending guests from his milieu to her and for including her in his celebrity. She was visited by Duchess Anna Amalia and Duke Carl August in her own home, and in June of 1803 she even met the Prussian royals.

> I was so tense that I may well could have laughed and cried at the same time ... Then the king came, too; the queen went to a cabinet and brought out a valuable golden necklace, and now you will be amazed!!! She fastened it around my neck with her own hands – moved to tears, I was not able to thank her properly.
>
> (HA Letters 2, p. 384: DS)

Goethe was extremely pleased to be able to give his mother enjoyments such as these, and he wrote to Zelter about her meeting with the king and queen: "Your beautiful Queen made several people happy on her journey, none more so than my mother; nothing could have given her more pleasure in her declining years" (Coleridge, p. 12).

When we look back over Goethe's development as a person and as an artist during the period 1788 to 1805, we are especially struck by his maturation, both the good sides and the bad. He was able to maintain a productive friendship with Schiller, but also with the Swiss painter and art historian Meyer, with the composers Reichardt and Zelter, and with the philosopher and linguist Wilhelm von Humboldt, who was not a well-known figure at that time. Stimulated by these diverse influences and sheltered by the working climate in Jena, Goethe was able to flesh out old themes he had been carrying around with him for some time and to turn them into works of some importance, giving us the masterful ballads "The Treasure-digger", "Legend", "The Bride of Corinth", "The God and the Bayadere", and "The Pupil in Magic", all composed in May and June of 1797. They show a mature poet, statesman, and citizen of the world, who faced the turbulence of life with creative aplomb. The didactic ballads "The Treasure-digger" and "The Pupil in Magic", though, are no longer passionately self-referential, as in the earlier poems and dramas. They have been purged of the turmoil of adolescence, sometimes even of empathetic feelings, and maintain a "healthy" distance.

This distance also had its dark aspects, though. It may have been partially responsible for his later inability to (or desire not to) see the violence employed by Napoleon, whom he uncritically admired. He – or at least one part of his personality – had become a government minister holding the opinion that he had to close his mind to human suffering. He had already exhibited a certain degree of ministerial coldness; he had shown no sympathy in 1783 for a desperate woman who had killed her illegitimate infant, despite his earlier sympathy for the unfortunate mothers he had in mind while writing the tragedy of Gretchen in *Faust*. As a member of the highest advisory body in Weimar, he was jointly responsible for the execution of the 24-year-old maidservant.

We can also observe a certain degree of detachment from immediate experiences in the sphere of art. Hence, he expected Schiller to provide an emotional impetus for Weimar that he himself had failed to do or no longer dared to do. He pushed for Schiller's involvement in the theater at Weimar, the central educational institution, reasoning as follows:

> Our Theater stands in need of such a new stimulus, which I myself cannot give it. Between him who has to command, and him who shall give to such an establishment aesthetic guidance, there is a very great difference. The latter must act upon the feelings, and must therefore show feeling; the former must close up all his avenues of sensibility in order to keep tight together the political and economic form.
>
> (Calvert, p. 371)

Goethe also found stability and a sense of direction in his scientific work in a world, both internal and external, that sometimes felt dangerous. Here we will allow ourselves a small digression on the topic.

Goethe as a natural scientist and researcher

Goethe's international renown, even today, was based primarily on his poetry and plays. And yet, if we measure his life's work quantitatively, his main area of activity was as a statesman and a scientist. His scientific writings are so extensive that his work in the area of optics alone rivals the oeuvre of any successful natural scientist today. Unlike modern practitioners of science, Goethe did not restrict himself to the rigid methods of objective research; rather, he attempted to incorporate his scientific findings into the bigger picture of his personal worldview. For him, natural history and the natural sciences provided reassurance about himself and his place in the world. This also led to serious errors, though, such as his sharp rejection of Newton's optics.

Goethe found "polarity" and "growth" to be the activating principles in nature, just as they were in his cultural and personal life; opposites give rise to the higher development of the nature and culture of mankind. Progress engendered by human striving would not lead to self-alienation, as feared by Rousseau, but to the realization of man's natural abilities. Nature and human physiology are closely related:

> The eye owes its existence to the light. Out of indifferent animal organs the light produces an organ corresponding to itself; and so the eye is formed by this light for the light so that the inner light may meet the outer.
>
> (Zajonc, p. 27)

Poetically Goethe resumes: "If the eye were not like sunlike/It never could behold the sun" (HA 1, p. 367: HH). This also applies to other phenomena in nature that are the basis for man's elevated status in his world.

Goethe had already been involved in the study of medicine and the natural sciences during his student days in Leipzig and Strasbourg. During his first few years in Weimar, this interest was reinforced by his practical and political activities. He was concerned about the destitute workers employed in local industries such as mining. He applied his studies of geology to improving unprofitable mines in Ilmenau and to carrying out his duties on the Roads and Waterways Commission. Later, he supervised the institutes of the university at Jena, which gave him the opportunity to carry out more thorough scientific studies. He was a member of numerous scientific societies and was at the forefront of research at that time (Cremer 2011). Much of his work continues to be applicable today, such as his phenomenological and morphological approach in biology.

Goethe's theory of optics continues to have a strong influence, yet he himself viewed his *Theory of Colours* as his most important work. Although it was not published until 1810, Goethe's interest in the topic dates back to his youth. He wrote to Friederike Öser in 1769,

Oh! my friend, light is truth; yet the sun is not the truth, although light flows from it. Night is untruth. And what is beauty? It is not light, and not night. Twilight, an offspring of truth and untruth – a middle thing ... for when I come to this subject I begin to ramble, and yet it is my favorite subject.

(Bell, p. 41)

Later, Goethe attempted to prove this poetical explanation by means of meticulous experiments. It is said that he carried out considerably more experiments in the field of optics over the course of his life than Isaac Newton did. His research in this area was characterized by an interdisciplinary network consisting of not only physicists and chemists but also painters and philosophers. This network inspired the work of the physicist Gustav Kirchhoff and the chemist Robert Bunsen, who developed spectral analysis, one of the most important discoveries in the history of science, in the early 1860s (Cremer 2011).

Light had been characterized as wavelike (Huygens) or corpuscular (Newton), but Goethe postulated "that to create color, light and dark, lightness and darkness – or if a more general formulation is preferred, light and non-light – are required" (letter to Eckermann, 2 May 1824: DS). This view was long considered erroneous, but experiments have shown that color is produced by shining a white light onto a surface. We will see that this basic principal is of eminently practical importance to this day.

Goethe's view that light is an elementary natural phenomenon that is not further reducible comes closer to the modern theory of light than Newton's naive particle theory. Quantum theory (Planck, Einstein) holds the photon to be the simplest and most homogeneous phenomenon currently known. The discovery of photons made it clear that the physical properties of light are not coincidentally connected to chemical colors, rather that they describe intrinsic properties of objects. Sommerfeld and Bohr explained that the structure of the atom is closely related to the creation of light. The Heidelberg physicist Christoph Cremer has written that

color arises from the interaction of light (photon) with a "dark" state A (atom/molecule in a low-energy state); this leads to a "light" state B (atom/ molecule in an excited high-energy state) and the subsequent transition of the "light" state B into the "dark" state A. In the process, a photon (an elementary particle of light) with a certain color is emitted.

(Cremer, p. 82)

From the perspective of modern nuclear physics and theories of optics, this description could easily refer to Goethe's intuitions. We know, for instance, that Werner Eisenberg, who made a substantial contribution to modern physics, worked intensively on color theory and that it is likely that he, like Christoph Cremer, was influenced by Goethe during a key phase of theory development.

Also noteworthy is Goethe's influence on the development of the modern optics industry. He made his own experimental observations with a microscope, often with the goal of disproving Newton's theory. For that reason, he promoted the manufacture of optical lenses with highly specific refractive properties. He sought and found private sponsors to fund the necessary infrastructure for his research, such as a glass foundry. As the Minister of Education, Science, and Technology, he promoted glass production and appointed renowned scholars to teach at the University of Jena. The director of his glass foundry, Körner, had a student whose name has reverberated down through the years in the fields of science and technology: Carl Zeiss. He was the godson of the main sponsor of Goethe's optics research. After completing his studies, he continued to work with Körner, and in 1846, he established a workshop for precision mechanics and optics that was the birthplace of the Zeiss Group, which is still a world leader in the field of optics today. Without Goethe's support for optics as a field of study, it is highly unlikely this company would exist today. Carl Zeiss recognized the significance of Goethe's theory for the construction of high-performance microscopes and won over scientists such as Ernst Abbe who provided him with support.

Modern cell biology was made possible by the new microscopes, but also present-day pathology and microbiology, leading to an explanation for bacterial illnesses such as anthrax, tuberculosis, cholera, and the plague. Cremer (2011) reckons that several billion people owe their lives to the development of the microscope. The new high-performance microscopes of the time only had a maximum resolution of 200nm, though. Below this limit, it was no longer possible to recognize structural details. This was not a technical problem, but rather a fundamental limit on what could be learned about nature by means of optics. It seemed that the secrets of the cosmic nanoworld would only be revealed using electron microscopes and x-ray microscopes, but in the 1990s there was a breakthrough in the supposedly unalterable limits of optical resolution; since then, localization microscopy has allowed researchers to analyze cellular nanostructures and viruses using visible light.

> This type of supermicroscopy is based on processes that separate Airy disks, which are formed from each illuminated molecule of an object by the microscope's lens, even if they lie close together, i.e., if they have a much smaller distance between them than the previously mentioned absolute limit of 200 nm for light microscopy.
>
> (Cremer, p. 88: DS)

Today, molecules can be put into a light state when the incident light is appropriate; when alternated with dark states, a high-resolution image is produced. This would appear to be an application of Goethe's idea "that the eye sees no form, inasmuch as light, shade, and colour together constitute that which to our vision distinguishes object from object, and the parts of an object from each other" (Eastlake, p. xxxviii).

In summary, we can say that the scientific and technical development of superresolution microscopy is a fascinating example of how ideas that arise from intuitive experiences of the world around us can lead to creative innovations. Individual disciplines incorporating theory and practice are normally isolated from one another; the previous example shows, though, how crossing boundaries between disciplines leads to scientific progress. Goethe, at any rate, "laid claim to the help of philosophers, naturalists, mathematicians, painters, mechanists, dyers, and heaven knows how many others" (Schmitz 1885, p. 286). Modern physicists like Cremer find Goethe's vision to be very timely and are basing their ideas for interdisciplinary research programs and academies on it.

Notes

1 Schiller's literary journal, *The Hours*.
2 Changing the meaning to "whores".
3 She always referred to Goethe by his title.

Chapter 12

Political changes and new passions
1806–1823

He who is not flayed does not learn.

After a decade of "Weimar Classicism", uninterrupted by the events of war, the military conflicts between Prussia and France represented a radical turning point. Napoleon crowned himself Emperor of the French in 1804 and began his campaign of conquest across Europe, which did not prevent Goethe from visiting Karlsbad for rest and relaxation, nor Christiane from spending some time in Bad Lauchstädt. But on 14 October, the Prussian troops were annihilated at the Battle of Jena–Auerstadt; afterwards, over 40,000 soldiers were quartered in Weimar, where they plundered and set fires. Goethe reacted with physical symptoms and was not able to participate in an audience with Napoleon on 16 October, where the other two privy councilors asked the emperor to cease the plundering. "In that horrible moment, I was assailed by my old malady. Please forgive my absence. I hardly know whether I will be able to send this note" (HA Letters 3, p. 27: DS). On that same day, though, he received a writ of protection, signed on behalf of Napoleon, to safeguard him and his home from invasion by marauding soldiers. It was only by dint of the courageous action of Duchess Louise, the only member of the ruling family to have remained in Weimar, and some lucky circumstances that the destruction ceased and the duchy survived. She was successfully able to advocate for the interests of the duchy against Napoleon, and Goethe recorded on 18 October the following in a letter to friends in Jena:

> In my house, nothing is damaged, I have lost nothing. The duchess is well and has conducted herself in such a way that demands the highest admiration. Wieland and I dined yesterday with the commandant. The good old man also had a lucky escape. The palace is undamaged. This we owe to our duchess alone.
>
> (HA Letters 3, p. 28: DS)

This period of unrest, plus Goethe's gratitude for Christiane living thorough "hours of trial" with him, led him to finally legitimize their relationship.

We are alive! Our house was spared from plundering and fire, as if by a miracle ... In order to brighten up these sad days with a celebration, I and my little cohabitant [literally, "house-friend"] came to the decision yesterday ... to officially enter into the holy state of matrimony.

(HA Letters 3, p. 29: DS)

They had a small, private wedding; the witnesses were his friend Riemer and their son August, now 16 years old. Nevertheless, Christiane was accepted only slowly and reluctantly into Weimar society, even after becoming Mrs. Goethe.

Goethe reacted to the terrible events of war and the chaos that followed by working for the common good:

Each of us must pull ourselves together in these initial moments and reconstruct as much as possible; in this way, all of us will be helped. We can start yet again to have an effect on ourselves and on others.

(HA Letters 3, pp. 29f.: DS)

Goethe attempted to get over the horrors of the events of October by throwing himself into his administrative and scientific work, which he also hoped would have an impact on his friends. He had a similar reaction to the death of Duchess Anna Amalia, whom he highly esteemed, on 10 April 1807:

Our Grand Duchess is a great loss, at a time when so much is turned upside down and chaotic. We must reflect no further on this subject, nor on anything else at the present time. We must live on from one day to another, and do and accomplish what is still possible.

(Bodley, p. 96)

During the summer, he was able to travel to Karlsbad again, informing Christiane that he felt quite well there. During his stay, he maintained his usual work rituals: he dictated short little stories and fairytales, began writing *Wilhelm Meister's Apprenticeship*, drew, and carried out geological investigations. He showed sympathy for individual sufferings caused by the war, but he vehemently rejected the patriotic remorse of the "Germans": "But when people lament over the whole thing that is supposed to be lost, but which no one in Germany has ever in his life seen, and much less cared about, – I have to conceal my impatience" (Coleridge, p. 48).

While taking the waters in Karlsbad, he met Count Reinhard, a German in the service of the French. His correspondence with Reinhard allowed him to remain within his sphere of activity in Weimar and yet to maintain contact with the happenings in the wider world. In fact, Goethe had become something of a homebody, enjoying the manageable size of his sphere of activity. He declined one of Zelter's many invitations with the following words: "but for several years past, I have felt a certain clinging to the place I live in; this has mainly arisen from the many interests awakened, but as yet undeveloped within me" (Coleridge, p. 50). As in his younger years, his drive to create things helped him to overcome terrible events. Too many new impressions, though, would prevent his internal work and damage his creativity. For this reason, he gladly acquiesced when the shadows of the past overtook him, allowing him to work on his "inner fairytale". In September of 1807, he received a letter of introduction from Elisabeth von Türkheim, née Schönemann, and he responded immediately to the woman who had once been so beloved, but whom he had left so hastily more than 30 years before:

> In conclusion permit me to say this—that it gave me infinite pleasure after such a long time once again to see a few lines by your dear hand, which I kiss a thousand times in memory of the days that I reckon among the happiest in my life.
>
> (Mann, p. 275)

In November, the pull of his "Jena canapé" was too great to resist. He was unable to be without an external stimulus, though, and became embroiled in a passionate attachment to the 18-year-old Minchen Herzlieb. This inspired him to compose new love poems.

The Friendly Meeting

In a broad mantle pulled up to my chin,
I trod the rocky path, so steep and grey,
Then down to the wintry plain,
Uneasy in my mind, intent on the nearby water.

But suddenly a new day was revealed:
A maiden came, heavenly to behold,
As ideal as those lovely women
In the realms of poetry. My yearning was quenched.

Yet I turned away and let her go
And pulled the folds of my mantle closer around me,
As though I wanted to warm myself in spite of myself;

But followed her nonetheless. She stood. Then it happened!
I could no longer remain within my mantle,
I cast it aside, she lay in my arms.

(HA 1, pp. 294f.: DS)

This sonnet, the second of 17, shows the aging, desperate man, who once again, "intent on the nearby water", entertains the idea of suicide. The poetical self is roused to new life by love, though: "But suddenly a new day was revealed". This can also be read as an allegory of Goethe's artistry, which found inspiration in erotic love. This love, though, is ambivalent, and the poetical self pulls back again in the third stanza. It "pulled the folds of its mantle closer" in order to seek warmth and security within itself. After retreating briefly, it is able to throw off its "mantle" in the last stanza and give itself over to love. The interaction between passionate attraction and dark rejection is the locus of the poetical self's erotic and creative realization. In the end, both passion and creativity remain unfathomable, even demonic.

The fifth and sixth sonnets describe how failure transforms unsettling erotic passion into art.

Growth

. . .
I feel the hot raging of love in my heart.
Should I embrace her to soothe the pain?

But alas! Now I must regard you as a princess:
You stand so starkly high above me;
I bend before your look, a passing glance.
. . .
If I should wean myself from the radiance of those looks,
They would no longer enhance the beauty of my life . . .

Now I can calmly travel through the world:
What I need may be had everywhere,
And that which I cannot do without I bring with me – love.
(HA 1, pp. 296f.: DS)

The poetical self feels its passion as "hot raging" and questions whether it can truly "soothe" its passion in the embrace of its beloved. The answer seems to be no, so the poetical self puts the beloved at an unattainable distance: "Now I must regard you as a princess". The beloved is so "high above me" that she is now beyond the reach of the poetical self. This appears to be a prerequisite for Goethe's art, but not just Goethe. Petrarch also wrote his famous sonnets to a woman, Laura, whom he would never be able to touch. Self-denial seems to have appeased the poetical self in Goethe's sonnets in a unique way: "Now I can calmly travel through the world". The interaction between passionate devotion and renunciation provides the poetical self with something indispensable, creative power. The poet, wandering through the world via his work, finds love and creativity: "What I need may be had everywhere". The strict form of the sonnet reminded Goethe of a passion that self-denial had transformed into creativity and that had hence been fulfilled on a different plane, which had been expressed more than 30 years previously in "Welcome and Departure".

Minchen Herzlieb was not the only one to inspire Goethe's new work. Beginning at this time, Goethe started showing an inclination for finding aesthetic inspiration in much younger women. Thus, this sonnet cycle is also connected to the young daughter, born in 1785, of Baron von Ziegesar, a court official and minister. Goethe had known her since she was a child and became better acquainted with her during the years 1802 and 1803. During the summer of 1808, while spending time in Karlsbad and Franzensbad, Goethe developed an ardent affection for her that spurred him to write more sonnets. His letters provide no hint of how far the relationship went, though. Immediately after his arrival in Franzensbad in July 1808, he wrote to Silvie von Ziegesar:

> How I came over, I don't quite know myself. The night was beautiful, the road as good as it could be, the horse vigorous, the coachman reliable. I was sunk in my thoughts of you and did not notice when we started; finally, I slept by turns, and your dear little oval face with all of its friendliness and gracefulness was before me.
>
> (HA Letters 3, pp. 82f.: DS)

Both this and the other letters to Silvie remain a mystery, yet they do reveal that this was when Goethe started searching for young women ("ogle-ees") for poetical inspiration. He wrote to his wife, who was going about Bad Lauchstädt "in a strange way":

> Fräulein Silvie is sweet and good, just as she always was; we have taken many walks together, and have always come away well from our excursions, even if it has rained every day ... What will you say, though, when I tell you that Riemer has found a pretty little thing [an "ogle-ee"], moreover a pretty little thing with a coach and horses, who takes him for drives. What will happen with you in this chapter, I will more than likely also discover.
>
> (HA Letters 3, p. 81: DS)

Silvie von Ziegesar was not a brief flirtation for Goethe; he developed a close relationship with the little girl and later the young woman. When his mother died on 13 September 1808, he wrote to Silvie straightaway:

> When the express message called me away from your friendly valley, dearest Silvie, I could not anticipate what lay in store for me. The death of my dear mother has clouded my return to Weimar. With only few words, I commend myself to your memory and hope that the cutting instruments accompanying this may not sever any of the fabric of your friendship.
>
> (HA Letters 3, p. 87: DS)

The passionate attraction a very young woman, one who has only recently left childhood behind, can exert on a mature man is one of the themes in the novel *Elective Affinities*. Goethe devised the novel during his stay at a spa town in the summer of 1808; in it, he also worked through his own conflicts, although without laying them bare: "I have put much in it, have hidden much in it. May this open secret be a joy to you" (HA Letters 3, p. 105: DS). Twenty years later, he told Eckermann, "There is not a line anywhere in the *Elective Affinities* that I did not experience myself, and there is more in there than anyone could comprehend on first reading it" (HA 6, pp. 644f.: DS).

With these comments, Goethe set his readers on a path that he knew would never lead them to a conclusive interpretation of the autobiographical contents of this work. It is likely that he himself wanted to avoid the knowledge of the psychological reality of his attraction to very young, very immature women. Nevertheless, he seems to have identified, at least in part, with Edward, the mature man who has fallen in love with the little-girlish Ottilie. In a letter to Reinhard, he thanked him for his understanding. "You accept my dear Ottilie so truly, so well, and so kindly, and you also do justice to Edward, who seems to me, at least, to be quite inestimable, because he loves unconditionally" (HA Letters 3, p. 120: DS). Goethe and Christiane's marriage had cooled during this period, and Goethe ensured that they spent a great deal of time apart. They continued to be fond of each other, though, and tolerant of entertaining relationships. In the summer of 1810, he wrote from Karlsbad to Christiane in Bad Lauchstädt,

> I doubt not that old and new objects of flirtation ["ogle-ees"] will abound and so I wish you luck. Make as many friends around there as possible; here there is always something strange and such a confusion that makes me almost annoyed with myself.
>
> (HA Letters 3, p. 134: DS)

In any case, something exceptional happened during this period that overshadowed, or rather, outshined, his marriage with Christiane, his philandering, and the death of his mother: His encounter with Napoleon.

In October of 1808, Goethe was given an audience with Napoleon during the Congress of Erfurt, a meeting between Alexander I of Russia and Napoleon, which was followed a short time later by Napoleon visiting Weimar. Goethe appeared dazzled by these meetings. He had already been an adamant admirer of Napoleon's before that, which seems quite out of place considering his usual sense of reality. In February of 1807, Riemer had noted the following comment by Goethe: "Extraordinary men, such as Napoleon, place themselves outside of morality. They act, after all, like physical causes such as fire and water" (Dombowsky, p. 10).

Goethe declared Napoleon a demonic genius who was entitled to defy common values, holding fast to this belief into old age. He viewed Napoleon as a "compendium of the world" and expressed the following with admiration to Eckermann in 1829: "Napoleon was in this especially great – that he was at all hours the same ... He was always in his element, and equal to each situation and each moment" (Oxenford, vol. 2, p. 166). Later Goethe expressed: "Daemonic beings of such sort the Greeks reckoned among their demigods" (Oxenford, vol. 2, p. 359). The circumstance that Napoleon carried a copy of *Werther* with him in his field library cannot be the only factor that blinded Goethe to the "awful and repulsive" aspects of the emperor, since he was able to perceive them in himself, in the form of Faust. He projected onto the despot an ideal of perfection and completeness that was missing from his own life. And yet his acceptance of his own imperfections and ambivalence and his insight that everyone is composed of both shadows and light had led him to live a creative, active life. His path, though, was shaken by crises and overshadowed by doubts about his self-worth. With Napoleon, he could be party to the splendor of an ideal genius, one who was "always in his element". In order to do this, though, he had to ignore Napoleon's dark side. At the time of his meeting with Napoleon, Goethe was feeling his own limits more clearly than ever. His marriage had become noticeably less warm, he was beset by illness, and there was no indication his love affairs would come to anything. This made him susceptible to creating a romanticized ideal of sovereignty and integrity. He could see himself reflected in the glory of this perfection and drawing the admiration of young women:

> The Emperor of France also gave me the Legion of Honour, and so you will find me decked in stars and ribbons when we meet again ... The lovely children at court were the most beautifully behaved, the most assured, you would have liked it, and the "ogle-ees" were countless.
>
> (HA Letters 3, pp. 90f.: DS).

Goethe appears to have shared a collective notion of grandeur that overshadowed the misery of the millions of dead and wounded, and the millions of orphaned and paupered. In October of 1808, he wrote the following to his friend Zelter:

> You will be astonished, I know, on reading the newspapers, that this flood of the mighty and the great ones of the earth has rolled as far as Weimar, and on to the battlefield of Jena ... The point where the Temple stands, is the farthest point, reached this time by Napoleon, towards the North-East. If you pay us a visit, (which Heaven grant you may!) I will place you on the very spot, where the little man here, is pointing to the world with his stick.
>
> (Coleridge, p. 64)

Goethe was not able to see through the notion of grandeur he was projecting onto Napoleon and then in turn identifying with, a delusion of grandeur that people have always been susceptible to and that has repeatedly led to the glorification of destructive violence. We can perhaps forgive Goethe for taking a benign view of the situation in 1808, and it is true that he was deserving of the order of merit he was awarded by Napoleon by dint of his service to the duchy. But the idea that he could not imagine anything greater in life really makes you think: "I gladly confess that nothing higher and more pleasing could have happened to me in all my life than to have stood before the French Emperor on such a footing" (Bielschowsky, vol. 2, pp. 414–415).

Goethe continued striving for social advancement may have clouded his apprehension of the horrors of the Napoleonic era; he basked in the glory of the great and mighty. After spending the summer in Karlsbad and Teplitz, he recorded the following: "Not remaining unknown by the Empress of Austria at the first location, and getting to know the King of Holland better at the second, were great gains, which I will always have to delight in" (HA Letters 3, p. 137: DS).

Once things calmed down, Goethe began writing his memoir, *Poetry and Truth*. He produced an initial outline in 1809, and the first three parts appeared between 1811 and 1814. He directed his gaze into the past and rekindled his early childhood and youth, perhaps in response, at least in part, to the death of his mother in September of 1808. He resumed the labor of dealing with unavoidable fate using his creativity. Once again, he retreated to Jena and asked for Christiane's patience:

> When you are together and enjoying yourselves, just think that I will be spending the next days working in order to soon be able to enjoy myself with you without interruption. I implore you to discourage all visits to me; real business can be handled in writing, especially if it is well thought out and presented well.
>
> (HA Letters 3, p. 108: DS)

In May of 1811, Goethe embarked on a new friendship. He received new creative energy from his intellectual exchanges with his new friend, Sulpiz Boiserée, 24 years Goethe's junior, culminating in a joint journey along the Rhine, Maine, and Neckar rivers. He was rejuvenated and felt especially productive, writing new poems while still underway and before reaching his destination. Looking back, he told Eckermann,

> Thence it comes that in men of superior endowments, even during their old age, we constantly perceive fresh epochs of singular productiveness; they seem constantly to grow young again for a time, and that is what I call a repeated puberty.
>
> (Oxenford, vol. 2, pp. 46–47)

At this time, Goethe was introduced to the world of the Persian poet Hafez, whose philosophically profound yet sensuously zestful works promoted

Goethe's revived powers of creativity. This led to the wonderful collection of poems *West-eastern Divan*. In the poem "Phenomenon", an aging man who feels newly imbued with the beauty of nature rediscovers his capacity for love:

Phenomenon

When Phoebus mingles
with the wall of rain,
immediately the edge of a bow appears,
shaded into colors.

In the mist I see
a similar arc drawn;
to be sure, the bow is white,
but still a heavenly bow.

And so, sprightly old man,
you should not be gloomy;
even if your hair is white,
still you'll fall in love.

(Appelbaum, p. 171)

During his travels, he met the former dancer Marianne von Willemer, who had recently married the banker Johann Jacob Willemer, in Frankfurt. This brief meeting in 1814 led one year later to a deep attachment. An erotic–poetical dialog developed between the two of them, spurring Marianne to write her own poems, which Goethe later included in his *West-eastern Divan*. This poetical love filled the 65-year-old with a new joie de vivre.

In September of 1815, Marianne and Goethe met again, this time in the grounds of the Heidelberg Castle; a third trip to visit Marianne was planned but never materialized. Their farewell was melancholy, and they never saw each other again. But having a relationship once again with a "distant lover" provided Goethe with an unforeseen degree of creative energy; he composed around 400 poems that addressed religious, philosophical, and political themes as easily as romantic yearnings and poetical self-reflection. Goethe's poetical experiences of himself and of the world resulted in the poem "Blissful Longing".

Blissful Longing

Tell nobody except the wise,
because the mob is immediately scornful;
I wish to praise that element of life
which longs for a fiery death.

In that coolness of nights of love
which begat you, where you begat,
an unfamiliar sensation comes over you
when the silent taper shines.

No longer do you remain embraced
by the shadow of the darkness,
but a new desire draws you
upward to a higher form of mating.

No degree of distance makes you doubtful;
you fly over and fall under a spell,
and, at last, lusting for the light,
like a moth you are burned to death.

And so long as you don't have it,
this "Die and be transformed!",
you will only be a gloomy guest
on the dark earth.

(Appelbaum, p. 173)

From a psychological standpoint, the poem seems to be a summary of Goethe's life experience. The first stanza declares that creativeness represents something disconcerting that many react deprecatingly to. For this reason, this knowledge should be shared with "nobody except the wise" and should not be surrendered to the derision – an expression of psychological defense – of the "mob". Creativity can destabilize personal boundaries to the point that it evokes a fear of death; the creative "element of life" inevitably finds itself near "fiery death".

In the second stanza, the solution to the hazards facing creativity is described. The "nights of love" (i.e. erotic encounters) lead to the creation of the creative self, which "begat you, where you begat". Yet the past touches us with "an unfamiliar sensation", even in the midst of erotic love and creative passion; the "silent taper" symbolizes temporality. In the third stanza, we are freed from "the shadow of the darkness" by erotic creative energy. It leads us to a "desire" for "a higher form of mating", i.e. to strive to become one with the natural and spiritual world. In this way, we rise up from the fear and darkness and grow wings, like the wings of desire in Plato's *Symposium*, that allow us to reach a higher level of being.

Everything seems possible in the fourth stanza: the poetical self is no longer "doubtful" due to any "degree of distance"; rather, it has fallen "under a spell" and has "flown over" for sexual union. The fulfillment of its yearning, "lusting for the light", leads it to cease to be like the "moth" in Chinese poetry. The fifth stanza reminds us that changing and dying – "this 'Die and be transformed!'" – are unavoidable for creative vitality. He who manages to avoid the tumult of passion and creativity will remain "a gloomy guest/on the dark earth".

Even though Goethe and Christiane each maintained many other relationships, and even though their once exuberant sexual love for each other had cooled, they remained connected by their ties as partners, but also by the ties of love. In the year before her death, in March of 1815, Christiane wrote to Goethe in Jena,

> My only thought now is to see you again and to tell you how much I love you. And how I am happy when each morning, when I wake up, I can thank you, that my energy has increased again.
>
> (Gräf, vol. 2, p. 362: DS)

Goethe was profoundly affected by Christiane's death in June of 1816. She died of kidney failure and suffered such immense pain before her death that she bit through her own tongue. The women caring for her had to leave her room, as they could no longer bear to hear her screams of pain. Goethe himself was confined to his bed with a high fever, and so she was alone during her final hours. He was also kept from her bedside by his dread of illness and death. Goethe recorded the following in his journal: "Approaching end of my wife. Final terrible battle of her constitution. She passed away about noon. Emptiness and deathly stillness in and around me" (qtd. in Friedenthal, p. 264). On the day of her death, he wrote the following verses for her epitaph:

> In vain you try, o sun,
> To shine through the dark clouds!
> The whole value of my life
> Is to weep for her loss.
>   (Ghibellino, p. 85)

After Christiane's death, Goethe sought refuge in his work both in the administration of the duchy and in the scientific and artistic institutes in Weimar and Jena, which included supervising libraries, parks, and the university at Jena. In addition, he kept up with his friends Boiserée, Zelter, and Wilhelm von Humboldt. A short time later, he also took up his own scientific research again.

During times of sorrow, Goethe was supported by his work and his friendships, but he was also assisted by his disciplined lifestyle. He woke up early, was careful to eat regularly and to get plenty of exercise out in the open air. This saw him through periods of crisis and also facilitated his administrative and scientific work, but it cut him off from the "pathological wellspring" of his poetry, hence his lack of productivity in writing poetry during this period.

Chapter 13

Love in old age and late creativity
1821–1832

And when mortals fall silent in their torment,
a god granted me the power of expressing my suffering.

Now in his eighth decade, Goethe once again experienced an unexpected change in his life. The renowned statesman, scientist, and poet had actually achieved everything he wanted to and could now calmly look on both his life and his death with the wisdom of age. The poem "The One and the All" reflects his independent worldview.

The One and the All

To find himself in the limitless,
the individual will gladly disappear;
there all satiety is overcome;
instead of ardent wishes, violent desires,
instead of burdensome demands, strict obligations,
self-surrender is a pleasure . . .

It must stir and act creatively,
first shaping itself, then transforming itself;
only seemingly does it stand still for a few moments.
The Eternal is constantly astir in all things:
for everything would have to crumble into nothingness
if it insisted on remaining in its momentary state.
(Appelbaum, pp. 195–197)

This poem was composed in Jena in 1821 and depicts a poetical self that is reconciled to its fate. The narrow boundaries of one's own person are dissolved in favor of being taken up in a greater cosmic whole. Inspired by ideas from the Far East, this dissolution is experienced not as a threat, but as bliss: "Self-surrender is a pleasure". As in Taoism, this does not mean cessation, but rather activity in a higher sense, where the creative being is not dispersed, but rather remains completely present while outside of himself. The "eternal", which is found in activity, will be one of Goethe's central themes in his poem *Legacy*, which we will look at more closely at the end of this book. In this poem, the permanence of being is emphasized – "no being can crumble into nothingness" – while in "The One and the All", the dialectical antithesis is declared: "everything [must] crumble into nothingness". Fading into the stream of life is a prerequisite for the eternal, "if it [insists] on remaining in its momentary state". In *Legacy*, this apparent paradox will be solved.

In the summer of 1823, out of a clear blue sky, Goethe experienced a romantic disappointment which plunged him into a deep crisis, as had happened 50 years earlier. While taking the waters in Marienbad, he fell in love with the 19-year-old Ulrike von Levetzow. Just as he had known Silvie von Ziegesar since childhood, so he knew Ulrike, and now he developed a burning passion for the young lady in the first bloom of womanhood. The 74-year-old Goethe seriously planned to marry the much younger woman. He even had his physician confirm that his advanced age did not preclude him from marrying, and Duke Carl August was prepared to solicit the bride. Amalie von Levetzow, Ulrike's mother, initially thought the whole thing was a joke, but once she realized that Goethe was serious, she practically fled Marienbad with her daughter. Goethe seemed to almost a demand an explicit rejection and followed the Levetzows. His proposal was rejected again; deeply disappointed and in despair, he composed the famous "Marienbad Elegy" during the arduous journey home to Weimar. He added to it the poems "To Werther" and "Reconciliation" to create the *Trilogy of Passion*. Remembering the emotional pain he had described almost 50 years earlier in *The Sufferings of Young Werther*, he titled the first poem "To Werther":

To Werther

Once again, much-lamented shade, you venture
out into the light of day ...
I was chosen as one to remain; you, as one chosen to depart,
left before me – and didn't lose much.

. . .

You smile, my friend, sentimentally, as is befitting:
a horrible departure made you famous;
we mourned your lamentable misfortune,
you left us behind for weal or woe.
Then the uncertain path of passions
drew us again into its labyrinth;
and we have been embroiled in repeated amorous plights,
finally in separation – separation is death!
How touching it sounds when the poet sings
in order to avoid the death that separation brings!

Entangled in such torments, half to blame,
may a god give him the power to express what he endures.
                                          (Appelbaum, pp. 215–219)

It is remarkable that Goethe was still so deeply connected to feelings he had experienced 50 years before. Werther's "much-lamented shade" is still quite near to him. The world of emotions in *Werther*, which mirrored Goethe's world of experience during the years 1772 to 1774, was still very present to the 74-year-old, as if he had experienced *The Sufferings of Young Werther* only a short while ago. Werther preceded him in death, "and didn't lose much". Goethe, on the other hand, continued to live, "for weal or woe"; he was plagued by his passions and "embroiled in repeated amorous plights". In the end, even the poetical self must face the inevitable: "separation is death!" But then the poet lifts up his voice to avoid death. He is "entangled in such torments" and calls out to a god, "to express what he endures". Ultimately, he expects to overcome separation and death in work.

Goethe's creative culture of work and of remembrance saved him again and again from suicide, and made it possible for him to produce timeless creations. In the *Trilogy of Passion*, he appeared deeply grateful for his ability to process his disappointments using his creativity. For that reason, he chose as the epigraph for "Elegy" the verses at the beginning of this chapter:

And when mortals fall silent in their torment,
a god granted me the power of expressing my suffering.
                                          (Appelbaum, p. 207)

In the poem "Elegy", Goethe recapitulated his relationship with Ulrike, with all of its highs and lows:

What am I now to hope for from this meeting,
from this day's blossom, still enclosed in its bud?
Both paradise and hell are open to you:
what changeable stirrings in my mind! –
No more doubts! She arrives at heaven's gate,
and raises you up to her arms.
                                          (Appelbaum, p. 207)

At first, the poetical self wavers, and everything – "paradise and hell" – are open to him until the transfigured beloved appears: "She arrives at heaven's gate,/and raises you up to her arms". Deified love allows the poetical self to feel liberated from earthly pain:

And so you were received in paradise
as if you were worthy of an eternal, beautiful life;

your every wish, hope, desire was fulfilled;
here was the goal of your most ardent striving;
and at the sight of that unique beauty
the fountain of yearning tears at once dried up.

(Appelbaum, p. 209)

In the next 20 stanzas, the poetical self takes the reader along on a journey to the most blessed zenith of erotic love, only to end at the nadir of despair:

I have lost the universe, I am even lost to myself,
I who recently was still the favorite of the gods;
they tested me, they lent me Pandora,
so rich in possessions, richer in danger,
they thrust me toward those gift-bestowing lips;
now they separate me from them and utterly destroy me.

(Appelbaum, p. 215)

In the third poem of the *Trilogy of Passion*, which is dedicated to the pianist Maria Szymanowska, Goethe appears once again to be reconciled to his fate.

Reconciliation

Passion brings suffering! – Uneasy heart,
who can soothe you, you that have lost too much?
Where are the hours, vanished too quickly?
The most beautiful thing was chosen for you in vain!
Sad is our mind, confused are our endeavors;
how the lofty world fades away from our senses!

And then music hovers by on its angel's wings,
interweaving one tone with another into millions,
in order to penetrate man's being through and through,
to fill him overabundantly with eternal beauty:
his eyes grow moist, in a higher yearning
they feel the divine worth of music and of tears.

And so the relieved heart quickly notices
that it still lives and beats and wishes to go on beating,
so it can offer itself willingly in return,
in sincerest thanks for that more than generous gift.
Then came the sensation – may it remain forever! –
of the double happiness of music and of love.

(Appelbaum, p. 207)

In the first stanza, the poetical self describes the pain of passionate love: "Passion brings suffering". On the one hand, love is "the most beautiful thing", but on the other, it afflicts us so strongly that "the lofty world fades away from our senses". In the second stanza, the poetical self is given new heart by artistic mastery, by "music ... on its angel's wings", and is filled with a feeling of "eternal beauty". In the third stanza, it feels reconciled to its fate by creativity and passion, "the double happiness of music and of love".

It almost seems as if Goethe had sought out an over-inflated, unrealizable romantic relationship in order to reignite his passion, allowing him to reach the pinnacle of his mature poetical powers. It was reported, though, that Goethe, exhausted by the pain of his final infatuation, became increasingly despondent (see Höfer 2002). And yet, soon after his paroxysms of grief and his outbreak of poetry passed, it was back to business as usual, and he resumed his normal rituals of work and life. He suffered another attack of the "pernicious catarrh" that had begun in November, yet it was not long before Goethe could get back to work on his two great works of his later years, *Wilhelm Meister's Travels* and *Faust II*. During this crisis period, he continued to correspond with his friends, and he enjoyed spending time with his grandchildren. He wrote to his daughter-in-law, Ottilie, in August,

> The children are well and cheerful; Walther, busied and preoccupied by lessons, piano practice, and visits at court. Wolf[gang] sticks especially close to me and has claimed a drawer in my desk for odds and ends and other toys, which he turns out every day; but he always does it with care and in a certain symmetrical order, which is delightful.
>
> (HA Letters 4, p. 119: DS)

Daily life with Ottilie and August and his three grandchildren was not too disruptive to his work and also provided him with a zest for life into old age. Family life also acted as a buffer against his melancholy moods. And yet he sometimes regarded both communal living and creative life as difficult, uncomfortable tasks. In a conversation with Eckermann, he summed up his life thusly:

> I have ever been esteemed one of Fortune's chiefest favourites; nor will I complain of or find fault with the course my life has taken. Yet, truly, there has been nothing but toil and care; and I may say that, in all my seventy-five years, I have never had a month of genuine comfort.
>
> (Oxenford, vol. 1, pp. 124–125)

Goethe's nurturing of his son began when he was just a child and continued into his adult years; Goethe's letters to him while a student are evidence of a concerned father trying to be supportive of his son. This support saw him through his law studies and afterwards his position in the administration of the duchy. According to probability theory, the likelihood that August would be as creatively active as his father is almost nil; the innate ability and environmental conditions contributing to a once-in-a-century talent are statistical outliers, so individuals in the succeeding generation will regress toward the mean, i.e. they will be of average ability. August had no recourse to creative work to counter his own moods, so he turned instead to alcohol, which his father had already warned him against while he was a student. He also had a rocky marriage, and his father had little success in mediating between August and his wife during their fights. Goethe felt the pull of affection toward his daughter-in-law, Ottilie, and seems to have been able to deal with her temperament better than with his son's.

In his later years, Goethe attached importance to his conversations with his secretary, Johann Peter Eckermann, who became one of his close confidants starting in 1823. Eckermann's recordings of these conversations are impressive, documenting the older Goethe's realm of thought and experience. They show how the elder statesman and poet continued to participate in contemporary developments in literature and science. He had long been familiar with European literature, and now works of Indian and Chinese literature came to his attention, paving the way for his *Chinese-German Hours and Seasons*. These poems appear light, breezy, and hopeful.

Goethe seems to have reconciled himself to his fate, and writing poetry seems to have calmed his latent fear of death: "Self-surrender is a pleasure". He was unable to avoid another stroke of fate, though: the death of his friend and patron Duke Carl August in June of 1828, ending a close-knit relationship that had lasted over 50 years. Although he knew it would be considered an affront, Goethe fled from the conventional funeral rites. Sequestered away in Dornburg, he wrote a poem in which he was able to give expression to his love for Carl August and the others he had lost or left behind, as well as for the world:

To the Rising Full Moon

Dornburg, 25th of August 1828

Do you wish to desert me at once?
A moment ago you were so close!
You are darkened by masses of cloud,
and now you are gone altogether.

But you feel how gloomy I am;
your rim looks upward like a star!
You bear witness to me that I am loved,
no matter how far away my sweetheart is.

And so, rise! Brighter and brighter,
on a clear course, in full splendor!

Even if my heart beats painfully faster,
the night is more than full of bliss.
                    (Appelbaum, pp. 225–227)

The poetical self laments its losses: "and now you are gone altogether". It is saddened and turns toward the cosmos: "your rim looks upward like a star!" Here it feels it has been assumed into a larger whole, which shows it that it is loved, "no matter how far away my sweetheart is". It feels connected to those who are far away and those who have passed away, and it feels filled with loved. Although these cosmic bonds are painful, they are also "more than full of bliss". Goethe was thankful for the love he had been able to feel for and from his parents, his sister, his friends of both genders, his wife Christiane, and Duke Carl August. It led him to create beauty "in full splendor" and also to experience a blissfulness in pain that has a timeless effect:

Dornburg, September 1828

In the morn, when valley, hill, and garden
Are hidden in veils of fog
And flowers are filled to overflowing
With deep yearning,

When the cloud-bearing ether
Contends with limpid day,
And a driving east wind
Clears the way for the sun's orbit across the blue,

Then you, feasting your eyes, will give thanks
To the pure heart of the great ones, the fair ones,
And the departing sun, cloaked in red,
Gilds the horizon.
                    (HA 1, p. 391: DS)

This measured celebration of nature in animated images is one of Goethe's last poems. It was composed against the backdrop of the 79-year-old's premonition of death. In November of 1830, Goethe received word of the unexpected death of his son, with whom Goethe had maintained a lively correspondence to the end. His initial reaction was calm, and he wrote to his friend Zelter,

"Expect trials up to the last" … The element in this trial that is really strange and significant is, that all those burdens which I thought to divest myself of immediately, – nay, with the New Year, – letting them devolve on one younger than myself, – I shall now have to drag on alone, and that too with more difficulty than ever. In such matters, it is the grand idea of duty that can alone uphold us.

(Coleridge, pp. 418–419)

However, 14 days later he suffered a violent hemorrhage, and it was thought he would not survive. He recovered quickly, though, and continued to fulfill his duties as head of the family. Despite the worry they caused him, Goethe's grandchildren were also a source of happiness and hope for him. In June of 1831, he wrote the following about the little girl and the two boys: They

> are really like sunny weather; wherever they go, it is bright. Joy in the moment, whatever it may be; that is then directly conveyed even to the oldest among us, and so we want to praise the good spirits who have lit just such a little light for us.

(FA 38, p. 407: DS)

In August of 1831, he took the two boys with him on a visit to his old workshops in Ilmenau, and it is interesting to note how sympathetic and loving the seemingly unapproachable statesman, scientist, and prince among poets was in his interactions with them (see Damm 2007). When alone, though, he was troubled by the imminence of death, alternating between despondent resignation and the hope of living on after death. In February of 1829, he commented to Eckermann, "Man should believe in immortality; he has a right to this belief; it corresponds with the wants of his nature" (Oxenford, vol. 2, p. 122). In addition to this belief, which sounds rather like a protest against the unavoidability of death, his literary work also kept him facing life. He dedicated his final years to completing *Wilhelm Meister's Travels* and *Faust II*, in which he worked through two aspects of his own ambitions: Wilhelm Meister recognizes his own boundaries but renounces them, while Faust strives to overcome his own earthly limitations. On 22 July 1831, the entry in his diary stated that he had completed *Faust*, and hence "the main business achieved". He considered *Faust* his legacy; with it, he gave lasting and universal expression to his mortal struggle with passion and creativity.

Like his life, Goethe's death was characterized by fear and desperation, hope and reconciliation. On 14 March 1832, he caught a chill, and three days later he dictated a letter to Wilhelm von Humboldt, the contents of which will be discussed in more detail in the last chapter of this book. He was bent on "augmenting, wherever possible, what is and has remained within me" (Gray) during the time he had left. Up until shortly before his death, he did not appear to have lost any of his mental clarity or desire to learn. On 20 March, he felt a crushing pain in his chest that was probably due to a heart attack. When the pain subsided, Goethe expressed his hope of being able to work again. He died on 22 March 1832, and his daughter-in-law reported the following in the death notice: "Mentally strong and very kind to the last breath, he departed from us in his eighty-third year of life".

Part II

Creativity, art of living, and illness

Chapter 14

Life as creative self-realization

The *Wilhelm Meister* project

> Do you know the land where the lemon trees blossom,
> where the golden oranges glow in the dark foliage . . .

Like Werther and Faust, the fictional character of Wilhelm Meister has some traits that are undeniably autobiographical. Goethe spoke of "his beloved dramatic likeness". The *Wilhelm Meister*-project – from the *Theatrical Mission* through *Wilhelm Meister's Apprenticeship* to *Wilhelm Meister's Travels* – was full of starts and stops, accompanying Goethe through more than 50 years of his life. The novels show the history of one man's education in his relationship to society. The risks involved in giving shape to his own life, including the possibilities of failure, are symbolically and allegorically portrayed by various figures.

Wilhelm Meister's Theatrical Mission

Wilhelm Meister's Theatrical Mission was begun in 1777 and abandoned, incomplete, in 1785 after the fourteenth chapter of the sixth book. It impressively documents Goethe's psychological development in these years. Unlike in *The Sufferings of Young Werther*, Goethe regards himself as more wise in the ways of the world and less torn by self-referential passions in this novel, his second, which contemplates his personal development at the junction of his familial and social environments. The novel begins with a description of a father who does not feel comfortable with his wife. It is his mother that he discusses pedagogical issues with, emphasizing that play – with puppets, fairy-tales, and "comedies" – is indispensable for children's development, in much the same vein as modern psychoanalysts, such as Donald W. Winnicott (1971).

The second chapter depicts how the biblical stories of Saul and David are acted out on Christmas Eve; later, Wilhelm sits alone in his room, ruminating on what has occurred. Wilhelm, pseudonymous with Goethe, is described as a child who was often unsatisfied and thus retreated into his own inner world. In the next chapter, this retreat into a fantasy world of his own making is linked to his disappointments in his mother:

He begged his mother to let him have it played over again, but only got a harsh answer, because she could find no joy in the fun provided by the grandmother for her children, which seemed like a reproach on her own unmotherliness. I am sorry to have to say it, but the fact is true, that this woman, who had borne her husband five children – two sons and three daughters, of whom Wilhelm was the eldest – had with advancing years conceived a passion for an insipid man, and her husband, who was aware of the truth, could not endure the fellow. As a natural consequence, neglect, trouble and mutual bickering crept into the household.

(Page, p. 8)

This shows how the mother's affair leads to a lack of interest in her son's games and also how it seriously impedes the family's ability to peacefully coexist. It seems that Wilhelm's, and hence Goethe's, creativity developed despite his mother's resistance. This is a circumstance that is often found among creative types. They may be carefully encouraged, but they may also develop their creative powers under adverse conditions.

Unlike in *Götz* and in *Werther*, where women are portrayed as fascinating and colorful but also dangerous and destructive figures, here Goethe's depiction of the mother's role in Wilhelm's emotional and artistic development is closer to reality:

in her dissatisfaction, their mother was generally in a bad temper, and even when this was not the case, was sure to rail against her husband ... Sometimes this hurt Wilhelm acutely ... Thus the boy became estranged from his mother, and was most unfortunately situated, because his father also was a hard man; so that nothing seemed left for him but to creep into himself, a fate with which children and old folks is of serious consequence.

(Page, pp. 8–9)

Goethe's alter ego, Wilhelm Meister, reacts to these difficult circumstances by devoting himself to his fantasies, in this way attempting to cope with painful experiences:

Thus for some time Wilhelm's childish existence pursued its way. His thoughts often turned back to that happy Christmas Eve, and he delighted to look at pictures or to read fairy and heroic stories. Meanwhile his grandmother, who did not wish to have taken so much pains for nothing, arranged that, on the long-delayed visit of some neighbours' children, the puppet theatre should again be erected and the play once more repeated.

(Page, p. 9)

His lively curiosity leads him to develop his fantasies within him while also exploring the reality around him. He wants to discover the secrets of the puppet theater and to take what he has seen to use in his own way. He spies on the maid while she is packing the puppets away, attempting to understand what is happening backstage in the theater, but also the events that are happening around him. He has an inner need to do this; the mood in the family is hostile. His father is increasingly distressed by his wife's horrible conduct:

> And had it not been for his children, a look at whom gave him courage and conviction that he still had something in the world to work for, it would hardly have been possible for him to endure it. In such moods men lose almost all taste for childish joys, the invention and arrangement of which are indeed rather the mother's affair, and not the father's; and when she is a wretch, then little consolation is left for the family in what should be its most blessed years. In the present case it was the grandmother who provided this consolation.
>
> (Page, p. 13)

Goethe will also acknowledge the important role his grandmother played in his personal development in *Poetry and Truth*. The puppet theater was associated with his grandmother, and a fantasy world arose from it that would be further developed in the theater. Nevertheless, he also emphasized the importance of solitude for personal development in the *Theatrical Mission*: "He often invited his brother, sisters and comrades to join him, but was much more frequently quite alone. His imagination and vivacity brooded over this little world, which necessarily soon assumed another form" (Page, p. 15).

Puberty is a difficult period for Wilhelm, yet he is able to draw on his power of imagination, which had been supported and challenged during his childhood, to creatively mold this critical phase in his life:

> Wilhelm had now reached those years in which the physical forces begin most to develop, and in which people are often unable to imagine why a smart and active child should appear outwardly stupid and impracticable. He now read a great deal, and still found his best satisfaction in comedies.
>
> (Page, p. 20)

He notices physical changes in himself and no longer feels comfortable in his own skin:

> The age of boyhood is, I believe, less amiable than that of childhood, because it is a middle, a half state. Although childishness still clings to our boys, and they are still childish, yet with its earlier limitation they have lost the lovable complacency of that former state ... they imitate and act things they neither can nor should be. It is just so with the inner state of their bodies, just so with their outward growth.
>
> (Page, p. 23)

Wilhelm evades these self-doubts and frictions by avoiding the upsets of little love affairs and withdrawing into the world of the theater:

> It was particularly fortunate under these circumstances that Wilhelm's good natural qualities came to his help, and that none of the girls for whom he soon enough began to feel a fancy were able to join his theatrical company; his love for the theatre therefore remained pure, and he could behold without rivalry how the others each sought to set his own princess upon the throne.
>
> (Page, p. 23)

He creates a conflict-free sphere for himself where he is able to deal, indirectly, with his problems. He succeeds in this for a time, until he meets a sexually experienced woman who sparks his desire:

> I name her here as Madame, though I remember having formerly spoken of her as a girl. To avoid all misunderstanding, let me then at once disclose the fact that she had contracted a "marriage of conscience" with a man without conscience. He soon after quitted the company, and she was, except for this trifle, a girl as before. She again used her former name, and passed first as maiden, then as wife, and now as widow. Wilhelm was anxious to hold her for the last, and found certainly the strongest reasons on this side. His embarrassment and agitation on beholding her did not but render him the more agreeable and vivacious.
>
> (Page, pp. 29–30)

In Madame, alias Mariana, there are echoes of many of Goethe's love affairs, reminding us of Gretchen, Käthchen Schönkopf, Charlotte Buff, and Lili Schönemann. Meeting Mariana transports Wilhelm to another world:

> and all night long and next day her image floated so often before him that he was very absent and clumsy at business. Next evening, as soon as he had closed the shop, an invisible hand seized him by the forelock, he felt that he was being led away, and found himself sitting, as in a dream, on the sofa beside his adored one.
>
> (Page, pp. 32–33)

He desires her and feels desired in turn, and he treats his beloved's previous sexual experiences with tolerance:

> A girl who wins herself a fresh lover in succession to several previous conquests is like the flame when a new log of wood is laid upon the burnt-out embers. Actively she flatters the newly arrived darling, plays with lambent heat around him until he glows in full blaze of splendour. Her

avidity seems to pass over him in play, but with every flash she pierces deeper and deeper, consuming his marrow to its very depths. Ere long, like his forsaken rivals, he will lie upon the ground and, inwardly glowing, extinguish in smoky agony.

(Page, p. 33)

Evidently Wilhelm, alias Goethe, fears more than abandonment; he also fears losing his creative potency if he were to engage in sexual love. What is remarkable about this passage, though, is a different aspect, namely, the likelihood that a man without any sexual experience could write so empathetically and knowledgeably about sexual love. In other words, how plausible is Eissler's (1963) opinion that Goethe was 38 years old before he had a sexual relationship with a woman? I will expand on this point from different perspectives in Chapter 18. Wilhelm's assessment of Mariana's sex life and his own stance toward it are depicted in the *Theatrical Mission* thusly:

In her early years she had beheld the childish joys of love too quickly scared away, was conscious of so many humiliations endured in the arms of one and another, and at the present time was sacrificed to the secret pleasures of a wealthy and unbearably dull milksop, and, being naturally a good-hearted creature, never felt quite comfortable when Wilhelm seized and kissed her hand in all sincerity, gazing into her eyes with the full, clear glance of youthful love. She could not endure that glance; she feared lest he might read experience in her own; her eyes sank in confusion, and the happy Wilhelm believed that he found therein an augury and sweet confession of love, so that his senses clashed against each other like the strings of a psaltery. O happy youth! O happy time of love's awakening fires!

(Page, pp. 33–34)

These lines speak of real experience, making it difficult to believe they could have come from the pen of someone inexperienced. What is most likely is that Goethe was doing more than accompanying Carl August while on the prowl in Weimar; he was probably maintaining longer-term sexual relationships, perhaps with one of Carl August's mistresses. An addition indicator of sexual experience is another one of Wilhelm's descriptions of Mariana:

In his arms Mariana first learned to know that bliss of love to which she had hitherto been a stranger; the heartiness wherewith he pressed her to his bosom, the thankfulness which often contented itself with her hand, penetrated her, and she daily recovered spirit ... But the lightness, animation and wit with which in the early stages of their passion they had sought to bind and entertain each other, and whose exercise gave zest to each caress, tended daily more and more to decay ... But when alone, when from the clouds amid which his passion bore her aloft she fell to recognition of her situation, then indeed was she to be pitied ... But now that the poor girl had felt herself uplifted for brief moments into a better world, had looked down, as from the skies, through light and joy upon the waste and refuse of her life, had realised what a wretched creature that woman is who cannot, with desire, also inspire love and respect ... With Wilhelm it was quite otherwise. For him a new world had arisen, a world rich in blissful prospects. If the excess of his first joys somewhat abated, yet the fact which formerly had but darkly burrowed in his soul now stood out as clear as light: She is thine! She has given herself to thee!

(Page, pp. 38–40)

Could a sexual novice write such a passage? It is perfectly clear that Goethe's alter ego is having a sexual relationship with Mariana: "Wilhelm's tenderness had triumphed over her prudence, and she began to feel that the undesired felicity of becoming a mother lay before her" (Page, p. 44). When it comes to all things sexual, shouldn't Goethe be reflected in his Wilhelm Meister? A seamless identification of Goethe with his protagonist would make this assumption completely implausible. Wilhelm Meister enjoys the pleasures of sexual love, thereby entering not merely the next phase of life, but a new version of his own self:

O, Mariana! to me, the happiest of men, it is as with a bridegroom, who, full of anticipation of the new world which shall unfold in and through him, stands thoughtful, longingly, upon the sacred threshold, before the mysterious curtains whence the ravishments of love whisper him their greeting.

(Page, pp. 48–49)

Wilhelm's first sexual love allows him to detach himself from his parental abode, as so frequently happens during late adolescence, while also helping him to create his own cultural world: "My heart has long since forsaken my parents' house. Even as my spirit hovers over the stage, so truly is my heart with you" (Page, p. 49). This happy love affair soon comes to an abrupt end, though, when Wilhelm erroneously comes to the conclusion that Mariana had been unfaithful to him. He is plunged into crisis, just as Goethe was at the age of 14 after separating from Gretchen and at the age of 18 after breaking things off with Käthchen Schönkopf. Goethe's reflection, Wilhelm, shares his same fate of becoming physically ill: "When misfortune overwhelmed our poor Wilhelm, his inward parts burned like a furnace ... Then followed a period of clamorous, ever-recurrent and insupportable anguish" (Page, p. 58).

Like Goethe, who found stability in his family and in his friend Behrisch, Wilhelm is able to accept the support of his siblings and his friend Werner during his grief-induced illness:

A virulent attack of fever, with its usual sequel of physic, weariness, anxious friends around his bed, the company and love of his relations, often first manifested in our hours of distress and weakness, were all now so many distractions of a changed condition.

(Page, p. 59)

Like Goethe after his return from Leipzig, Wilhelm withdraws from social contact:

He fled from the face of man, and confined himself to his room, which he could never make warm enough ... He was plagued by spurious moods, his opinions grew confused and exaggerated, so that one could hardly recognise him for the youth of earlier days.

(Page, p. 60)

In the end, Wilhelm's emotional and physical crisis leads to a productive regression and to an improved state of health, just as Goethe experienced after his collapse in Leipzig. Wilhelm also develops an exceptional amount of creative energy from this crisis; he acquires the works of the great masters, delving into questions of poetry, and becomes a poet himself. This allows him to cope with his everyday sufferings and cares:

He partakes the sorrows and joys of every human destiny. As the man of the world crawls through his days in gnawing melancholy over grievous loss, or meets his fate with extravagant rapture, so does the receptive, quickly-stirred spirit of the poet step like the wandering sun from night to day, and tune, with easy transfer, his harp to joy or grief. Native-born upon the soil of his heart blooms the lovely flower of wisdom, and while others dream awake, and whatever marvels may happen, they are to him both past and future.

(Page, pp. 73–74)

In the theory of poetics developed in the novel, which at the same time is also an introduction to his art of living, we hear from a mature poet who has overcome many crises. Unlike the poetical self in "Odes to Behrisch" and "Journey to the Harz in Winter", Wilhelm finds inner peace and a certain distance from himself in daily work and art, thereby reflecting Goethe's state during his first period in Weimar, albeit while ignoring its dark aspects. Wilhelm creates an idealized image, well knowing that he will have to wrest it from fate anew each day. The hazards of poetical life follow hard on the heels of unbridled enthusiasm:

Now first can I understand the laments of the poets – of the wretched, who through anguish became wise. Until now I regarded myself as indestructible, invulnerable: and now, alas! I see that an early and heavy injury can never be washed out, never again made good. I feel that I must carry it with me to the grave, that not for a single day of life may it leave me, this agony

which now at last destroys me–yea, and HER memory also shall remain
with me, the memory of the worthless.

(Page, pp. 77–78)

Once again, this underscores the importance of remembering for creative
productivity, even if the experiences remembered are painful. To Eissler (1963),
this approach is evidence of Goethe's masochistic tendencies. He may well call it
that, but in pathologizing it, he is overlooking the fact that working through
painful, guilt-ridden, and shameful experiences is an essential aspect of creativity.

In the last two passages cited, we find a wonderfully condensed psychological theory of creativity. The poet gives himself over to "the sorrows and joys of
every human destiny", frequently finding himself at the very limit of what he
can bear. Sometimes he experiences a poetical triumph and is able to lift himself
above the pain of reality, only to immediately have "an early ... injury" catch
up with him. The psychoanalyst and philosopher Jacques Lacan (1949) speaks
of a "primordial lack" (*manque primordial*), an initial deficiency that prevails at
the beginning of all creative endeavors. Like Goethe, Wilhelm senses the danger
of falling into the emptiness and annihilation of the primordial lack. Whether
the tendency to gravitate toward chaos obeys a biological law, which Freud
referred to as the "death drive" (1923), or if it is basically due to ubiquitous
frustrations and traumas is of secondary importance here. A creative person
masters the pull of destruction by shaping new realities, yet this does not
prevent him from repeatedly suffering new injuries that then require new
efforts; he is unable to find true equanimity.

Like Goethe, Wilhelm is doomed to wander. Nevertheless, he is calmer and
more wise than Goethe's earlier condensations, in particular Werther. He is
integrated into a social group, where he seeks a place for himself, and the
history of his personal education is more tightly interwoven with his social
relationships. Werther seeks ecstatic experiences of becoming one, but Wilhelm
Meister learns to accept his own limitations and those of his environment; in
this respect, he reflects the adult Goethe. He defends the danger of losing the
creative forces of adolescence while growing older by using his artistic work to
maintain his pubescent follies.

Wilhelm is able to bear social isolation to some degree, and after his sister
marries his best friend Werner, he begins to travel. Immersing himself in nature,
being alone, and working creatively all lead him back to himself. During all of
this, he comes to grips with a number of people who are typical of different
conceptions of life; in the following, we will consider them from the perspective
of Goethe's personal development. We will gain special insights if we start from
the assumption that many characters are not simply reflections of the whole
Goethe, but rather are expressions of various aspects of not only him, but also
his conflicts and his personal relationships. From this perspective, the devoted
Mignon, the easygoing Philina, and the lugubrious harper appear especially
significant:

The attachment of the child [Mignon], this mysterious creature, gave his being a sort of consistency, more strength and weight, which is ever the case when two good souls become united, or even draw together. His fugitive fancy for Philina excited his vital spirits to an agreeable desire, while the old man [the harper] with his harping and his songs aroused the noblest sentiments, so that for brief moments he enjoyed a more real and worthy blessedness than he could remember during his whole life.

(Page, pp. 227–228)

These passages underscore the importance of the three characters mentioned above for Wilhelm and for Goethe himself. Let us begin with Mignon, the most mysterious character created for the *Theatrical Mission*. Goethe introduces her as a "young creature" of approximately 12 or 13 years of age and of uncertain gender. For the most part, Wilhelm thinks of her as a girl, although he occasionally refers to her using male pronouns. Mignon behaves strangely:

"What is your name?" said he. "They call me Mignon," answered she. "How old are you?" "No one has ever counted my years." "Who was your father?" "The great devil is dead." ... She gave her answers in broken German and with an air which quite bewildered Wilhelm, laying each time her hands on breast and head and profoundly bowing.

(Page, p. 181)

Mignon wants to buy her way out of her indentured servitude with a troupe of actors and to serve Wilhelm for reasons that are not initially clear. He is rather diffident at first, but soon begins to feel an interest in her. The mysterious Mignon directs Wilhelm's attention to something enigmatic he senses in himself. Having just escaped the turbulence of adolescence, he can remember the early days of puberty. The author of the *Theatrical Mission* would naturally be familiar with the self-states connected to this time of life – unformed, standing athwart the world, sexually indeterminate – and he placed these aspects of his own development in the character Mignon. Certain descriptions give readers the feeling they are sharing memories of Goethe's own vulnerability during the early phase of puberty. Oddly enough, Wilhelm feels a strong pull toward the strange and the different in Mignon, as if sensing in her both an aspect of his own unconscious self and, probably, a side to his relationship with his sister.

Usually, these unconscious aspects must remain hidden and are only able to emerge under special circumstances, such as in poetry. Wilhelm is closely identified with Mignon, as his reaction to her song shows:

Wilhelm did not notice how she spoke the first few lines, but when she reached the last, they were uttered with such an emphasis of sincerity and truth that she aroused him from his dreams, and it sounded to him as though another person were speaking.

(Page, p. 158)

He comes into contact with unconscious aspects of himself in Mignon as if in a dream; ultimately, they can only be unlocked through poetry. Goethe wrote Mignon's famous song in November of 1783; in it, her fears and longings are condensed:

Do you know the land where the lemon trees blossom,
where the golden oranges glow in the dark foliage,
where a gentle breeze blows from a blue sky,
where the myrtle stands silently and the laurel grows tall,
do you know it?
   There! There
I would like to go with you, my beloved!

Do you know the house? Its roof rests on columns,
its great hall shines, its rooms glitter,
and marble statues stand looking at me:
"What have they done to you, poor child?"
Do you know it?
   There! There
I would like to go with you, my protector!

Do you know the mountain and its footbridge amid the clouds?
The mule seeks its way in the mist;
in caves the ancient brood of the dragons dwells;
the crag plummets and, over it, the waters:
do you know it?
   There! There
our path leads! O Father, let us go!

(Appelbaum, p. 77)

The first stanza takes us to Italy, the yearned-for land, which Goethe had not yet visited at the time of writing, despite his long-cherished dream to go there. It appears as a land of fresh beauty and natural eroticism, and we discover a longing for Arcadia: in the classical tradition, "myrtle" refers to Venus, and the "laurel" to Apollo. The German philologist Peter von Matt (1993) has interpreted the oranges, myrtle, and laurel as sexual symbols. From a psychological perspective, the first stanza portrays a young couple's longing for love, which becomes especially obvious when, in a later version, the word "protector" is replaced with "beloved".

In the second stanza, the couple is now at home, and it is implied that they live in a sumptuous palace; Goethe probably had the Villa Rotonda in Vicenza in mind. Psychologically, the house represents a steadfast, protected connection, one that the couple is settling into. The "marble statues", which we can take to be ancestral images, indicate that the couple is entering into the genealogy of their own past. However, in this respect, Mignon is damaged. Something was done to her that made it impossible for her to have a serious relationship or fulfilling marriage. Peter von Matt has surmised that this refers to sexual abuse, which is not unlikely, considering the previously portrayed theme of sexual assault.

The inhospitable mountainous landscape of the third stanza is reminiscent of the Saint-Gotthard Massif, which Goethe climbed on his first journey to Switzerland. There are echoes of the feelings of being lost and under threat that we recognize from "Journey to the Harz in Winter", and the poem ends with an image of destruction. In *Wilhelm Meister's Apprenticeship*, the word "protector" is replaced with "O, Father", and the last stanza has taken on a Christian tinge. The motif in the third stanza will be reappear later in *Travels* and can be understood there in more depth.

A vague, mysterious yearning connects Wilhelm to Mignon, a yearning that finds expression in a poem written in June of 1785:

Mignon

Only one familiar with yearning
knows what I suffer!
Alone and sundered
from all joy,
I look up at the sky
seeking the world beyond.
Ah, the man who loves me and knows me
is far away.
I'm dizzy, my heart
is burning.
Only one familiar with yearning
knows what I suffer!
(Appelbaum, p. 85)

Goethe's never-ending yearning can be detected in Mignon's song. It is very revealing that Wilhelm, Goethe's reflection, is deeply touched by the song at a time when he has become involved with different women. He has gotten closer to the easygoing Philina, his old love for Mariana is stirring again, and his brief encounter with a "beautiful and strange amazon" has kindled his fantasy:

For a few days, Wilhelm felt the lack of Philina's presence. He had lost in her a careful nurse and cheerful companion, and was no longer accustomed to be alone ... Hardly even to himself did he confess this inward longing to find her [Mariana] once again ... the image of the beneficent beauty [the beautiful and strange amazon] again floated before his fancy; he indulged in the sweetest imaginations, and a yearning passion rushed upon him such as his bosom had never before experienced.

(Page, pp. 303–305)

In this situation, Mignon's song articulates Wilhelm's own yearning and describes his creative appetite. We have seen that Goethe drew amazing creative energy from unfulfilled passion. These dangers are personified in the form of the harper. The harper is introduced as a peculiar stranger, and his song speaks to Wilhelm's feelings of loneliness and guilt:

The man who never ate his bread with tears,
who never sat weeping on his bed
through the sorrowful nights,
does not know you, heavenly powers.

You lead us into life,
you let a poor man acquire guilt,
then you abandon him to his pain:
for all guilt is avenged here on earth.

(Appelbaum, p. 73)

In this song, the harper expresses Goethe's creative credo. Loneliness, sadness, and self-denial are necessary for developing personal and artistic capabilities and for tapping into the "heavenly powers" of creativity. In the process, that person cannot remain an innocent child, but is thrown "into life" and is allowed to "acquire guilt". He must actively overcome the struggles of life with all of its joys and pains, ultimately paying the price for all of his actions in death, "for all guilt is avenged here on earth". He can only become reconciled to this fate through art, which provides him with pleasant, comforting moments. Thus, the harper's song also fills Wilhelm with happiness:

All the sorrows which oppressed his own soul melted away; he yielded to his feelings, pushed open the chamber-door and stood before the old man ... "What emotions have you not quickened within me, good old man!" he exclaimed. "All that stagnated in my heart you have set afresh in motion".

(Page, p. 216)

The harper embodies the dark sides of living and creating while detached from the world and also the dangers of self-flagellating contemplation. Society and erotic pleasure are effective remedies against depressing solitude. These sides are epitomized in a young, spirited actress. Goethe gave her the name

Philina, bringing to mind the Greek dancers and servants of Love. Wilhelm is both attracted and repulsed by Philina:

> and it was true also that he regarded her with indulgence and a kind of deference, although he could neither esteem nor like her. From the very earliest times she had lived with incredible levity, carelessly devoting every day and night to joy, as though it had been her first and last.
>
> (Page, p. 200)

Wilhelm feels a strange sympathy for Philina, who could be described as a floozy. He is equally fascinated and disgusted by her and resists her diverse attempts at seduction. Her easygoing nature attracts him while also unsettling him. This is one of Goethe's own fundamental conflicts: on the one hand, a lust for life, but on the other hand, a fear of becoming superficial, dull, and uncreative if he were to indulge in the pleasures of life. Wilhelm finds himself being pushed and pulled by Philina's song about the lightness of being:

> Sing no more in mournful tones
> Of the loneliness of night;
> For 'tis made, ye beauteous ones,
> For all social pleasures bright.
>
> As of old to man a wife
> As his better half was given,
> So the night is half our life,
> And the fairest under heaven.
>
> How can ye enjoy the day,
> Which obstructs our rapture's tide?
> Let it waste itself away;
> Worthless 'tis for aught beside.
>
> But when in the darkling hours
> From the lamp soft rays are glowing,
> And from mouth to mouth sweet showers,
> Now of jest, now love, are flowing, –
>
> When the nimble, wanton boy,
> Who so wildly spends his days,
> Oft amid light sports with joy
> O'er some trifling gift delays, –
>
> When the nightingale is singing
> Strains the lover holds so dear,

Though like sighs and wailings ringing
In the mournful captive's ear, –

With what heart-emotion blest
Do ye hearken to the bell,
Wont of safety and of rest
With twelve solemn strokes to tell!

Therefore in each heavy hour,
Let this precept fill your heart:
O'er each day will sorrow lour,
Rapture ev'ry night impart.
                    (Bowring, pp. 436–437)

Goethe wrote this poem long after he had returned from Rome and had been living with Christiane, but he had already conceived of the character of Philina beforehand, and the preceding descriptions had been written before his Italian journey. They show a surprising openness to "amor levis", or flirtation. In the *Theatrical Mission*, Wilhelm finally succumbs to Philina's attempts at seduction; he then describes her as a "pretty sinner". We have already shown the improbability of Goethe's not seeking or enjoying such temptations in real life. Having said that, ambivalence consistently pervades both Wilhelm's and Goethe's love lives; this is repeatedly expressed in Wilhelm's relationship with Philina:

> One morning, when Wilhelm awoke, he found himself in strange proximity to her. During his sleep he had slipped quite to the further side of his wide couch, and Philina lay diagonally across the nearer side ... The disorder of sleep enhanced her charms more than any art or design, and the smiling calm of childhood hovered about her face. For a time he gazed upon her, and seemed to blame himself for the pleasure with which he beheld her, yea, we cannot tell whether he blessed or cursed his present condition.
>
> (Page, p. 299)

After Philina's departure, Wilhelm is both relieved to be free of the temptress and regretful at being alone again. His yearning leads him to remember the "beautiful amazon", and he repeatedly pictures her riding out of the bushes towards him, coming nearer, and letting the surcoat she is wearing fall from her shoulders. This is completely Goethean. In her absence, Wilhelm romanticizes the distant lover, using her to spark his fantasy and his creativity. But what a difference compared to the young Goethe of the Frankfurt, Leipzig, Strasbourg, and Wetzlar periods! Wilhelm's flights of fancy did not prevent him from maintaining real relationships; there is the easygoing Philina, but also, and especially, Mariana, who will be placed center stage at the beginning of *Apprenticeship*. The *Theatrical Mission* already includes a description of

Wilhelm's sexually fulfilling love for her that was destroyed by her relationship with an older lover who supported her financially. Wilhelm leaves her, but his yearning continues to tie him to her. "Hardly even to himself did he confess this inward longing to find her once again, and beg forgiveness for his harshness" (Page, p. 304).

These are not the words of the adolescent dreamer in *Werther*, rather of a mature, though even younger, man, one who is seeking partnerships, where he is willing to take the good with the bad, and who is willing to take on parental responsibility for their child. He is able to recognize his own mistakes, to feel guilt, and to assume responsibility. Wilhelm (Goethe) no longer uses women in order to fall in love with them, to experience exaltation, to "rest in their eyes", only to flee at the first sign of real attachment; instead, he has become a sympathetic partner, one who is able to be responsive to other people's feelings. He is also able to ignore his own joys and sorrows and to lend a sympathetic ear to others.

There are several places in the novel where Wilhelm has the task of helping those who are suffering emotionally, fulfilling some of the functions of psychotherapy. In doing so, he shows a remarkable level of empathy, especially for women whose love has had disastrous results for them. The topic of suicide appears repeatedly, not in relation to himself, but rather as other people's approach toward their problems. Mignon and the young widow Aurelia both entertain thoughts of suicide, which he is able to dissuade them from. However, he is also aware of the limits of his ability to understand others:

> "I confess my state of schoolboy innocence," he answered, "and beg for forgiveness. From my youth up I have always looked more within than without, and it is therefore quite natural that I should learn to know mankind up to a certain point without understanding men in the least".
>
> (Page, p. 323)

Wilhelm recognizes that he still has much to learn. He tries to be guided by more experienced men and women and to develop himself further. He is convinced that he will only be able to successfully cultivate his personality if he remains in contact with those who are immature (Mignon), despairing (the harper), deserted and unhappy (Aurelia), seeking and artistic (Serlo), and easygoing (Philina). All of this is colored by an unending yearning for the "distant lover", for the one who is neither fulfilled nor fulfilling. After Wilhelm has reached his primary goals and been accepted into a friendly, ethically minded community, the *Theatrical Mission* ends with the following words:

> He could give nothing in return, for he stood as one struck dumb and, in spite of their presence, fell into a state of silent musing. His thoughts roamed hither and thither, till suddenly the wood-encompassed meadow filled his imagination, and from the bushes, mounted on a white horse, the

lovely amazon rode to greet him, approached, dismounted, moved to and fro with humane solicitude, stood still–the mantle fell from her shoulders and covered the wounded man, her face, her form gleamed once more resplendently before him and–vanished!

(Page, p. 342)

Wilhelm Meister's Apprenticeship

Goethe had been working on *Wilhelm Meister* since 1777, but the first volume did not appear until January of 1795. He often despaired over his doppelganger, and it was only his friendship with Friedrich Schiller that allowed him to complete *Apprenticeship*. Schiller emphasized the portrayal of subjective experiences, which, admittedly, would be expressed in a more artistically mature way compared to *The Sufferings of Young Werther*. Unlike *Wilhelm Meister's Theatrical Mission*, which began with Wilhelm's birth, *Apprenticeship* begins with Wilhelm detaching himself from the family home and his first love. Otherwise, the two novels are mainly in agreement, especially from a psychological perspective. It is only in the fifth book of *Apprenticeship* that new psychological themes are introduced, such as the significance of a father's death and one's paternal responsibility for a child. Moreover, Wilhelm and Werner's opposing conceptions of life are further explained. Werner would like to convince Wilhelm of the value of a well-ordered, bourgeois existence, but Wilhelm does not feel ready to conclude his personal development: "What good were it for me to manufacture perfect iron while my own breast is full of dross? What would it stead me to put properties of land in order, while I am at variance with myself?" (Carlyle, vol. 2, p. 8). This is followed by a criticism of bourgeois lifestyles, which make comprehensive personal development impossible. With an astounding degree of self-assurance, Wilhelm feels called to something better:

Now, this harmonious cultivation of my nature, which has been denied me by birth, is exactly what I most long for ... But I will not conceal from thee, that my inclination to become a public person, and to please and influence in a larger circle ... that so, in this enjoyment henceforth indispensable, I may esteem as good the good alone, as beautiful the beautiful alone.

(Carlyle, vol. 2, p. 10)

He hopes to find these opportunities for development, which are actually reserved for people of rank, in the theater, yet he is disappointed once again. At a deeper level, Goethe is reflecting on the tension between the reality of coping with life and the fantasy of satisfying desires.

While searching for that which is good and beautiful, Wilhelm encounters various types of failure. Mental disorders, in particular, attract his interest. He devotes himself to the topic of insanity and studies the treatment methods used by a country clergyman with his mentally ill charges. These therapeutic applications are simple yet effective:

> They are the very means by which you hinder sane persons from becoming mad. Awaken their activity; accustom them to order; bring them to perceive that they hold their being and fate in common with many millions; that extraordinary talents, the highest happiness, the deepest misery, are but slight variations from the general lot.
>
> (Carlyle, vol. 2, p. 58)

This is a striking summary of psychotherapeutic principles that are still valid today: guiding patients toward self-efficacy, helping them to structure their own lifeworlds, and reflecting on experiences in their social environment. Wilhelm is impressed by the teachings of the country clergyman and a physician who emphasizes that man's main source of unhappiness is "when some idea lays hold of him, which exerts no influence upon active life, or, still more, which withdraws him from it" (Carlyle, vol. 2, p. 59). Here we are able to discern Goethe's own philosophy of health again, which states that no one should give himself over to solitude too thoroughly, nor should he avoid an active life within society. The connection between religion and mental health is explained in "Confessions of a Fair Saint", the sixth book of *Apprenticeship*. Goethe describes pietism as a lifestyle that is primarily inward-facing and that leads through self-denial to spiritual equilibrium. Katharina von Klettenberg's way of life was a clear example of this for him; she arguably had a strong influence on "Confessions" (see Boyle 2000).

In the seventh book, the preparations are laid for the events of the novel that are to be disentangled and resolved. Wilhelm arrives at Lothario's estate, which is central to the Society of the Tower. This society, like the Freemasons, cultivates enlightenment virtues. From an individual psychology point of view, he is continuing his formative process, which also consists of self-enlightenment. He learns of Mariana's fate and her death, which causes him to develop deep, well-founded feelings of remorse. Now he is able to assume parental responsibility for the child that was the result of his love with Mariana. The maxims of the Society of the Tower lead to active employment, much like those of the Freemasons, to whom Goethe belonged. These principles increasingly bring Wilhelm, with his "wandering" way of life into conflict. In the end, he chooses the Society of the Tower and ends his career in the theater. The confirmation of his role as a father symbolizes a break in his life: the unlimited, uncertain phase of youth has ended, and Wilhelm is now an adult. Nevertheless, the fact that earlier stages of development were not simply completed and left behind, but are repeatedly given new form in more developed stages, remains a requirement for his inner vitality: "'everything that happens to us leaves some trace behind it; everything contributes imperceptibly to form us' ... 'The history of every person paints his character'" (Carlyle, vol. 2, p. 125, 143).

After coming to these general insights, Wilhelm reflects on his behavior more consciously, which leads him to develop mature attitudes toward love, commitment, and the performance of his duties. He is able to retreat into the background with his own wishes and to concur with the principles of the Society of the Tower:

> It is right that a man, when he first enters upon life, should think highly of himself, should determine to attain many eminent distinctions, should endeavour to make all things possible; but, when his education has proceeded to a certain pitch, it is advantageous for him, that he learn to lose himself among a mass of men, that he learn to live for the sake of others, and to forget himself in an activity prescribed by duty.
>
> (Carlyle, vol. 2, p. 185)

In the eighth book, themes and motifs from the earlier books are taken up and condensed. Wilhelm and Werner meet up again and note that the difference between them has deepened. Werner has developed poorly; he has become pale and feeble, symbolizing the price paid for a life that did not embrace and actively shape developmental crises. In contrast to Werner, the limitations of bourgeois society do not have a blunting effect on Wilhelm because he allows himself to become involved in a complex formative process and consciously lives through painful memories, humiliating experiences, and culpable entanglements. This educational ideal of Wilhelm's corresponds with Goethe's self-treatment program, which interprets crises as transitions and not as illnesses. This process is never complete; after breaking off his love affairs and taking leave of the theater, Wilhelm is accepted into the Society of the Tower, knowing that his future life will continue to be a formative process: "'Oh, who knows,' cried he, 'what trials are before me! who knows how sharply bygone errors will yet punish me, how often good and reasonable projects for the future shall miscarry!'" (Carlyle, vol. 2, p. 200).

At the end of *Apprenticeship*, Wilhelm and the "beautiful amazon" find their way to one another, resolving his convoluted relationships with women like in a fairytale. He marries her, but reality and fantasy will only be in consonance for a short time. The Society of the Tower pressures him to undertake a journey in order to fulfill his "higher" duties. Once again, renunciation will be one of the conditions for further advancement. Wilhelm's path to a life that is socially responsible and meaningful is not yet over. The goal of implementing a community of active "citizens of this world", one which would achieve prosperity, freedom, and equality without revolutionary violence, still appears to be far away.

Wilhelm Meister's Travels

In May of 1807, Goethe began dictating the first chapter of *Wilhelm Meister's Travels*. He would work on this novel for many years, trying to affirm his self and his place in the world. Compared to the *Theatrical Mission* and other early works, the tone of this piece is tranquil and wise. The aging Goethe had developed a style in which the impulsive outbursts of youth had given way to a contemplative distance to himself. At the age of 71, he completed the last chapter and sent the manuscript off with the following poem:

> To travel now the Apprentice does assay,
> And every step is girt with doubt and danger:
> In truth, he uses not to sing or pray;
> But, in his path perplexed, this toilsome ranger
> Does turn an earnest eye, when mist's above him,
> To his own heart, and to the hearts that love him.
>   (Carlyle, vol. 3, p. 3)

Goethe had remained a wanderer as well. At the same time, he took a more relaxed view of his actions and allowed himself to be led along difficult paths by self-reflection, i.e. the glimpse into "his own heart", and by empathy for his fellow man, i.e. the glimpse into "the hearts that love him". Thus, *Travels* is the continuation of a lifelong attempt to develop himself and his relationships. This work can never be completed, and at the age of 79, he was still engaged with his novel. In November of 1829, he wrote the following: "Now with such books, it's as with life itself: in the complex of the whole there is that which is necessary and aleatory, planned and unplanned, successful and flawed, whereby the book is endowed with a sort of endlessness" (qtd. in Redfield, p. 102). In the same letter, he noted that the axiom "act prudently" is simply the practical side of "know thyself". Accordingly, Wilhelm's practical activities in and for the Society are at the forefront of the events involved in finding himself. We find meaning in our lives when we are productively active in our communities.

The frame story in *Wilhelm Meister's Travels or The Renunciants* builds on the events of *Apprenticeship*. The Society of the Tower, which busied itself with the education of young people in *Apprenticeship*, has now dedicated itself to more comprehensive social and political functions. It is trying to open up new possibilities for the poor, who have been economically doomed by the introduction of machines in manufacturing, by encouraging them to emigrate. While planning this undertaking, Wilhelm comes into contact with a wide range of people. First, there is a nobleman and large landowner who has inherited further property from his father in America. Then he encounters a woman of wisdom, whom he calls on in her castle. At her behest, he seeks out her nephew Lenardo, who is supposed to inherit and cultivate property in America. Lenardo and the Society of the Tower join forces, and a large emigration enterprise is planned, including settlements for farmers and craftsmen and also industrial facilities. Lenardo is dynamic, technologically and organizationally skilled, and the right man to lead the enterprise. While he is dealing with the logistics, an abbot is in charge of the philosophy of the organization. Capable people are courted from a special academy of training, the Pedagogic Province, which is described in detail as an ideal model of education. But new opportunities have also emerged in their own country. A German prince has provided the opportunity to settle in his province. Hence, part of the emigrants leave for America, and part of them proceed with the European project.

The novel's main characters are the leading men in these enterprises. They recognize their own limits and know that they most forego much for productive activity. Their life experience and their objective makes them "renunciants". They have learned from their own struggles and are therefore able to lead people who have not even been made aware of their own limits. Despite the emphasis on their abilities and accomplishments, the male central characters pale in comparison to their female counterparts, especially in comparison to Makaria, who has been gifted with the highest wisdom.

From a psychological perspective, Wilhelm – still a reflection of Goethe – appears mature, world-wise, and open to communal objectives. When the novel begins, Wilhelm is no longer educating himself, but is now raising his son, Felix, and rediscovering the world through his eyes. In a letter, he describes the duties and ordeals he has taken on, but he also expresses his approval of their perpetual wanderings and the constant changes they experience: "Life belongs to the living, and he who lives must be prepared for vicissitudes" (Carlyle, vol. 3, p. 25). However, we are able to discern, more than once, that Wilhelm also longs for domesticity and a stable relationship with a wife. But first he has to wander. His wanderings full of privations, symbolize both the individual's and society's journey through life, something that is essential in order to be able to act ethically and responsibly.

Life is a journey, developing actively from beginning to end. Along the way, Wilhelm meets people who accompany and support him during the process of maturation. Makaria has been given a central role; she is depicted as a "holy figure", but is also grounded in daily life. She is brilliant and intuitive and helps people find their own way to their selves by reflecting how they could be. Goethe paints a picture of an empathetic companion who fulfills many different psychotherapeutic functions, much like Auguste zu Stolberg and Charlotte von Stein, but she is also transported into the transcendental realm. Wilhelm dreams of Makaria:

> I was lying in soft but deep sleep, when I felt transported into the saloon as yesterday, but alone. The green curtain went up, Makaria's chair moved forward of its own accord, like an animated being; it shone with gold, her dress seemed sacerdotal, her glance sparkled mildly; I was on the point of throwing myself down. Clouds spread forth around her feet, and ascending they bore like wings the holy form upwards: instead of her glorious countenance I beheld through the parting clouds a shining star, that was ever carried upwards, and through the opening roof united itself with the whole firmament, which seemed to be ever expanding and to embrace everything.
>
> (Boyesen, vol. 5, pp. 65–66)

This apotheosis of femininity, which we also find at the end of *Faust*, stands in remarkable tension with everyday love relationships in *Travels* as well as in the other *Wilhelm Meister* novels; on the morning after he has had this transfiguring dream, Wilhelm comes across his son in the garden, "which to his astonishment he saw being tilled by a number of girls. If not all beautiful, not one was ugly, and none seemed to have reached her twentieth year" (Boyesen, vol. 5, p. 66).

In many parts of the novel, Wilhelm appears friendly and relaxed as he observes his son's erotic activities, and we get the impression that Goethe himself would describe the light-hearted sides of sexuality with a certain degree of unconcernedness now that he had attained a certain grandfatherly distance. But the dangerous and inscrutable aspects of sexuality remain a shocking theme, even in a novel like *Travels*, with its wisdom gleaned from age and experience of the world. Wilhelm describes an experience he had in his youth, when he was invited to go fishing by an adolescent slightly older than him, "a boy who had at once attracted me by his serious demeanor". This new friend was tempted by the coolness of the water to undress and swim in the river. "Quite a strange feeling" fell over Wilhelm, who was looking on:

> It was so warm and sultry all around, one yearned to be out of the sun and in the shade, out of the cool shade in the still cooler water below. So it was easy for him to entice me down; I found an invitation, not often repeated, irresistible, and what with fear of my parents, and timidity about the unfamiliar element in addition, I was quite strangely excited. But soon undressed upon the gravel, I ventured gently into the water, but not deeper than was due to the gradually sloping bottom. Here he let me linger, went to some distance in the sustaining element, came back, and when he got out and stood up to dry himself in the fuller sunshine, my eyes seemed to be dazzled by a triple sun; so fair was the human form, of which I had never had any idea. He seemed to look at me with equal attention. Though quickly dressed, we still seemed to stand unclothed before each other; our spirits drew together, and amidst the most ardent kisses we swore eternal friendship.
>
> (Boyesen, vol. 5, pp. 145–146)

This depiction of young love is especially magical. Wilhelm (Goethe) describes the physical beauty of his friend, but he also discovers his own physical excitement in this encounter. Immediately following this scene, he meets the daughter of his host and falls in love with her:

> a stroll in a well-kept pleasure-garden, in which the daughter, who was somewhat younger than I, accompanied me to show me the way, was very agreeable to me … My companion was beautiful, fair-haired, and gentle; we walked confidentially together, soon held each other by the hand, and

seemed to wish for nothing better ... When I look back, after so many years, at my situation on that occasion, it seems to me really enviable. Unexpectedly, at the same moment, the premonition of friendship and love seized me: for when I unwillingly took leave of the beautiful child, I comforted myself with the thought of disclosing these feelings to my young friend, of confiding in him, and of enjoying his sympathy together with these fresh sentiments.

(Boyesen, vol. 5, pp. 146–147)

These new sensations are due to his discovery of the beauty of his own sexuality. To Wilhelm, his blossoming erotic power seems to be the appearance of his "real original nature": "How we must have despaired at seeing so cold, so lifeless an outward life, had not something revealed itself in our heart that glorifies nature in quite another way, whilst manifesting a creative power, to beautify ourselves in her" (Boyesen, vol. 5, p. 147). The burgeoning sexual and creative power of adolescence is already under threat, though: The pastor's wife will not allow Wilhelm's new friend in the house because she finds him indecorous; instead, she gives him the task of catching crayfish for her guests. Wilhelm waits for his friend at the edge of the woods at dusk and becomes restless and concerned when the friend does not appear. Then comes the news that Wilhelm's new friend and four other boys have drowned while attempting to carry out the task given to them by the pastor's wife of fishing crayfish out of the river. Some of the boys were weak swimmers, and when they were pulled under, Wilhelm's friend tried to save them and was himself pulled down into the deep water.

The only survivor was the youngest boy, who had remained on the shore, and who now stepped forward and dutifully held out the bag of crayfish to the pastor's wife. Wilhelm, despondent, sneaks into where the dead children lay:

In the large room, where meetings of all kinds are held, lay the unfortunates, stretched naked upon straw, dazzling white corpses, shining also in the dim lamplight. I threw myself upon the tallest—my friend. I had no words to express my condition; I wept bitterly, and deluged his broad breast with unceasing tears. I had heard something of rubbing, which in such a case was said to be of use. I rubbed in my tears, and cheated myself with the warmth that I excited. Amidst my confusion, I thought of breathing breath into him.

(Boyesen, vol. 5, p. 148)

Wilhelm's awkward attempts to revive his friend, reminiscent of Goethe's attempts to revive his brother Hermann and other siblings through literature, are put an end to, and rather ungraciously, by his parents. The next morning, he awakens in a dark mood. He is surprised to find his mother, aunt, and the cook "in weighty consultation". Their discussion centers on the fact that they should not boil and serve the crayfish to avoid reminding his father of the accident that had just occurred. His aunt is not distressed about this, because she plans to fatten up the crayfish in order to serve them to her patron. On reading this scene, we get an image of a peculiar mourning ritual. On the one hand, the mothers appear dangerous, because, like the pastor's wife, they have contributed to the boys' death. On the other hand, they also seem uncaring and cruel, going right back to their daily lives so soon after the accident. We are reminded of Goethe's description of treacherous "woman's favor", which "abandons the infant brood to death and decay".

Wilhelm, though, does not try to repress his sadness and pain by throwing himself into his everyday activities. If he had once sought a solution to his problems in the theater, he now seeks to cope with the calamity by means of practical activity. He acquires medical knowledge and plans to become a physician, thereby creating new hope for the future. His interest in medicine has a foundation in the wish to be of practical help. We can see how Goethe had changed as well. As a youth, he employed poetry as his primary means of dealing with his grief and fear of death, but now, in old age, he was more likely to turn to practical, effective action: "How can a man come to know himself? Never by thinking, but by doing. Try to do your duty, and you will know at once what you are worth" (Saunders, p. 59).

This is only one side of the coin, though. Social activity also requires personal development. It is only when we have gone through a time-intensive process of self-formation, one accompanying us our whole lives long, that we are able to act effectively. As a consequence, we are able to leave behind our everyday desires and pains and to allow them to dissipate in a higher spirituality. A perfect example of this is found in *Wilhelm Meister's Travels* in the character of Makaria. She has a great deal of good sense, but also "seems born only to disengage herself from the earthly, to penetrate the nearest and most distant spaces of existence" (Boyesen, vol. 5, p. 222).

Goethe retains his sense of youthful libidinousness on his path to wisdom, but its dangers are also retained. Wilhelm tells of how his son was courting Hersilia, and in his state of passionate agitation had an accident, horse and all. He appears to be dead, but his father is able to use his medical arts to revive him. Once again, passion and death, as well as the means of overcoming them, are condensed by Goethe in a striking manner. The aging author's ability to understand a youthful experience is remarkable. We have frequently noted that Goethe's ability to keep earlier stages of his life alive within himself was an essential aspect of his creative energy and mental health. In the relationship between Wilhelm and Felix, we find two aspects of Goethe's own self divided between two characters: the passionate buoyancy of youth and the creative power of a mature man aware of his limits. It appears as though Goethe had found a solution to these conflicts in Wilhelm and Felix and had overcome the hazards posed by the feminine. As a consequence, a composed worldview opened itself up to him, one that contained worldly connections while simultaneously transcending them.

Chapter 15

Goethe's creativity from the perspective of modern creativity research

The word "creativity" is derived from the Latin word *creare*, meaning "to bring forth, produce, make, beget". It is closely related to the word *crescere*, which we will translate as "to arise, become, be born, come forth". Two very important aspects of creativity are found in the original meanings of *creare* and *crescere*: The conscious creation of something new, and the development of unconscious potential. I have given this topic a thorough treatment in my books *Kreativität – Konzept und Lebensstil* (*Creativity – Concept and Lifestyle*, 2010) and *Kreativität zwischen Schöpfung und Zerstörung* (*Creativity between Construction and Destruction*, 2011). Also my papers entitled "Goethe's Anxieties, Depressive Episodes and (Self-)Therapeutic Strategies" (2012), "The Dialectics of Creativity" (2013), and "Bipolar Disorder and/or Creative Bipolarity: The Case of Robert Schumann" (2017) form the background of the following considerations. Here, I will start with a short outline of the findings of creativity research, after which I will show how they apply to Goethe.

Biologists do not consider creativity to be merely a feature of gifted individuals, but rather a fundamental characteristic of all living things. For them, life is a continual process of adaptation, where the individuals develop in their environment. Like the most simple living organisms, biologically highly developed human beings also require the steady action of creativity in order to be able to survive. Briefly, we can say that, in all of the higher organisms, there is a continuous interplay between the establishment and maintenance of structures and their destabilization, which leads to new and usable forms. From an evolutionary biology perspective, creativity can be defined as the continuous recombination and transformation of that which already exists. This process is determined not only by the gene, but also by the so-called "meme" (Dawkins 1989). Memes are units of information that contain our cultural inheritance and that induce a more complex evolution of individuals and society than the genes.

Those studying the cultural and social sciences view the creative shaping of reality as the most basic task of human development. Creativity is not simply a way of killing time for those with time to kill, but rather a necessity for every social entity. Without creativity, not only is the world boring, it is at the mercy of forces that can destroy it (see Holm-Hadulla 2010, 2011).

Developmental psychologists and psychoanalysts see a basic model of creative behavior in the play of children (e.g. Freud 1908; Klein 1957; Winnicott 1971). Infants are already able to create an inner world by means of early forms of thoughts and ideas; this inner world then gives a certain degree of coherence and structure to chaotic emotions. Later, the child uses play to develop his own individual world, which is made up of various ideas and fantasies. In adult life, the playful joy of childhood is rediscovered in creative, productive work.

Because it is such a multifaceted concept, creativity can only be defined in rather vague terms: *Creativity is the ability to create something new, whether a new solution to a problem, a discovery, or a new product.* In order to be classified as creative, these new solutions, discoveries, and products must represent important contributions to a specific domain. We can derive the basic conditions for a creative personality from this definition and from the work of creativity researcher Mihalyi Cszikszentmihalyi (1996): *A gifted person can be considered creative if he is productively active in a promising area and in a sociocultural context that is supportive.*

Based on the above definitions, we can declare without a doubt that Goethe was eminently creative. He produced a diverse array of new literary forms and expressions that have had a lasting influence on the German language. But where does such an exceptional creative power and originality come from? To answer that question, we must look at the five conditions for creativity: talent, knowledge, motivation, personality, and environmental conditions (see Holm-Hadulla 2010).

Talent

Based on current research, we can divide talent into at least seven areas, often referred to as types of intelligence (Gardner 2002): linguistic, logical-mathematical, musical, physical-kinesthetic, spatial, interpersonal, and intrapersonal. Goethe exhibited linguistic intelligence at a very young age. He was not a prodigy like Mozart, but he took an early delight in language. His exceptional memory was useful to him when reciting, which won him special notice that later became admiration. He was probably only average in logical-mathematical and musical intelligence. He was physically adept and was good, but not great, at riding, dancing, and ice skating. It is likely that his spatial thinking was also not exceptional, if we take his sketches as a benchmark. He was very empathetic toward himself and others, with a considerable degree of intra- and interpersonal intelligence. This must have contributed to his poetic creativity.

Creativity researchers like Mark Runco (2007) have also worked out specific modes of thinking that are beneficial to creativity: fluent, associative, divergent, and original. Goethe's thinking was certainly fluent, and he made associative connections between ideas starting at a young age. But the emphasis then was on traditional learning, at least until he was 16 years old. According to his writings, his early learning was primarily focused on acquiring the traditional body of knowledge. Divergent and original solutions would only appear later. Nevertheless, he was already inclined to use his imagination at an early age. He loved to imagine scenarios and to speak with imaginary people. It is possible that Goethe's diligent learning allowed him to acquire figures of speech and structures he would later combine with his experiences – after going through severe emotional turbulences – and the moods of his emergent self, which then led him down the path to originality. At this point, we could speak of significant emotional intelligence (Goleman 2005). This was not something which just floated into being; instead, it was only made possible by his enormous knowledge and vibrant fantasy.

Modern research in the area of psychotherapy has given us the term "mentalization" for the ability to understand the thoughts, feelings, and actions of one's own self and others (Fonagy, Gergely, Jurist, and Target 2005). It goes beyond empathy, though. Mentalization is a continuous process that enables relationships, and it encompasses both emotional and cognitive processes. The wish to mentalize was an essential element of Goethe's ability and necessity to work creatively.

Knowledge and ability

The importance of intellectual knowledge and practical ability for creativity is often underappreciated. And yet, these factors have a special significance. These days, it must be stressed that data only becomes information when interpreted by knowledge. Starting in early childhood, Goethe acquired a broad range of knowledge, and his first-rate memory came to his aid when combining information in novel ways. Biographical research has shown how important practical ability, memory, and knowledge are for the arts, for instance in music and painting, even if these factors are considered to be of secondary importance. This is illustrated by the life and work of both Picasso and Mozart, for example (see Holm-Hadulla 2010). Even in modern pop-music, idols like Amy Winehouse and Madonna Ciccone, Jim Morrison and Mick Jagger show that technical skills are essential for creative achievements (see Holm-Hadulla 2017).

Motivation

Different motivations are necessary that talents and skills can flourish. We can differentiate between three motivational factors that are essential for creativity: curiosity, interest, and ambition.

Curiosity is an elementary motivation that can be observed in almost everyone, starting from birth. A child's inquisitive behavior is innate, but environmental influences also have a decisive influence on it. Curiosity is an expression of vitality, but it only leads to creative accomplishments if the person feels secure in himself and in his environment. This can be observed in the exploratory behavior of infants. They allow their inquisitive side free rein and play more creatively when they have sufficiently secure bonds. Every creative person, and his environment as well, must repeatedly reconfigure not only the interaction between the traditional and the new, but also the balance between a desire for change and a feeling of security. Goethe was decidedly curious and was to discover a family environment that provided a rich source of fuel for his curiosity. His mother and grandmother enjoyed playing with him as a child, his father was constantly offering him books, pictures, and musical compositions, and his sister was usually available to converse and play with him.

Interest means the need and the ability to be engrossed completely by an object or an activity. Goethe displayed this type motivation even as a small child, as exhibited in his diligence in learning and his years-long preoccupation with his puppet theater. This primary interest does not have to be created, only given nourishment and space. Until old age, Goethe took a vivid interest in political, scientific, and literary issues. His last works, which we will refer to in the last chapter of this book, document his tireless engagement in various aspects of public and private life.

Striving for recognition is an expression of the elementary human pursuit of being seen and responded to. Goethe's lifelong need for recognition and acknowledgement was quite striking. As a child, he was prone to showing off, even if it sometimes made him look ridiculous. We could classify the incident of crockery-throwing to the cheers of the neighborhood children to be the first indication of his propensity to render himself conspicuous and to place himself in the public eye. At the age of 14, he endeavored – without success – to be accepted into the "Arcadian Society of Phylandria", probably in order to find a public forum for his fledging literary attempts. Humiliations and injuries to his ambition – such as when his first love, Gretchen, did not take him seriously, or his fellow students in Leipzig made fun of him – did not lead him to retreat; instead, they caused him to redouble his efforts to improve himself. He also told himself, "People shouldn't be treated the way they are, but rather the way they could be."

The one thing the different types of motivation in creativity have in common is passion. This term describes a strong drive and a fixed intention that allow us to take a particular path or reach a certain goal while suffering privations. Curiosity, interest, and recognition become factors in creativity when they lead to a passionate engagement with the task at hand.

Personality traits

The following personality traits are frequently associated with creativity: flexibility, originality, self-confidence, resilience, authenticity, and transcendence.

Flexibility refers to the ability and readiness to have new experiences. Children perceive new events with openness and amazement; this is also the way in which creative people abandon themselves to unusual ideas, with playful enjoyment. Goethe has described how fantasies, poems, and literary figures developed with his conscious assistance, and how he himself was merely a malleable medium for their realization. He was able to abandon himself to an inner play space in which unusual ideas could occur. Goethe's flexibility was aided by clear structures. In general, openness and readiness to change are only possible on a sufficiently secure foundation; in Goethe's particular case, his grounding in his family and friends was a secure basis on which he was able to flexibly play.

For Goethe, *originality* only developed after he had learned classical languages, read Shakespeare in the original, and worked to achieve a broad educational foundation. While it is true that he had a special ability to engage in imaginative games at an early age, he only became a non-conformist at a much later age. His originality grew out of his creative work and was thus not available to him before that. This is a message that I wish many believers in superficial fun would get. Mozart, Picasso, Einstein (see Holm-Hadulla 2010), and hundreds of other eminent creative people only gained creative fun and originality *after* they had gotten involved in their material, their technique, and their work, not before.

Self-confidence was something Goethe had in spades. But his feelings were also easily hurt, and when he felt he had made a fool of himself, he could react by being very out of sorts. However, humiliations and rejections did not lead to apathy, withdrawal, and accusations, but to a sort of creative protest. His intensive preoccupation with slights, such as from Käthchen Schönkopf during his student days, and with rejections, such as from Charlotte Buff and Maximiliane von Brentano, had a majorly destabilizing effect on his self-esteem. Others might have gone on the attack and deprecated the women; Goethe, though, used this destabilization to produce lasting works of art.

Resilience is necessary for the creative process because the self becomes destabilized, even endangered, by intensive creative work. The creative person steps out of his everyday relationships, whether as "Prometheus" or a "mad scientist". Original people frequently suffer from the loss of their accustomed certainties; they are strikingly different and require a certain degree of resilience to overcome the challenges from their environment. In Goethe's case, the challenges to his sense of self primarily came from within. While writing *Werther*, it was as if he were out of his senses, and in his seventies, he wrote the following verse: "I am myself, I am lost to the world". A sympathetic environment, clear working structures, and a sense of resilience acquired through struggle helped him to stabilize himself during creative phases.

Goethe's *authenticity*, the feeling of finding and portraying oneself in a meaningful contribution, was very pronounced, even though his first exercises in poetry appear conventional and conformist. It was only after his experience of suffering as a student that his authentic self spoke out, such as in his "Odes to Behrisch". Most people seek authentic self-efficacy in their activities. Early on, Goethe sensed the longing to give expression to his self and to reify himself. This is also an essential part of the passion that leads to creativity.

Transcendence, the realization of values that lie beyond egotistical needs, is an essential prerequisite for creativity. Mothers employ it when they join their children's games; lovers practice it when they open themselves up to their beloved. For Goethe, it was centrally important for him to go beyond himself in his work, and he was continuously seeking a greater whole. He was able to lose himself in nature, and this personified nature thought and lived in him. His dedication to fantasies that transcend the narrow limits of the individual, socially normed self was an essential basic requirement for his creative power.

In his poetry, Goethe wrote out the most essential aspects of what it means to be creative. On the one hand, he defines creativity as the creation of something new that revolts against conventions. Prometheus rebels against tradition, replacing it with original creation. Accordingly, the genius demands special rights; his aggressiveness subjugates, even destroys, the traditional. Reckless-ness is a feature of both the individual creator and the creative process. The creative person feels a passionate duty only to himself and to his task.

On the other hand, Goethe juxtaposes the aggressive, unfettered aspect of creativity with the natural development of creative potency. When the politician, the artist, and the scientist are embedded in the natural processes of "becoming and dying", this leads them to a higher awareness. Both must understand and humbly follow the laws of nature and of history. The creative person is not like Prometheus, who places himself about the divine and natural orders; rather, he is of this world, integrating himself into the great cycle of natural and world history and only then becoming creative. Empathetically and respectfully allowing that which is dormant in natural history and tradition to take place – in the sense of *crescere* – is juxtaposed against willfully, aggressively creating something new – in the sense of *creare*.

Environmental conditions supporting creativity

Goethe's talents, skills, motivations and personality traits already became evident during his childhood. None of these things would have been able to develop without favorable environmental conditions, though. First, there was his loving and cheerful mother. It would seem that her fondness and admiration encouraged his creativity. At a deeper level, though, his coming to grips with the frightening aspects of his mother image were of even more importance for his creative development. However, he was only able to do this to the degree and the intensity I have described because his real mother also provided him with security and affection. His sister was always a faithful, understanding playmate, and she also showed him love and admiration. He was able to show off in front of her without fearing her derision. Their education-minded father sought to realize in his son everything that he himself had not achieved. Goethe was both nurtured and challenged from an early age, in an atmosphere that was apparently loving but also strict. His family's financial circumstances were also favorable, and he was spared the effects of war and adversity for many years.

We have previously discussed Goethe's emotional crises in detail. Not only were they were the reason for his creative attempts at coping, but they also fueled these attempts, allowing us to say that Goethe drew impulses for his work from rejections and slights. He perceived disappointments, accepted deficits, and consoled himself with activities he could shine in. He was also able to immerse himself in his authorial experiments with patience and dedication. Of great importance to his creativity were his teachers, friends, and the women he loved, all of whom he open-heartedly confided in.

Creative work

Creative work can be divided into five phases, which interact with each other: preparation, incubation, illumination, realization, and verification (Holm-Hadulla 2010).

In the *preparatory phase*, the problem or the subject is examined and a goal develops, although sometimes it is an unconscious or vague goal. Strictly speaking, the years of childhood, school, and college should also be counted as part of the preparatory phase. During this period, talents develop that will someday lead to creative achievements. Like Mozart, Picasso, and Einstein, Goethe had a broad education, and like the above-mentioned notables of music, painting, and science, he was urged to practice patiently. As we saw in the explanation of creative personalities, it is not enough to cultivate people's talents. The potentially creative person must also develop enough passion to be able to dedicate himself to something with curiosity, excitement, and persistence. Goethe's motivations were bolstered by the approval he continuously received from his grandmother, mother, sister, and father for his progress. His family's support also made it possible for him to bear the grueling, boring periods of learning, with the result that he could say, later in his life, "Genius is diligence".

The term *incubation* is derived from the Latin word *incubatio*, meaning "to lie on something", "to brood or hatch". A more biological definition of incubation is "the act of warming to promote development". In antiquity, incubation described the act of sleeping at a cult site in order to receive an oracle, healing, or a higher insight. This custom was also common at Christian pilgrimage sites. From this, we can see that what characterizes the incubation period is that the task is laid aside and given over to the unconscious mind to work on. Like the preparatory phase, the incubation phase is a complex phenomenon. The long preparatory period has left its marks on the creator, who then combines what he has learned, often unconsciously, in an original way, and abandons himself to his subject for a longer period of time. This is not always simple and can lead to major emotional tensions. During the incubation phase, it is necessary to allow one's thoughts to wander, even if it does not lead to tangible results, and to patiently cultivate the right balance between goal-oriented activity and unbounded imagination. For instance, Goethe described how he put *Werther* to paper after a long preparatory and incubation phase, "almost unconsciously, like a somnambulist".

The third phase is *illumination*. We can perceive the teachings of Augustine behind this term; according to him, human perception is enabled by a divine light. Within the creative process, illumination seldom appears as a sudden inspiration; rather, it is usually a complex perceptual gestalt that develops gradually. Usually, the creative spark has long been in preparation, repeatedly appearing and then disappearing again like a smoke signal, only to finally be consciously perceived in a tangible form at some point. Sudden inspirations, such as Kekulé's dream of the snake biting its own tail as his inspiration for discovering the benzene ring, are rare exceptions. There is even doubt that the above example was a sudden illumination; rather, it seems that Kekulé's story was simply an anecdotal condensation of his yearslong process of creation. Even Goethe's poems, which often appeared before his eyes in finished form upon waking, underwent a long period of preparation, developing in this and that direction and constantly being worked on, both consciously and unconsciously, until the final product appeared, seemingly "of its own accord". It is not only ideas that are creative, though; implementing the ideas in the form of a complex literary product is also creative. However, it is important to be on the lookout for illumination and to hold on to whatever it has condensed into an idea. Goethe describes the relationship between preparation, inspiration, and implementation as follows: "Everything that we call invention or discovery in the higher sense of the word is the serious exercise and activity of an original feeling for truth, which, after a long course of silent cultivation, suddenly flashes out into fruitful knowledge" (Saunders, p. 193).

Many poems, meldings of linguistic forms and unconscious fantasies, appeared to Goethe as if in a vision. Goethe described how these poems "suddenly came to him whole … often spontaneously, even against his will … when waking during the night" (HA 1, p. 417: DS). Discussing the origins of his poem "At Midnight Hour", Goethe said that he found it that much more worthy and dear to him "because I could not say whence it came and whither it wished to go" (HA 1, p. 419: DS). He was aided by his good memory in retaining the offshoots of his unconscious mind. He was loathe to divulge which of his poems were the most personal, the ones that were "still attached to" his heart. On the other hand, it was exactly those spontaneous poems, the ones "close to [his] heart", that he liked best. He felt so close to some of his poems that he did not publish them until decades after writing them, for example, "Over All Mountain Peaks".

During the *realization phase*, themes that have already gone through the earlier phases – a long period of preparation leading to slow growth before becoming perceptible, sometimes suddenly – are now worked out. Many talented people are well educated, dedicate themselves fully to a task, and receive a creative spark, but it takes more than preparation, incubation, and illumination in order to realize an idea. Passion, curiosity, and originality may already be in play, but now resilience is required in order to endure the work's often slow progress and the disappointment of comprehending that an illuminating idea is not an accomplishment in and of itself. Goethe, like Thomas Edison after him, was basically saying that his works contained 1 percent inspiration and 99 percent perspiration.

Many creative people fail during the realization phase. They often do not have the patience or the resilience to continue their difficult work, which follows their insights at a snail's pace; this then has a negative effect on their self-esteem. Most creative people report experiencing challenges during the long period when their work is being realized. They feel destabilized, reject ideas, even good ones, and find wrestling with their task and with themselves in solitude to be difficult. Their dedication to their work demands that they withdraw from everyday activities and loosen their connections to their environments. During crucial periods in the realization phase, they sense that they are alone in a very radical way, but also that they must remain alone. This can create fear and lead to a loss of self-worth. For these reasons, some creative types pull back from their work, remaining unproductive despite a passionate interest and original ideas. Goethe employed strict work rituals to combat such challenges, including a regular daily routine in which time was planned for both work and recreation and plans were clearly laid out. This was not a symptom of a compulsive tendency, but was rather a means of protecting himself from the emotional turbulence that is connected to creative work, something common to many creative types (see Holm-Hadulla 2010).

The last phase of the creative process is *verification*, i.e. review and confirmation. The creative person reviews his own work, and others inspect the quality of that work. He is often full of doubts when he views his product, and he may hesitate to allow the larger community of experts to assess it. This is the climax of the creative process, though. Goethe was in the happy position of having people respond positively to his inclination for self-expression as a child, with result that this inclination was directed toward productive channels. They enjoyed his recitation of poems he had memorized and later allowed him to entertain them by reciting parts of plays. Cornelia was a curious and supportive listener, and his friends were an appreciated audience. Goethe was also undeterred by the fact that some people found him annoying; the Arcadian Society, for instance, rejected his application for admission because they thought he was a "blabbermouth".

Later, from his first days at university, starting with Behrisch in Leipzig, then Herder in Strasbourg, Lavater in Frankfurt and Zurich, and eventually Schiller in Weimar, Goethe found friends to show his work to, friends who sympathetically supported, but also critically challenged, his creative process. Goethe played with his self, especially in his love relationships, and received the answers he needed. This gave him a sense of resonance and increased his feelings of self-worth, with the result that he found himself inspired and driven to better his accomplishments and to achieve more.

Chapter 16

Goethe's creative art of living and self-treatment strategies

Goethe has shown us that we cannot discover happiness, we must make it. Starting as children, we have the task of actively shaping our own lives. From this perspective, creativity is part of the art of living; it develops when we actively observe ourselves and others. Goethe had a special way of showing how the creative exchange between a person and his environment occurs. It does not happen spontaneously; rather, it must be wrested from the inertia prevalent in everyday life, a type of destructiveness. Effective communication is a central element of the art of living and is connected to creative self-actualization. Goethe's life and work underscore the great importance of memories, fantasies, and actions. It is only through mental representation and active actualization that we are able to achieve a certain degree of coherence, which is essential for us (see Holm-Hadulla 2013).

In the everyday art of living, feelings, ideas, and communicative activities fulfill this quasi-biological need for coherence, the basis of human identity. The North American philosopher Richard Rorty formulated this idea so:

> We pragmatists think that the reason people try to make their beliefs coherent is not that they love truth but because they cannot help doing so. Our minds can no more stand incoherence than our brains can stand whatever neuro-chemical imbalance is the physiological correlate of such incoherence ... So our minds are constrained (and in part constructed) by the need to tie our beliefs and desires together into a reasonably perspicuous whole.

> (2001, p. 15)

In this respect, Goethe, through his creations, was able to experience reality as coherent and meaningful. This does not mean that his works simply ensued from what he had experienced, but rather that his works made it possible for things that were portrayed to become what they were. The verse "And when mortals fall silent in their torment,/a god granted me the power of expressing my suffering" does not simply mean relief from painful experiences; rather, distressing occurrences are placed in the larger context of all experiences. In this way, poetry makes it possible to experience reality in a structured way, taking into account the need to experience the world around us – despite its many faults – as coherent. This is also an essential element of psychotherapy (see Holm-Hadulla 2004a, 2004b).

Creativity encompasses more than just the original act of production; it also includes hearing, seeing, and feeling. The enjoyment of art is not simply a pleasant luxury; it is also an essential element in shaping our lives. Moreover, art fulfills a social function. Greek tragedies and modern films capture the imagination of viewers, but more than that, they create collective fantasies and values. A common culture, whether good or bad, is the result of cathartic communication.

In addition to the outline for an artistic art of living found in Goethe's life and work, we also find interesting clues about how to live a rational life and how to deal with illness, nutrition, exercise, and hygiene. We will concentrate on the importance of the creative art of living for mental health. Goethe developed and used psychotherapeutic strategies that continue to be used today, which we can summarize using an ABCDE model (Holm-Hadulla 2017). "Alliance" refers to the importance of supportive relationships. This is a decisive factor, one that scientific studies have shown to be essential to success. The dimension "Behavior" focuses on correcting dysfunctional modes of behavior. "Cognition" deals with the processing of irrational meanings and beliefs. "Dynamics" includes the processing of unconscious conflicts, and "Existentials" the consideration of significant existential themes.

These five elements were very important for Goethe. Dependable relationships, self-aware behavior, cognitive clarification, processing of unconscious conflicts, and shaping existential themes were his personal therapeutic principles. He frequently considered himself to be at risk and had to overcome some depressive episodes. A summary of Goethe's self-therapeutic principles would show that he repeatedly sought, and found, supportive relationships, first with his parents, and then with his grandmother and sister. After leaving home for the first time, he succeeded in finding friendships in a new environment that gave him a sense of stability and safety. Looking back, he wrote the following about the depressive episode that began while he was a student in Leipzig:

> But what particularly revived me at this time was to see how many eminent men had, undeservedly, given me their affection. Undeservedly, I say; for there was not one among them whom I had not troubled by my tiresome vagaries, not one whom I had not more than once wounded by a morbid spirit of contradiction, and whom I had not stubbornly avoided for a time, from a consciousness of my own misbehaviour.
>
> (Smith, vol. 1, pp. 295–296)

Later, Goethe was able to cope with his conflicts thanks to his relationships with women such as Friederike Brion, Lilli Schönemann, Charlotte Buff, Auguste zu

Stolberg, Charlotte von Stein, and Christiane Vulpius, and with men such as Herder, Karl August, Wieland, Schiller, and Riemer.

We have had a thorough introduction to his behavioral and cognitive strategies. What sticks out is his principle of transforming both positive and negative experiences into language, a principle he followed his entire life, starting as a young boy. This allowed him to find intellectual clarity and emotional equilibrium during periods of melancholia.

Looking at the dynamics of his conflicts, we notice he was open to unconscious psychological processes, approaching them with curiosity and interest. Freely soaring fantasies and dreams were his important companions, helping him to orient himself in the world. His artistic work made him what he had the potential to be, much like the importance of a particular gene only being discovered when it is expressed as a characteristic. His creative playing with experiences, memories, ideas, and fantasies helped him to maintain his mental health in the face of repeated threats to it. His life seems to be an illustration of Schiller's famous adage that man "is only wholly human when he is at play". Goethe was able to give himself over to playing with his perceptions, memories, ideas, fantasies, and imaginary beings his whole life long, from his imaginative play with the puppet theater as a small child to his great works.

Modern developmental psychology has shown that play is essential for healthy human development. Donald W. Winnicott (1971), the English pediatrician and psychoanalyst, has described how completely unremarkable toys, such as a soft cloth or corner of a duvet, can have distinctive significance for children. The importance of these objects is frequently only discovered when the preferred pacifier, the beloved doll, or the teddy bear is misplaced. Then the child is inconsolable because something irreplaceable has been lost. Almost all children are capable of imbuing their toys with life. The child plays with anything and everything – a blanket, the sounds he makes, even the moon when he sees a face in it. Playing continues to be an element of adult life: science, art, and religion all develop from the process of the child learning to understand himself within his environment. Psychoanalytical research has found that there is an almost biological need for creative play:

> It is assumed here that the task of reality-acceptance is never completed, that no human being is free from the strain of relating inner and outer reality, and that relief from this strain is provided by an intermediate area of experience which is not challenged (arts, religion, etc.). This intermediate area is in direct continuity with the play area of the small child who is "lost" in play.
>
> (Winnicott, p. 13)

Thus, play, fantasy, and art are not contrasted with reality; rather, they have an indispensable role in coping with reality. Playing creatively with ideas, images, and musical impressions confers structure and coherence on chaotic human emotions. Sigmund Freud showed that every person shapes his world using his imagination in order to experience himself as a consistent being. This creative process of structure formation begins in early childhood and is used to cope with all experiences, whether pleasant or unpleasant:

> In the play of children we seem to arrive at the conclusion that the child repeats even the unpleasant experiences because through his own activity he gains a far more thorough mastery of the strong impression than was possible by mere passive experience.

(Freud 1920, p. 14)

In this respect, the emotional life of adults has the same function: It works to integrate thoughts, feelings, and experiences. Goethe's particular mode of integration made it possible for him to have productivity, a sense of coherence, and a successful life. What separates him from the crowd, though, is his exceptional ability to capture both his joys and sorrows in language that is unique and to express them in a way that is universal. Thus was the artist created whose work continues to show us how to cope with the gravitation toward chaos inherent in life.

It is often claimed that art is the search for a lost paradise. However, and just as importantly, art is also a way of dealing with tragic events in life. This is something Goethe shows us quite impressively. He was frequently struck by blows of fate and pushed to the brink of despair. Ultimately, though, he reacted, time and again, by turning to (a) people who were supportive of him, (b) his scholarly, artistic, and practical work, (c) intellectual sense-making, (d) clarification of his turbulent feelings, and (e) creative processing of existential themes (see Holm-Hadulla 2012).

From the perspective of psychoanalysis, creativity always serves the additional purpose of coping with pain, powerlessness, and death. In the face of destruction and chaos, the artist attempts to recreate the experience of finally being whole again, if only for a moment. Goethe spent his entire life laboring at this task.

Chapter 17

Goethe's creative bipolarity and "healthy illness"

Since ancient Greek philosophy, the connection between creativity and mental illness has been a theme in Western culture (see Holm-Hadulla 2011). Plato believed that politicians, artists, and philosophers were capable of exceptional accomplishments while in a state of ecstasy, i.e. while outside of themselves. He differentiated between four types of divine madness: poetic, prophetic, ritual, and erotic. Aristotle and his student Theophrastus found a tendency toward melancholy among the great thinkers and artists. The politician, scientist, and poet Johann W. von Goethe may well be the one thinker with the most extensive experience with this problem, which he dealt with in his work, from *Werther* and *Torquato Tasso* to *Wilhelm Meister* and *Faust*.

In 1862, as psychiatry was becoming established as a serious discipline in the field of medicine, Cesare Lombroso's deplorable book *Man of Genius* (lit. *Genius and Insanity*) appeared, which claimed that genius was connected to degeneration in the brain. Later, a whole array of illnesses including schizophrenia and manic depression, but also alcohol and drug abuse, would be attributed to creative personalities. Modern research has shown, though, that mental illness is not more prevalent among exceptional people than among the general population (Ludwig 1997). Many creativity researchers have even come to the conclusion that creativity provides protection against mental illness (see Runco 2007).

Nevertheless, the mental health of creative people is strongly dependent on their field of activity. While scientists, politicians, economists, explorers, painters, musicians, and essay writers tend to have good mental health, there are two groups of creative types who are more likely to exhibit mental illness: poets and performing artists. The poets are approximately three times more likely to suffer from a depressive disorder than the general population (Ludwig 1997). Alcohol and drug abuse is especially common among singers, dancers, and stage actors. Despite the popular belief that drugs can have a creativity-enhancing effect, studies have shown the opposite: high levels of drug and alcohol consumption normally have a negative effect on creativity. Alcohol and drug abuse are rarely found during periods of creative productivity; instead, they may be found before or after a working phase.

What about Goethe? As we have seen, he was prone to pronounced mood swings. Also his father was sometimes described as being melancholic or hypochondriac, although not to such an extent that it could be called a disease. His sister was described as being severely depressed during and after her pregnancies. For a long time after the birth of her first child, she was physically weak, sad, discontented, listless, and hopeless, and she found herself in this state again during her second pregnancy; she died shortly after giving birth to her second child.

Goethe's own birth was difficult, and this was followed by nightmares in infancy. The first emotional crisis he was himself conscious of occurred when he was 14 years old. After his first sexual ventures, disappointed love, and humiliating interrogations by the authorities, he was out of sorts and retreated from his usual social activities. He experienced a more profound emotional crisis during his student days in Leipzig. For the second time, disappointed love contributed to a state of depression that lasted, this time, for months and led not only to suicidal thoughts but even to suicide plans. In *Poetry and Truth*, Goethe described his condition thusly:

> I had brought with me from home a certain tendency to hypochondria, which, in this new sedentary and lounging life, was strengthened rather than diminished. The pain in my breast, which I had felt from time to time ever since the accident at Auerstedt, and which had perceptibly increased after a fall from horseback, made me dejected. By an unfortunate diet I destroyed my powers of digestion; the heavy Merseburg beer clouded my brain; the coffee, which produced a peculiar depression, especially when taken with milk after dinner, paralyzed my bowels, and seemed completely to suspend their functions, so that I experienced great uneasiness on this account, without having sufficient resolution to adopt a more rational mode of life. My spirits, sustained by ample youthful strength, fluctuated between the extremes of unrestrained gaiety and melancholy discomfort.
>
> (Smith, vol. 1, pp. 294–295)

The physician, painter, and natural philosopher Carl Gustav Carus, a friend of Goethe's, spoke in 1842 of a "healthy illness", while the psychiatrist Wilhelm Lange-Eichbaum (1928) took Goethe's descriptions literally and diagnosed him with manic depression. Ernst Kretschmer (1929), on the other hand, conjectured that he had a cyclical form of psychopathy. The psychiatrist and psychoanalyst Kurt Eissler, in his very interesting, very detailed study (1963), whose findings were nevertheless problematic, even went so far as to infer a psychotic disorder, in the sense of schizophrenia.

The following can be said about the diagnoses mentioned above: Depressive disorders are defined by a combination of depressed mood, lack of drive, loss of interests, hopelessness, and anhedonia. Other symptoms include somatic disorders such as circadian rhythm disorders, sleep disorders, abnormal physical sensations, loss of appetite, and listlessness. These are frequently accompanied by feelings of guilt and a sense of worthlessness. A differentiation is made between mild, moderate, and severe depressive episodes.

If we apply the above criteria to Goethe, we will see that he experienced several mild to moderate depressive episodes over the course of his life. Starting at the age of 14, he experienced depression that would often last several months and was accompanied by lack of drive, loss of motivation and interest, anhedonia, social withdrawal, reduced self-esteem, and suicidal thoughts. From the perspective of modern psychiatry typical "depressive episodes" can be diagnosed four or five times in his lifetime (see Holm-Hadulla, Roussel, and Hofmann 2010). They are only superficially similar to the "melancholy" attitude attributed to poets. Frequently, Goethe's depressive phases co-occur with severe physical ailments. Moreover, we can see that Goethe was describing a hidden chronic depression that could be classified today as "dysthymia", or persistent depressive disorder (PDD).

Goethe's depression was closely connected to his creativity, though. As described above, he was able to use his creative activity to overcome his dysthymic and depressive moods as well his intermittent suicidal tendencies. His works acted as an "inner fairytale" for him, in the sense of a transitional object. They helped him to endure an existential lack, to cope with sadness, and to assume a "depressive position" that he then transformed within his artistic work. This led him to experience self-efficacy (Bandura 1997), mindfulness, and a sense of coherence (Antonovsky 1987), which are of primary importance in modern psychotherapy, along with the acceptance of helpful relationships and the therapeutic principles of remembering, repeating, and working-through (see Holm-Hadulla 2017).

Manic phases are defined by elevated mood, increased drive, and a sense one has special mental and physical capabilities. If the ability to work and maintain social contact are not affected while someone is in this state, we would refer to it as hypomania. True manic phases are usually accompanied by attention and concentration deficits, leading to irritability, overconfidence, and an inability to engage in one's usual work. The affected person's mood and behavior are not appropriate to the situation, and he loses his social inhibitions. In the case of severe mania, people become incapable of functioning in their work and in their social lives, and they frequently also develop delusional symptoms and hallucinations.

If we consider Goethe with these criteria in mind, we can determine that, at most, he experienced some mild hypomania, although not to the extent we could call it a disease. For this reason, we can reject Lange-Eichbaum's assessment that Goethe suffered from manic depression. At the utmost, Goethe's mood swings during depressive periods could be said to be clinical manifestations of depression. A more detailed psychopathological analysis can be found in our 2010 article on Goethe (Holm-Hadulla, Hofmann, and Roussel).

Let us now look at Eissler's diagnosis of schizophrenia-like psychosis. The following symptoms are characteristic of schizophrenia:

Ego disorders: These manifest as a conviction that one's own thoughts have been beamed into one's mind or are being broadcast to others. Patients report phenomena such as audible thoughts, thought withdrawal, thought broadcast, and thought insertion. They can also experience physical sensations as having been externally created and manipulated. These patients are convinced that all of these things are really happening to them and are not fantasies.

Delusion of influence: Patients are certain they are being influenced by external actors who are controlling their thoughts and feelings. They are convinced of the reality of these experiences. One patient believed that the nightly newsreader was turning over a page to signal that he would now be reading a message meant just for the patient. Afterward, he sensed a beam of light shining into his head and has been absolutely convinced ever since that the newsreader is able to read and control his thoughts and behavior.

Hallucinations: The patients hear voices that comment on their behavior, that talk about them, and that give them commands. They can also hallucinate about their own bodies; thus, one patient said that his tormentors took away his thoughts and burned them. He became aware of this fire "in his heart, little pieces of which break off and move back and forth".

Thought disorders: One thought disorder that is typical in schizophrenia is incoherence, something that is difficult for those with little experience of psychiatry to understand. For example, a patient with schizophrenia who is asked to interpret the idiom "One swallow does not make a summer" might respond by saying,

> Yes, of course, swallows fly in the summer – lots, lots – this morning during the rounds – birds – my friend is coming to visit – oh, yeah, swallows – go on, fly – my head – who has my thoughts – the tormentors are black though – swallows are white – no, no tormentors.

When assessing this answer, it is important to remember that the patient's intention was not to create a Dadaist text; rather, he was making a real effort to interpret the idiom correctly.

Negative symptoms: These manifest as inexplicable apathy, social withdrawal, personality changes, and a severely reduced ability to begin or sustain activities. Negative symptoms can only be ascribed to schizophrenia when the other symptoms are also present or have been present before.

When we review the list of characteristic symptoms of schizophrenia, we find no evidence that Goethe could have had such a disease. Goethe suffered from mood swings, diverse mild anxieties, and hypochondriac fears, but certainly not from a psychosis. That being said, it is possible to detect some histrionic and narcissistic tendencies in his behavior.

Someone is described as having a hysterical or histrionic personality if they dramatize themselves, behave theatrically, and have a tendency to express their feelings in an exaggerated way. In addition, such people typically demand recognition and have a tendency to place themselves at the center of attention. These could all be imputed to Goethe, but there is much more to histrionic personality disorder (HPD). People with HPD are easily influenced, are emotionally labile and shallow, and are incapable of being alone. Goethe was certainly able to manage the last one, though; moreover, a smidge of hysteria, in the sense described above, can make perfect sense in a social setting, for instance, when socializing.

Narcissistic personalities are characterized by extraordinary self-referentiality. This is readily discernible in Goethe – in most artists, for that matter – but what is missing is the coldness in personal relationships that is so characteristic of narcissistic personality disorders and that was never evident in any phase of his life. He could be crude or dismissive, but he always maintained close personal contacts. Even if we wished to ascribe to him hysterical or narcissistic personality tendencies, we must admit that they could never be called clinical manifestations of HPD or NPD.

In summary, we can say that Goethe experienced several depressive episodes and suffered frequently from dysthymic moods. If he had received modern treatment with antidepressants, his mood swings would probably have been alleviated. It is likely that the chief effect of these medications – shielding the patient from uncomfortable sensations – would have led to one of the greatest geniuses of all time being cut off from the source of his creativity. Antidepressants are a blessing only for those patients with depressive disorders who are unable to creatively transform their suffering. As we have shown, Goethe's psychotherapeutic treatment of himself was quite effective, but he also allowed others to help him to overcome psychological crises (Holm-Hadulla 2012).

Let us return to Eissler's suspicion of schizophrenia. His argument relies heavily on a letter from Goethe to Behrisch in October of 1767, in which he bemoans Käthchen's supposed infidelity:

She asked me under the most passionate caresses not to torment her with jealousy, she swore to me always to be mine. And what does one not believe if one is in love? But what can she swear? Can she swear never to see differently, can she swear that her heart shall beat no more? Yet I want to believe that she can do so. But suppose – suppose nothing, it sounds as if I did not want to come out with it. – Today – a glance at a lover lifts him into Heaven, but his beautiful one can soon pull him down again; she need only turn her eyes upon someone else. An aphorism. You must forgive me my confused mind. Today I was standing next to her, talking, and she was playing with the ribbons of her bonnet. Presently, the younger one entered and asked my girl's mother for a playing card, the mother went to the desk and the daughter lifted her hand up to her eye and wiped it, as if something had got into it. This is what drives me mad. I am crazy, you think. Now listen further. I know this gesture of my girl very well. How often has she done this to hide her blushes, her confusion, from her mother, done this very thing as a pretext to bring her hand decently up to her face. Should she not do just that to betray her lover which she had done to deceive her mother? It is a suspicion that to me has a high degree of certainty. Put it as certain, and – I tremble to hear your answer – how should I excuse her? Yes, this is what I want – to excuse her. Tell me reasons in her favor, none against her. You would – enough – eyes in love see sharper than the eyes of the Lord, but often too sharply. Advise me all around, and comfort me because of this matter. Only do not mock me, even if I have deserved it.

(Eissler, vol. 1, pp. 56–57)

This letter reveals Goethe's perturbed state of mind and burning jealousy, which were surely not unwarranted. Käthchen was three years older than him and at an eminently marriageable age. Goethe had ruled out a marital bond, and neither of them was at liberty to go on an erotic adventure, for both internal and external reasons. In this situation, Käthchen was increasingly unnerved by Goethe's infatuation with her, and she was doubtlessly on the lookout for a bridegroom she could take seriously. It was not long before she was out of patience with Goethe and forbade him from contacting her. A few months later, when the opportunity presented itself, she married.

Eissler found the letter "uncanny" and thought Goethe was gradually losing control and fearing to "be smashed under the pressure of the impending cataclysm" (Eissler, vol. 1, pp. 57–58). There was one detail in this letter, that

permits – almost requires – the diagnosis of an acute paranoid psychotic episode. Goethe refers to his sweetheart's gesture of putting her hand to her eye. He isolates this gesture from the total content and imputes to it a meaning that is clearly a derivative of his own unconscious. This is a typical behavior pattern that is generally found in patients suffering from schizophrenic disorders.

(Eissler, vol. 1, pp. 57–58)

In response, the following can be said: Most interpretations of other people's actions are colored by our own conscious and unconscious preconceptions. Goethe is jealous and interprets Käthchen's gesture in the context of that jealousy. Moreover, there is not a single schizophrenic symptom described at any point in the letter. Eissler seems to have sensed that his argument was weak and resorted to the following justification: Unlike a hysterical person, the schizophrenic person lives "in a predominantly, if not exclusively, emotional world" (Eissler, vol. 1, pp. 57–58). Such a claim is not backed by any empirical scientific or clinical evidence. Second, Eissler holds that schizophrenia "lifts the pertinent gesture or emotional manifestation out of its proper context and attaches it to a broad segment of his own emotional life" (Eissler, vol. 1, pp. 57–58). This is a description of the common psychological mechanism of associative thinking, which does not justify the conclusion of a psychotic disorder.

Eissler then develops the following theory, based on a sophisticated interpretation of the letter we have been discussing and the poem "To Sleep":

> The paranoid symptom, in so far as it is connected with imagery about a mother, derives its momentum from a murderous impulse against his own mother. (This impulse stemmed – if its deepest layers are considered – from rivalry with her over whether she or he would mother Cornelia and the subsequent babies).
>
> (Eissler, vol. 1, pp. 58f.)

Eissler does take into account the fact that Goethe's interpretation of Käthchen's gesture was simply a suspicion, one he was deliberating on and had shared with a friend for his assessment. All of these criteria would rule out a delusion, defined as a false, fixed belief that cannot be corrected by reason and that stretches reality to the limit. Eissler's misunderstanding of Goethe's psychopathology is illustrated by his interpretation of one of the poet's dreams. Goethe wrote to his friend Behrisch in October of 1767,

> Another night like this, Behrisch, and, in spite of all my sins, I shan't have to go to hell. You may have slept peacefully, but a jealous lover, who has drunk as much champagne as is necessary to put his blood in a pleasant heat and to inflame his imagination to the highest point! At first I could not sleep, I tossed about in my bed, sprang up, raved; then I grew weary and fell asleep, but before long I had silly dreams, of tall people, hats trimmed with feathers, tobacco pipes, sleight-of-hand and jugglers' tricks, and thereupon I woke up and consigned it all to the devil. After that I had a quiet hour, nice dreams. The habitual looks, the beckoning at the door, the kisses snatched in flying past ... And then all at once, she had stuck me into a sack! A real sleight-of-hand trick! Guinea pigs one tricks into sacks at carnivals, but a human being like me – that is unheard of. But improbable soever though it appeared to me, just so real did I sense it. I philosophized in the sack and I wailed a dozen allegories in the style of Shakespeare when he rhymes. After that it seemed to me as if I had gone, gone from her, but not out of the sack. I wished myself set free, and woke up.
>
> (Brown, vol. 1, p. 31; Eissler, vol. 1, pp. 60–61)

Eissler was of the opinion that the first part of the dream consisted of phallic symbols in the form of "tall people, hats trimmed with feathers, tobacco pipes". He wondered whether these symbols arose from Goethe's own arousal or whether he was imagining Behrisch's erect penis. The dream occurred on Behrisch's last night in Leipzig, and Goethe must have had a strong desire for him. We could view it that way, but it has nothing to do with a psychotic disorder. When a young man has a nocturnal erection, it signals he is healthy; the fact that he incorporates this erection into his dreams is natural, according to psychology and neurobiology. But the claim that this must indicate he had a very strong sexual desire for Behrisch is unfounded. Even if this were the case, though, it would not have any interpretative significance for Goethe's alleged psychosis. I will come back to the topic of homosexuality in a moment.

Eissler's interpretation of Goethe "being stuck in the sack" seems to me to be more plausible and more closely related to the phenomena under discussion. Eissler pointed out that Goethe experienced Behrisch's departure as a great loss. As we can see in his letters and poems, Goethe actually thought of Behrisch as a protector, who helped him to control his feelings, to structure them by means of writing, and also to quiet his fears about women. After Behrisch left Leipzig, it is quite likely that Goethe's fear of a woman ensnaring him and neutralizing his power increased. This is followed by the idea – an idea I find reasonable – that a sexual encounter would have brought Goethe into contact with pregnancy, birth, and the threat of death, and that he therefore avoided such contact. Eissler quotes from a letter Goethe wrote to Cornelia at Easter in 1766:

And so from hour to hour we ripe and ripe,
And then from hour to hour we rot and rot.
(Eissler, vol. 1, p. 63)

This Shakespeare quote sounds like the threat of death is being evoked. In his dream, trapped in a sack, Goethe rhymes in a Shakespearean manner, using poetry to keep himself alive. Goethe feared that this remedy would no longer be accessible to him if he were to enter into a real sexual relationship. For a psychiatric assessment, this line of reasoning is only of secondary significance. What is relevant for a diagnosis, though, is working through emotional conflicts in dreams in this way is far from delusional.

One defining aspect of delusion is the treatment of thoughts and ideas as if they were real. It would therefore have been delusional if Goethe had believed in the days and weeks following his dream that tall people were following him in the street and that Käthchen Schönkopf was colluding with them to really put him in a sack. Goethe's dream is almost the antithesis of a delusion; it expresses a deep concern in the form of a story. Delusional and schizophrenic patients, though, are unable to sufficiently articulate their subjective impressions and to differentiate them from objective reality, which causes them suffering. They have difficulty confiding in others and are unable to find adequate words to describe their psychological trauma. They labor under an impaired ability to mentalize and to symbolize, which often reduces them to despair. When a patient in treatment is able to symbolize a personal experience and to stop reifying a delusion, he is on the path to recovery. In other words, dreams, fantasies, and stories that express personal experience are signs of mental health.

Eissler would admit this, even while raising the objection that Goethe's dreams, fantasies, and stories were actually a defense against latent psychosis or schizophrenia. This conception of psychosis is problematic, though, because then all human behavior could be understood as a defense against psychosis. Even if you agree with this, the idea of "latent psychosis" would be just as valid as the idea of "latent cancer", something we would all be at the mercy of since our immune systems constantly defend against cancer cells.

Eissler's second mistake comes from his appraisal of Goethe's homosexuality. Eissler's stance was within the psychoanalytical tradition of attributing a significant role to latent homosexuality in the genesis of jealousy and delusion. In *The Schreber Case*, Freud (1911) provided a detailed analysis of the autobiographical *Memoirs of My Nervous Illness* by Daniel Paul Schreber. In it, Freud construes a connection between homosexuality and paranoia, a connection that has not been empirically attested. Freudian analysis emerged during a time when homosexuality was ostracized by society and persecuted by the law. When homosexual tendencies manifested themselves, those affected often chose to take their own lives. Even in the New York of the 1950s and 1960s, Eissler belonged to a homophobic culture that continued to view homosexuality as a pathological perversion, hence his scandalized tone when speaking of homosexuality. Thus, his takeaway from the letter cited above was that Goethe was staving off strong homosexual impulses. Today – at least among the scientifically enlightened – any evidence of homosexual tendencies in Goethe would be considered banal. It is possible to go even farther and state that Goethe dealt amazingly openly with the tender and erotic aspects of his friendships with men. In addition, during the Age of Sensibility, it was quite common for men to express tender feelings for their same-sex friends. But even Eissler was unable to find any evidence for a sexual attraction, in the narrower sense, or a penchant for sex with men.

Something deserving of mention, though, is Goethe's interest in love triangles: Käthchen and Behrisch, Charlotte Buff and her fiancé, and Charlotte von Stein and her husband. As we have shown, these relationships were very multifaceted and cannot be adequately explained by any attempts at repressing homosexuality.

Eissler's third mistake is the result of misunderstanding Goethe's erotic relationship to Cornelia, a relationship which Eissler characterized as being incestuous, which then led him to draw far-reaching conclusions about Goethe's creativity. His argument went like this: Before writing *Werther*, he experienced Cornelia's engagement as a "catastrophic trauma". Her marriage in November of 1773 strengthened his fear of loss. It was only after her marriage that Goethe's creative eruption took place, in the form of his novel *Werther*, which deals with the trauma of the loss of a sister. The central argument supporting this hypothesis is the fact that the rival Albert in *Werther* does not resemble Kestner, Lotte's fiancé, but instead resembles Schlosser, Cornelia's husband. Goethe experienced Cornelia marrying as an act of betrayal that was a renewal of his mother's betrayal of not having additional children. In his interpretation, Eissler establishes a connection between Goethe's creativeness, especially the birth of *Werther*, and the pregnancies of Cornelia, Maximiliane, and Charlotte

Buff. *Werther* was Goethe's offspring, the most beautiful to ever be created and born in the whole world.

The theme of birth is a very important one in *Werther*, as well as in many of Goethe's other works, both as a theme from his personal background and as an explicit problem. Goethe's pain over the real loss of Cornelia also played an important role during this period of emotional processing and literary shaping. Eissler, however, postulated a causal relationship between purportedly incestuous desires and literary composition. For him, the birth of *Werther* is not metaphorical, but in reality is a concrete outcome of Goethe's sexual desire for Cornelia. Despite quoting Goethe's assertion to Eckermann that Lili Schönemann was his first love, Eissler did not correct himself. Even so, Eissler believed that the incestuous fixation became Cornelia's doom, whereas for Goethe it was the spur that drove him to creativity.

An error had crept into Eissler's argument, one that is often responsible for narrowing psychological misunderstanding: The motifs the poet was playing with were misunderstood as a causal explanation. *Reasons* are being confused with *causes*. Metaphorical and structural similarities are being taken as real conditions. But a devoted, tender love for a sister, which could also contain erotic fantasies, is not the same thing as an incestuous relationship. A consensus can be reached with Eissler's perspective if we avoid his pathologizing overtones and simply sum up that Cornelia was extraordinarily important for Goethe's creative development.

All in all, we can determine that Goethe's path to creativity was characterized by a passion that pushed the boundaries of the pathological but eventually led to a higher degree of health. Thus the diagnosis of Goethe's last physician Carl Gustav Carus (1842), "healthy illness", is right in some respect. This will become especially clear in his poem "Legacy", in his last letter, and in *Faust II*.

Part III

Goethe's legacy

Chapter 18

Goethe's late poem *Legacy*

In *Legacy*, one of Goethe's last poems, which he wrote in February of 1829, we receive a lasting impression of hope, truth, and love, as well as self-knowledge, sensuousness, and joie de vivre.

Legacy

No being can crumble into nothingness!
The Eternal continues to stir within all things;
nourish yourself on Being, and be happy!
Being is eternal: for laws
preserve the living treasures
with which the universe has adorned itself.

The truth was discovered long since,
and has created an alliance of noble minds;
hold on to the old truth!
Son of earth, thank the wise man
who showed it the path by which it circles the sun,
and showed that path to its siblings.

Now immediately turn your thoughts inward:
there you will find the central point
about which no noble-minded man can have doubts.
There you will find no rule missing.
For the independent conscience
plays the role of the sun to your ethical day.

Next, you have to trust your senses;
they do not allow you to observe anything incorrect
if your understanding keeps you alert.
Cheerfully make observations with fresh eyes
and walk, firmly but with suppleness,
through the meadows of a richly endowed world.

Make moderate use of abundance and plenty;
let reason be at hand in every place
where life enjoys life.
Then the past will be of permanence,
the future will come to life in advance,
and the present moment will be eternity.

And once you've finally succeeded,
and have been permeated with the feeling
"Only what is productive is true,"
you can probe the doings of society,
which will operate according to its own rules;
associate yourself with the smallest number of people.

And, as of old, the philosopher
and the poet created, in silent seclusion,
a labor of love in pursuance of their own will,
so you, too, will obtain the highest favor:
for to have a presentiment of what noble souls will someday accomplish
is the most desirable function of man.

                                    (Appelbaum, pp. 227–229)

Goethe's impetus for *Legacy* was a misunderstanding of one of his poems, "The One and the All" (1821). To his annoyance, the last two lines were displayed in gold letters at a conference of naturalists in Berlin:

For everything would have to crumble into nothingness
if it insisted on remaining in its momentary state.
                                    (Appelbaum, p. 197)

The 79- year-old felt compelled to compose a lyrical retraction, resulting in a summary of his artistic and life experiences.

Legacy begins with a description of his belief that beings cannot disintegrate, that they exist forever, and that they continue to live on in new forms: "The Eternal continues to stir within all things". This expresses a deeply rooted outlook, one that only appears to be a lyrical retraction of the last lines of "The One and the All"; instead, it is a variation on Goethe's old theme of life as a continuous process of development, one that takes place in the space between tension and relaxation, dedication and retreat, activity and composure, changing and dying. In Faust's study, Mephistopheles, "the spirit of perpetual negation", stresses the following:

    . . . for all
    That's made is fit to be destroyed.
    Far better if it were an empty void!
                (Vs. 1338–1341)

By way of contrast, in the first act of *Faust II*, which was completed at the end of 1829, Mephistopheles describes the activities of the primordial mothers as never-ending.

> ... formation, transformation,
> Of mind eternal, eternal recreation!
> (Vs. 6287–6288)

In the dialectic of "Die and be transformed", Goethe draws conclusions in *Legacy* that are of practical importance for living and provides recommendations for successfully shaping our lives, ideas gleaned from his own passionate search. Before we further develop this theme, though, we should briefly examine his belief in life after death. This belief is present throughout all of religious and cultural history; for Goethe it is connected to the idea of an indestructible entelechy. In a conversation with Eckermann in May of 1824, he comforted himself about his inevitable death with the following words:

> "At the age of seventy-five", continued he, with much cheerfulness, "one must, of course, think sometimes of death. But this thought never gives me the least uneasiness, for I am fully convinced that our spirit is a being of a nature quite indestructible, and that its activity continues from eternity to eternity".
>
> (Oxenford, vol. 1, p. 161)

In the second line of *Legacy*, the active aspect of the living is brought up: "The Eternal continues to stir within all things". Existence is constantly transformed, which gives it permanence; if it were to remain static, its doom would be certain. Next, Goethe addresses the reader directly, commanding him to exhaust the possibilities of life and to take his fate in his own hands: "Nourish yourself on Being, and be happy!" This is not a moral imperative; rather, it is a recommendation of his everyday art of living. After this, the poem reintroduces a philosophical point of view. The eternalness of being is founded on laws, and these laws give permanence to the living, in all of their manifestations. What kinds of laws are being referred to? We might think of natural laws, or even moral or legal laws. From a psychological perspective, which is what our interpretation is based on, we can see that this stanza expresses hope and a zest for life. The mental tendency toward chaos and destruction is balanced by a belief in continued existence. The aging poet inspires confidence that he will be subsumed in the continuity of life. Here we are reminded of the hope cherished by many people that they will somehow continue to have an effect through their achievements. This includes, first and foremost, the idea that one will continue to live through one's own children. In addition, many people are confident that they have made a lasting contribution to their communities through their careers and their social activities.

Despite his hopeful glorification of human striving, Goethe remained realistic. During the period when he was composing *Legacy*, he learned that his friend Zelter was going to receive an award; he wrote the following words on it on 26 January 1829: "These marks of honour are really nothing but magnified encumbrances, upon which, notwithstanding, we must congratulate ourselves and others, because life–if it goes well–should ever be considered as a perpetual fight and a perpetual conquest" (Coleridge, p. 348). In light of this resignation, we can say that *Legacy* shows a fresh side of human striving, one turned toward life. Thus, the "truth" in the second stanza is not raised to the level of the didactic but is instead discovered in lively activity. Goethe conceives of the truth as a phenomenon that "was discovered long since", meaning that man has been inclined toward the truth since time immemorial and that his efforts must necessarily be turned toward achieving it. The pursuit of truth is the collaborative task of all those who are in "an alliance of noble minds". It is within his community that the individual finds his way to himself.

In the next verse, the reader is again commanded to remain active and to acquire the treasures of tradition: "Hold on to the old truth!" Each individual should adopt the knowledge passed down in the areas of religion, philosophy, and cultural history. In this way, each individual person not only fulfills his own intellectual duty, but he also realizes his own potential within a social and historical context. Furthermore, the reader and "son of earth" is called upon to show his gratitude to the superior being that created the laws of nature. As Boyle (2000) has argued, it seems as though Goethe were speaking here of a wise, personal god who presides over creation. At the same time, though, he is referring to the scientists who investigated the orbits of the sun and moon and who dedicated their lives to the discovery of truth, scientists such as Copernicus. Goethe bows before him because his work in the natural sciences established an age of human introspection that has made it possible for us to look beyond surface appearances.

From a psychological perspective, the second stanza expresses the fundamental hope that there is something good and true governing our individual and social lives. For the modern reader, this appears quite idealistic. Wars, social injustice, strokes of fate, illness, and personal shortcomings can cause people to lose their belief in goodness, truth, and beauty. Goethe himself often despaired during his lifetime, and the goodness, truth, and beauty found in his works is always pervaded by a negative force. Goethe grappled with these negative forces in many of his works – from *Werther* to *Faust* – his whole life long. Evil arises within the individual himself and, like the Freudian death drive, it can only be overcome by means of constant activity. From the transfiguring view of *Legacy*, these remain background aspects.

The third stanza starts by calling for introspection in the reader: "Turn your thoughts inward". Here we are reminded of the Socratic "know thyself", but we cannot understand it solely by means of the intellect; rather, we must recognize that it portrays a way of life that joins together cultivated people, whom Goethe refers to as "noble". Natural and social events are reflected in their inner world as in a monad: "There you will find no rule missing". The manifestation of the individual's morals, his "independent conscience", plays just as much of a role in this as in fulfilling the laws of morality. From a psychological perspective, we could interpret the third stanza as follows: Biological processes and social experiences are represented and processed within our conscious and unconscious mental lives. Ideally, this inner activity would be under the control of an "independent conscience". In terms of the Freudian theory of id, ego, and superego, we would understand "independent conscience" to be a mental construct that, under the direction of the rational ego, mediates between the instincts of the id and reality or social demands and finds expression in the superego. When it is successfully able to reconcile inner and external reality, it makes possible a life that is moral, but also bright and beautiful: It "plays the role of the sun to your ethical day". This is reminiscent of a famous line in Kant's *Critique of Practical Reason*: "Two things fill the mind with ever new and increasing admiration and awe, the oftener and the more steadily we reflect on them: *the starry heavens above and the moral law within*" (p. 260).

This lofty concept of freedom and necessity crowns both Goethe's and Kant's treatments of nature and man. The "sun to your ethical day" is also reminiscent of Plato, who compared human goodness with cosmic harmony, using the sun to symbolize the idea of goodness. This stanza does not address the dangerous aspects of the path to morality. One thing Goethe himself had frequently experienced and also portrayed in his works, particularly in *Faust*, was the way that self-reflection can lead to self-referentiality, loneliness, and despondency. But he also repeatedly showed that the other extreme, unconditional capitulation to the demands of the external world, leads to failure. Thus, there is a dialectic concept of human self-reflection just under the surface of this stanza. It is only when the conflicting tendencies of inner and external reality are recognized and continuously developed that a person will achieve a type of personal freedom that is meaningfully related to his social community.

Accordingly, in the fourth stanza, Goethe recommends turning your eye outward. "Next, you have to trust your senses" is a typically Goethean rejection of abstract speculation. Openness to the life-world that is experienced through the senses leads to true experiences, and "they do not allow you to observe anything incorrect". This aesthetic evidence only serves the truth, though, "if your understanding keeps you alert", that is, if the certainty of your senses can hold its ground against examination by critical thinking. Translated into psychological terms, this means that a meaningful connection must be established between emotional and aesthetic experiences and intellectual insights. Experience via the senses also requires consistency and coherence, which can only come about if it is mentally structured (see Holm-Hadulla 2013). Sensuousness and reason stand in a dialectic relationship of recognition to each other, similar to in Hegel's *Phenomenology of Mind* (1807). But unlike Hegel, for whom human development culminates in absolute mind or spirit, for Goethe, humans manifest themselves after all of their intellectual reflection in the world of the senses. This world imparts enjoyment, security, and courage whenever someone wanders through the "richly endowed world ... firmly but with suppleness".

Complete enjoyment of life also requires structures in order to develop more fully. For this reason, the beginning of the fifth stanza points to the necessity of acting reasonably while also enjoying "abundance and plenty". Reasonable enjoyment means comprehending sensory stimuli and creatively shaping it. It is only in the interplay between sensuousness and reason that "life can enjoy life" and that the treasures of the past can be saved and the events of the future anticipated with hope: "Then the past will be of permanence,/the future will come to life in advance". This leads to happy moments in which it can be said, "and the present moment will be eternity". From a psychological perspective, we can say that satisfying experiences preserve both the pain of the past and anxious expectations of the future. If we dedicate ourselves with passion to those experiences that comprehend the present, the past, and the future, a transformation can occur, if only for a brief time, giving us a feeling of fulfillment and immortality. Many other poets have spoken of this, of course; we are reminded, for example, of the wonderful poem "To the Fates" by Friedrich Hölderlin:

To the Fates

Grant me just one summer, powerful ones,
  And just one autumn for ripe songs,
    That my heart, filled with that sweet
      Music, may more willingly die within me.

The soul, denied its divine heritage in life,
  Won't find rest down in Hades either.
    But if what is holy to me, the poem
      That rests in my heart, succeeds—

Then welcome, silent world of shadows!
  I'll be content, even though it's not my own lyre
    That leads me downwards. Once I'll have
      Lived like the gods, and more isn't necessary.
                                        (Mitchell, p. 16)

Unlike Hölderlin, who was unable to fulfill his own potential in the world and whose light was extinguished early, Goethe's lifelong productivity was the result of moments of being "permeated with feeling". The eternity of the moment becomes accessible despite suffering, or perhaps more accurately, due to the passionate turmoil that has been lived through. In the process, the poetical self remains conscious of danger, just as Goethe himself experienced the convulsions of world history and lived through revolutionary technological innovations such as the railway and the steam ship. It is clear in *Faust II* that there was an awareness of the psychological and social dangers inherent in unfettered science and economics. Today, we attempt to escape the desensitization of our experience of life, something Goethe greatly feared, in our "velociferous"[1] age by fleeing to substitute worlds provided by modern media. In doing so, we run the risk of becoming helplessly entangled in the instrumentalization of body and mind. Goethe countered this by holding up the ideal of being present in the moment, both sensuously and sensibly.

In the sixth stanza, to be "permeated with feeling" is formulated as the ideal for human striving. In this state of mindfulness and being present in the moment, "Only what is productive is true". Goethe was concerned with more than the utilization and mastery of nature, whose dark sides are portrayed so frightfully in *Faust II*. Sensory experience and intellectual understanding are reified by means of propagating activities. The self-directed aspect of creative passion is thus expanded by a communal, reality-based perspective. It is unavoidable that someone, faced with moments filled with sensuousness, would repeatedly examine the "doings of society"; that is, that person would view himself as part of a whole larger than himself and would come to an understanding with the "smallest number of people" about himself. What this primarily refers to is a society of knowledgeable people who have the necessary fundamentals to judge and act competently. This aspect of the "smallest number of people" receives a thorough treatment in *Wilhelm Meister*. In *Torquato Tasso*, we find the following:

Who doth not in his friends behold the world,
Deserves not that of him the world should hear.
(*Works* 11, p. 115)

The injunction to "associate ... with the smallest number of people" is not an anti-democratic rejection of politics, but rather a warning to put one's moral values and approach to life into practice within the personal sphere of friends and relations.

Seen from the perspective of psychology, the admonition to "associate yourself with the smallest number of people" could also be understood as a connection to the experiences of childhood and the primary attachment figures who accompany us through life in the form of moods, feelings, and memories. At first glance, this interpretation may seem surprising, but it is legitimized by the view that hermeneutical and psychological textual interpretation permit the reader to approach a text with his own prior understanding and to "transfer" his own experiences onto the text (Gadamer 1989). I have shown the critical influence that childhood experiences had on Goethe's life and work, beginning with his own traumatic birth and including the death of his brother Hermann Jakob. Although he used his creativity for many different purposes, it also aided him in coping with his fear of death and his continual framing of life as rebirth.

For this reason, it seems to me, based on my experience as a psychotherapist, that we can conclude that Goethe's belief in an eternal spirituality affecting the future corresponds to a backward-looking conviction that the past is eternal, similar to what Freud called the "indestructibility of the unconscious". Viewed from this perspective, people live on in their children and their works, but this also allows them to remain in contact with their own childhoods and pasts. Thus we could also read the following lines in the "Dedication" of Faust as evidence that far-distant memories of "the smallest number of people" have colored both individual and poetical experiences:

> Once more I sense uncertain shapes appearing,
> Dimly perceived in days of youth long past.
> Now in my heart I feel the moment nearing
> When I can hold those phantom figures fast.
>
> (Vs. 1–4)

Memory and the active transformation of memory may be tasks of the poet and the philosopher, but they are also used to shape everyday life and relationships. In a letter to Marianne von Willemer, Goethe, now 82 years old, wrote the following while on a journey to Ilmenau with his two grandsons, Wolfgang and Walther: "These insights, tying the past to the present, were heightened and animated and the landscape was exquisitely embellished because I had brought my grandsons with me" (FA 39, p. 468: DS).

We know from many psychological studies that emotional health and enjoyment of life are established when people are able to maintain contact with their unconscious and conscious memories. This leads to a stable experience of coherence and a feeling of identity that is reflected in the ability to be procreatively active and to enjoy one's children and grandchildren. Goethe has shown us the importance of integrating memories, even painful ones, into the self. Modern authors – for instance, Marcel Proust, Thomas Mann, James Joyce, Jorge Semprún, Jonathan Franzen, and Steven Spielberg – also proceed on the assumption that a key component of their creative work is the integration of their early experiences. When, at an advanced age, Picasso noted with satisfaction that he was improving at painting like a child, he meant that he was able to portray all of the aspects of his self from his childhood, including his joys and fears. In much the same way, Goethe, although well advanced in years, was able to compose poetry of simple beauty, to enjoy his life, and to experience the eternity in the present moment.

The seventh stanza describes the activity of coping with life, an achievement both poetical and philosophical, as a work of love. Here we can discern a reference to the New Testament:

> "I may speak in tongues of men or of angels, but if I have no love, I am a sounding gong or a clanging cymbal".
>
> (1 Corinthians 13:1)

True fertility can only arise from a spirit of love. "As of old ... the poet created, in silent seclusion" according to his own will. This means that all creative work is subjective and is wrung from one's own experiences. But it is also a labor of love for others. Each of us "will obtain the highest favor" when we act on the maxim to take our personal development in our own hands and to conceive of ourselves as desiring and striving until our dying day. Then the reader will make a connection to an intellectual community and will be able to "have a presentiment of what noble souls will someday accomplish". This summarizes an idea that was developed in the previous stanzas, that creativity is a leitmotif not only in art and science, but also in everyday life, and that it leads to the manifestation of the individual self and the social self. This striving is "the most desirable function of man", with which he "will obtain the highest favor".

The sovereign worldview of *Legacy* was won over a lifetime of battling fear and desperation. From birth to death, Goethe experienced highs and lows, and his life and work show us how we can deal with the fateful crises winding through our pasts, presents, and futures. To put it briefly, his message is to embrace and creatively transform our existence with passion. Then we will be fruitful in our ability to love and work, but we will also be able to let go and, as Goethe said in *The One and the All*, "self-surrender will be a pleasure". This hope allowed Goethe to view his death with subtle irony, serenely and composedly: "To me, the eternal existence of my soul is proved from my idea of activity; if I work on incessantly till my death, nature is bound to give me another form of existence when the present one can no longer sustain my spirit" (Oxenford, vol. 2, p. 122).

Note

1 A word coined by Goethe, joining "velocity" and "Lucifer", and meaning something like "diabolical haste" (Kirby, p. xx, note 20).

Chapter 19

Goethe's final letter

In his final letter, dated 17 March 1832 and addressed to his friend Wilhelm von Humboldt, Goethe condensed his ideas about creativity in a way that is still applicable today. He put these lines to paper only five days before his death, and they show once again how important he found conversation with his friends, here in the form of a letter, for the development of his intuitions and ideas. He begins with the traditional view that animals are "taught by their organs", something that is also true of humans, but they have the advantage of also being able to teach their organs. What he means by this is the interrelationship between body and mind, anticipating the modern psychosomatic concepts of "embodiment" and "corporealization" (see Fuchs 2016).

Then Goethe turns to the role of innate talents. He explains that every action depends on inherited abilities, which work automatically and unconsciously. A set of rules is also inherited with these abilities, which initially proceed randomly and without a purpose. One's natural talents are enhanced by handicrafts and art, and the earlier this occurs, the happier the person. For one's "innate individuality" to develop, external influences are necessary. These lines are a summary of Goethe's dialectic view of the importance of predisposition and environment, and also of spontaneous development and directed education. The "best genius" accepts everything and makes it his own. A proper education enables and elevates one's original character; it does not twist or malform it.

The next part of the letter is dedicated to the role of unconscious creative processes. Consciously doing something and unconsciously allowing something to happen are connected to each other in many different ways. Goethe took the example of someone musically talented wanting to compose a musical score. Conscious work and unconscious material act like the "warp and woof" of the process. Goethe alludes to this comparison in *Faust I*:

The mind, however, needs more room;
It's like a master-weaver's loom.
A thousand warps move as he treads,
The shuttle flies, and to and fro

The fibres into patterns flow –
One stamp combines a thousand threads.
(Vs. 1922–1927)

This is a lovely description of what we would today refer to as the formation of a neural network. What we now call combinatory and associative thinking occurs mostly unconsciously, something Goethe recognized: "the organs of man unconsciously unite, in a free activity, the acquired and the innate, so that this process creates a unity which sets the world in amaze[ment]" (Gray, p. 490). Nevertheless, he emphasizes the necessity of certain activities: "practice, teaching, reflection, failure, furtherance, opposition, and renewed reflection" (Gray, p. 490). A mixture of success and failure is unavoidable.

These general reflections are followed by a discussion of *Faust*, which Goethe had worked on for over 60 years: "Here, I must admit, appeared the great difficulty of attaining through resolution and character what should properly belong only to a nature voluntarily active" (Gray, p. 490). Here he is addressing a fundamental conflict within creative productivity: The tension between spontaneous activity and goal-directed work.

Finally, he brings up the topic of friendship. Companions were of the utmost importance for Goethe's life and work. The most well known is his friendship with Schiller, but it is not the most significant friendship. His entire biography can be recounted alongside two lists, one of his love affairs and one of his friendships. During his university days, it was Behrisch and Herder who helped him to deal with his emotional turmoil and who gave his creative impulses direction. Merck was the next one to give him support, and at the age of 25 he made the acquaintance of someone whose friendship would turn out to be the most important of all, Duke Carl August. With him, Goethe was able to relive the turbulence of adolescence from the perspective of someone older and wiser. The business of state, the horrors of war, and shared passions connected the two men for more than 50 years. In his old age, Goethe's correspondence, especially with the musician Zelter, gave him the opportunity to formulate his thoughts and feelings.

Goethe's last correspondence was with the statesman, scientist, and author Wilhelm von Humboldt. They began to exchange letters in November of 1794. Both cultivated a culture of letter-writing in which the addressee assumed the role of the "ideal audience". Goethe's final letter was preceded by a missive from von Humboldt dated 1 December 1831, in which he asked Goethe about the factors involved in the production of *Faust*. Goethe responded with "infinite pleasure" to his "valued, ever thankfully recognized, and widely scattered friends" and dedicated these "very serious jests" to them. Summing up, he hoped for a response: "In theory and practice confusion rules the world, and I have no more urgent task than to augment, wherever possible, what is and has remained within me and to redistill my peculiarities". And yet he found "there is seldom an hour when these mysteries of life may be realized" (Gray, p. 491).

These were the last words he wrote before ending the letter with "Weimar, the 17th of March 1832, yours faithfully, J. W. v. Goethe".

It is astonishing that Goethe continued his work on the "mysteries of life" until shortly before his death, in order "to augment, wherever possible" himself and "to redistill [his] peculiarities", a metaphor from the world of alchemy and the associated processes of mixing and amalgamating, which is used here to characterize the intellectual exchange taking place among friends. Goethe left us something very special here: His courage to work on himself actively and in open exchange with others into old age.

Chapter 20

Goethe's "inner fairytale"

The psychological messages of *Faust II*

Goethe worked on *Faust* for more than 60 years. The tragedy became his "inner fairytale", accompanying him like a favored toy, always the same but always new. For this reason, the play is considered ingenious, or in modern terms, extraordinarily creative, because it portrays an unbelievably rich array of phenomena from life using unique language. This is also the reason why the play can still mean so much to us today. For Goethe himself, this "inner fairytale" was a means of understanding and poetically shaping his political, economic, and scientific experiences. It also had a major psychological significance for him. Goethe always drew on his own experiences but seldom stopped there; instead, he took the individual and the practical together with the general and the theoretical, turning their dialectics into universals, especially in *Faust II*. In many places, he challenges us to find that which is most significant for us in the play. And indeed, it is worthwhile to address the psychological messages in the second part of the tragedy.

In the first act of the second part of the play, after Faust's disgraceful deeds that led to the death of Gretchen, he finds himself in a "pleasant landscape". Ariel, a spirit of the air, expects that the elves will mollify Faust and free him from his recriminations: "And purge from deep within the burning dart/Of self-reproach and bitter suffering". A chorus of elves extol the blessing of sleep. It frees one from "joy and grief" and makes a sort of rebirth possible. Goethe was familiar with the classical physicians who, under the banner of Asclepius, prescribed healing sleep for the sick and the weary, allowing them not only to forget negative emotional reactions, but also, and more importantly, to discover higher insights while in a state of sleep. This is not so distant from the findings of modern sleep research. There are reliable indicators that neural networks are dissolved and reformed in new combinations during sleep. Through psycho-analysis, we have been able to repeatedly confirm that the dreams that occur during sleep serve the purpose of processing and dealing with experiences. Dreams can have a healing effect. Thus, Faust wakes from his healing sleep, re-energized.

The pulse of life now quickens, as before me
Ethereal light of dawn from night emerges.

You, Earth, were constant through the dark hours for me;
Beneath my feet new life within you surges.
I feel such joy in your embrace, deriving
New strength that with fresh resolution urges
My spirit on to ever higher striving.

(Vs. 4679–4685)

For the present, Faust has forgotten his iniquities and feelings of guilt and returns to his journey of self-improvement and hubris. Here Goethe describes a psychological dynamic that is characterized in modern psychoanalysis as the interplay between the depressive position and the manic defense. We have already discussed the depressive position as a psychological development, where realistic feelings of guilt are developed and transformed into constructive activities. This is also relevant for the modern reader. Goethe showed us how we can find our way to creative activities by "remembering, repeating, and working-through" our conflicts and accepting the "depressive position".

Yet, we cannot be constantly remembering, and the depressive position is not a permanent state; it is part of a complementary relationship with forgetting and manic defense, but at the opposite pole. Actions in which we "forget" ourselves interplay with periods of contemplation and self-reflection. Something new is discovered and created. This is something Goethe shows us in *Faust II*. The recuperated hero feels emboldened to commence new activity. In the "imperial palace" scene, he solves political and economic problems using Mephistopheles' magical powers. Money is issued but is not backed by capital, and all find themselves giving in to the temptation of unwarranted boldness and hubris. There is a sumptuous celebration, and a *pandemonium mundi* is unfolded before the delighted emperor and his vassals, who no longer recognize reality and allow themselves to be blinded by unexpected wealth. They all find themselves in a manic position, and Faust even agrees to conjure up Paris and Helen of Troy, the timeless embodiments of beauty. We have already seen where that leads in the "gloomy gallery" scene.

Denying one's limitations is part of the manic position. Faust exemplifies both this and the depressive position. His productive drive is seized on and perverted by his assistant Wagner in order to accomplish nothing less than the creation of new human beings. In the "laboratory" scene, a homunculus is created in a test tube with Mephistopheles' assistance. The unsuccessful creation proves to be hubris. Naturally, Faust does not respond to this failure by giving up; rather, he gathers the courage to continue and to seek the crowning achievement of his creativeness, the love of the divine Helen: "All hail then to Eros, the lord of creation!" (Vs. 8479).

The oscillation between the manic and depressive positions is concentrated in the figure of Helen. Helen is either the most beautiful queen or only "a sacrifice for all [Menelaus's] hurt" (Vs. 8528). She is "so much admired", yet "so much reviled" (Vs. 8488). Even though she is wavering between the most precious hopes and horrible fears, "base fear does not become the daughter of great Zeus"; nevertheless, she perceives the "horror that emerges from the primal womb/ Of ancient night, that in a myriad shapes rolls forth" (Vs. 8647–8650). Helen unconsciously senses that, as the messenger and the incarnation of Aphrodite, disaster accompanies her everywhere, like all of the children of Uranus and Kronos, the fathers of the gods. The "horrid spawn/Of night" are repulsed by Apollonian forces, yet they continue to act subliminally. Her poetic and erotic encounter with Faust is short-lived, and latent destructive forces draw near:

> Spelling out your love-sick pleasure,
> Cooing to your lovers' measure,
> Idly wooing at your leisure –
> But you have no time to spare.
> Can you hear a muffled pounding?
> Can you hear the trumpets sounding? –
> Danger threatens everywhere.
> (Vs. 9419–9425)

Poetry and eroticism do not allow Helen and Faust to have a lasting creative relationship. Faust feels obligated to do battle, because "no man deserves a woman's favour/Who cannot shield her from the foe" (Vs. 9444–9445). However, this is immediately followed by a countermovement, and the erotic and poetical ideal of a successful union is reaffirmed. Faust depicts the union of classical beauty and harmony with modern satisfaction and health:

> Contentment is a birthright here, a blessing
> That shines in every creature's face;
> Such bliss, such health and happiness possessing,
> Each is immortal in its place.
> (Vs. 9550–9554)

The natural exhilaration of poetic and erotic creativity is manifested in the form of Euphorion, the child of Helen and Faust. But what happens then? The lovely child grows into an expansive youth who surrenders himself to destructive forces and calls out:

> You dream of peace? Then stay,
> Dreaming of peace one day.
> War! is the call for me,
> Onward to victory!
> (Vs. 9835–9839)

In his adolescent boundlessness – "undaunting, free and brave,/Gladly their lives they gave" – he courts disaster, falling to his death like Icarus. His desperate voice can be heard from below: "Mother, must I remain/Here in the dark alone?" (Vs. 9905–9906). The creative joy Helen and Faust found in Euphorion has lasted only a short time and "bliss must give way to pain". Helen feels the pull of dark forces again and follows her son into the underworld.

The poet is left to mourn the loss and to transfigure it within the intellectual sphere. In this way, the horrors are transformed and the destructive forces overcome. This is where Goethe's idea of a life after death comes into play. He believed in a force intrinsic to life that strives for perfection and that survives the death of the physical body. Creativity also continues to operate within living nature; it "continues to stir within all things". The Arcadian scene also ends with a celebration of creative activity with singing, dancing, and intoxication, as in the Cult of Dionysus in antiquity. This joyful celebration soon takes a different turn, though, and new destructive conflicts announce themselves. At the end of the scene, Mephistopheles reveals himself as having been in disguise as Phorkyas. He reminds us of the evil and destruction that will be shown in the next act, not on the plane of the poetic and the erotic, but once again on the plane of the military, politics, and economics. In the "high mountains" scene, Faust strives for economic and political power: "I'll rule in territories I can call/My own; fame's nothing, but the deed is all" (Vs. 10187–10189).

We can also view this turn toward politics and economics as a reaction to his erotic failure. His attempts to win a wife, to have children, and to raise those children were unsuccessful. Thus, he rededicates himself to striving for political and economic power, where creation and destruction are found side by side. He wants to dominate nature, the "aimless play of elemental might". The creative element of water drives him to desperation with its natural wave motion, endlessly coming and going. He wants to combat this, and striving for dominance over nature and economics leads him to intervene in a new war. Through trickery and a pact with ruthless helpers, he is granted a piece of land, but he wants to expand it. His ruthless, insatiable desire for expansion results in the murder of Philemon and Baucis, who personify goodness, traditional values, and a culture of remembrance. His creative drive and his political and economic ruthlessness lead him to find everything that reminds him of slow, natural, civilized development hateful:

A curse on *here*! It preys
Upon my mind and sours my days . . .
That aged couple must give way!
Those lindens shall be mine alone;
Those few trees taunt me day by day,
Pollute my joy in all I own.
How can I halt that mocking sound?
I rage, and yet I hear [that clanging bell] still . . .
Then get them both out of my sight!
(Vs. 11233–11275)

Lynceus the watchman extols the destruction of the world, he who had "found such delight/In all I have seen!" (Vs. 11302–11304):

> What appalling horrors loom
> Out of the surrounding gloom! ...
> That vision that delighted me,
> For evermore has ceased to be.
> (Vs. 11306–11307; 11336–11337)

In the end, we see that Faust has some scruples about his work of destruction and is now full of concerns. Finally, he becomes blind, and yet he is unable to bid goodbye to his megalomaniacal plans for domination. While his grave is being dug, he speaks of making living space for millions of people. Despite his work of destruction, Faust expresses his approval of his creative drive to expand at the last minute: "they/Who must defend their freedom every day/Deserve to live lives that are truly free" (Vs. 11575–11576).

In summary, the conflict between constructive and destructive impulses are condensed in *Faust* in a unique way. The tragedy serves as a warning to respect the limits of human creativity in politics, economics, and the sciences. From a psychological perspective, creative activity seems to be the only possibility for fully experiencing the interplay of light and dark in life while retaining some degree of sanguineness. And so let us think back again on the final verse of the poem "Blissful Longing":

> And so long as you don't have it,
> this "Die and become!",
> you will only be a gloomy guest
> on the dark earth.

Bibliography

Literature

Abbot, T. K. (trans.) 1889. *Kant's Critique of Practical Reason and Other Works on the Theory of Ethics*. London: Longmans, Green & Co.

Andreasen, N. 2005. *The Creating Brain*. New York and Washington, DC: Dana Press.

Antonovsky, A. 1987. *Unraveling the Mystery of Health: How People Manage Stress and Stay Well*. San Francisco, CA: Jossey-Bass.

Bandura, A. 1997. *Self-efficacy: The Exercise of Control*. New York: Freeman.

Bielschowsky, A. 1969. *The Life of Goethe*, trans. by W. A. Cooper. 3 vols. New York: Haskell House Publishers.

Bion, W. 1962. *Learning from Experience*. London: Heinemann.

Bodley, L. B. 2009. *Goethe and Zelter: Musical Dialogues*. Farnham, UK: Ashgate.

Borchmeyer, D. 1999a. *Goethe – der Zeitbürger*. Munich: Hanser.

Borchmeyer, D. 1999b. *Weimarer Klassik*. Weinheim: Beltz Athenäum.

Bowlby, J. 1988. *A Secure Base*. London: Routledge.

Boyle, N. 1991. *Goethe: The Poet and the Age*. Volume I, Oxford: Oxford University Press.

Boyle, N. 2000. *Goethe: The Poet and the Age*. Volume II, Oxford: Oxford University Press.

Brown, P. H. 1920. *Life of Goethe*. 2 vols. New York: Henry Holt & Company.

Carus, C. G. 1842. *Goethe. Zu dessen näheren Verständnis*. Leipzig.

Cornish Rev., F. F. 1894. "Goethe's Weimar Life, 1775–1786". In *Transactions of the Manchester Goethe Society, 1886–1893*. pp. 1–20.

Cremer, C. 2011. "Vom Farbenkreis zum Supermikroskop". Bayrische Akademie der schoenen Kuenste, Jahrbuch 25. Wallstein Verlag, pp. 74–96.

Csikszentmihalyi, M. 1996. *Creativity*. New York: HarperCollins.

Damm, S. 1992. *Cornelia Goethe*. Frankfurt am Main: Insel.

Damm, S. 1998. *Christiane und Goethe*. Frankfurt am Main: Insel.

Damm, S. 2007. *Goethes letzte Reise*. Frankfurt am Main: Insel.

Dawkins, R. 1989. *The Selfish Gene*. Oxford: Oxford University Press

Dombowsky, D. 2014. *Nietzsche and Napoleon: The Dionysian Conspiracy*. Cardiff: University of Wales Press.

Dörr Zegers, O. 2004. "El legado de Goethe". In *Artes y Letras*. Mercurio: Santiago de Chile. n.p.

Düntzer, H. 1883. *Life of Goethe*, trans. by T. W. Lyster. Vol. 2 (1786–1832). London: Macmillan & Co.

Eissler, K. R. 1963. *Goethe: A Psychoanalytic Study, 1757–1786*. 2 vols. Detroit: Wayne State University Press.

Fonagy, P., Gergely, G., Jurist, E., and Target, M. 2005. *Affect Regulation, Mentalization, and the Development of Self*. New York: Other Press.

Fuchs, T. 2016. "The brain – a relational organ". *Journal of Consciousness Studies*, 18, pp. 196–221.

Freud, S. 1908. "Creative writers and day-dreaming". *Standard Edition*, vol. 9. London: Hogarth, pp. 141–154.

Freud, S. 1911. "The case of Schreber". *Standard Edition*, vol. 12. London: Hogarth, pp. 3–84.

Freud, S. 1914. "Remembrance, repeating, working through". *Standard Edition*, vol. 12. London: Hogarth, pp. 145–157.

Freud, S. 1917. "A childhood recollection from *Dichtung und Wahrheit*". *Standard Edition*, vol. 17. London: Hogarth, pp. 145–156.

Freud, S. 1920. "Beyond the pleasure principle". *Standard Edition*, vol. 18. London: Hogarth, pp. 7–66.

Freud, S. 1923. "The id and the ego". *Standard Edition*, vol. 19. London: Hogarth, pp. 1–66.

Freud, S. 1933. "Why war?" *Standard Edition*, vol. 22. London: Hogarth, p. 276.

Friedenthal, R. 2010. *Goethe: His Life and Times*, trans. by J. Nowell. New Brunswick: Transaction Publishers.

Gadamer, H. G. 1989. *Truth and Method*. New York: Crossroad.

Gardner, H. 2006. *Multiple Intelligences: New Horizons in Theory and Praxis*. New York: Basic Books.

Ghibellino, E. 2007. *Goethe and Anna Amalia: A Forbidden Love?*, trans. by Daniel J. Farrelly. Dublin: Carysfort Press.

Goleman, D. 2005. *Emotional Intelligence*. New York: Bantam Books.

Gray, L. H. (trans.) c. 1913. "Letters to Wilhelm von Humboldt and his wife". In *The German Classics of the Nineteenth and Twentieth Centuries*, vol. 2, ed. by K. Francke. New York: German Publication Society, pp. 469–491.

Gundolf, F. 1916. *Goethe*. Berlin: Bondi.

Hawking, S. 2004. "The black hole information loss problem". Dublin, 17th General Relativity Conference.

Hegel, G. F. W. 1807 [1970]. *Phänomenologie des Geistes*. Frankfurt: Suhrkamp. English edition (1979): *Phenomenology of spirit*. Oxford: Oxford University Press.

Höfer, A. 2002. *Goethe*. Munich: dtv.

Hölderlin, F. 1969. *Werke und Briefe*. Frankfurt: Insel.

Holm-Hadulla, R. M. 2004a. "Psychoanalysis as a creative act of shaping". *International Journal of Psychoanalysis*, 84, pp. 1203–1230.

Holm-Hadulla, R. M. 2004b. *The Art of Counselling and Psychotherapy*. London and New York: Karnac Books.

Holm-Hadulla, R. M. 2010. *Kreativität – Konzept und Lebensstil*. Göttingen: Vandenhoeck & Ruprecht.

Holm-Hadulla, R. M. 2011. *Kreativität zwischen Schöpfung und Zerstörung*. Göttingen: Vandenhoeck & Ruprecht.

Holm-Hadulla R. M. 2012. "Goethe's anxieties, depressive episodes and (self-) therapeutic strategies: A contribution to method integration in psychotherapy". *Psychopathology*, 46, pp. 266–274.

Holm-Hadulla, R. M. 2013. "The dialectic of creativity: Towards an integration of neurobiological, psychological, socio-cultural and practical aspects of the creative process". *Creativity Research Journal*, 25, pp. 293–299.

Holm-Hadulla, R. M. 2017a. *The Recovered Voice: Tales of Practical Psychotherapy.* London: Karnac Books.

Holm-Hadulla, R. M. 2017b. "Bipolar disorder and/or creative bipolarity: Robert Schumann's exemplary psychopathology". *Psychopathology*, 50, pp. 379–388.

Holm-Hadulla, R. M., Roussel, M., and Hofmann, F.-H. 2010. "Depression and creativity: The case of the German scientist, poet, and statesman J.W. von Goethe". *Journal of Affective Disorders*, 127, pp. 43–49.

Kandel, E. R. 2012. *The Age of Insight*. New York: Random House.

Kant, I. 1799. *Kritik der praktischen Vernunft* [*Critique of Practical Reason*]. Hamburg: Meiner.

Kernberg, O. F. 1980. *Internal World and External Reality*. New York: Jason Aronson.

Klein, M. 1957. *Envy and Gratitude*. London: Hogarth Press.

Kohut, H. 1971. *The Analysis of the Self*. New York: International Universities Press.

Kretschmer, E. 1929. *Geniale Menschen*. Berlin: Springer.

Lacan, J. 1949. *Ecrits*. Paris: Editions du Seuil. English edition (2001): *Writings*. London: Routledge.

Lange-Eichbaum, W. 1928 (1979). *Genie, Irrsinn und Ruhm*. Munich: Verlag Ernst Reinhardt.

Langer, M. 1987. *Das gebratene Kind und andere Mythen*. Freiburg: Kore.

Ludwig, A. 1997. "Creative achievement and psychopathology". In *Eminent Creativity, Everyday Creativity, and Health*, ed. by M. Runco and R. Richards. Greenwich: Ablex.

Matt, P. v. 1993. "Lied der Mignon". In *Verweile doch*, ed. by M. Reich-Ranicki. Frankfurt: Insel.

Maugham, W. S. 2000. *Points of View*. London: Vintage Books.

Meltzer, D. 1988. *The Apprehension of Beauty*. Worchester: Billing & Sons.

Mitchell, J. (trans.) 2004. *Poems of Friedrich Hölderlin*. San Francisco: Ithuriel's Spear.

Nager, F. 1999. *Der heilkundige Dichter. Goethe und die Medizin*. Zurich: Artemis & Winkler.

Parry, I. 1991. "Tell me about your work". *PN Review* 80, vol. 17, no. 6, July–August.

Peters, U. H. 1982. *Hölderlin*. Reinbek: Rowohlt TB.

Redfield, M. 1996. *Phantom Formations: Aesthetic Ideology and the* Bildungsroman. Ithaca and London: Cornell University Press.

Richards, R. J. 2003. "The erotic authority of nature: Science, art, and the female during Goethe's Italian journey". In *The Moral Authority of Nature*, ed. by L. Daston and F. Vidal. Chicago: University of Chicago Press, pp. 127–154.

Richards, R. J. 2010. *The Romantic Conception of Life: Science and Philosophy in the Age of Goethe*. Chicago: University of Chicago Press.

Rorty, R. 2001. "Universality and truth". In *Rorty and His Critics*, ed. by R. B. Brandom. Oxford: Blackwell, pp. 1–30.

Runco, M. A. 2007. *Creativity*. San Diego: Elsevier Academic Press.

Runco M. and Richards, R. 1997. *Eminent Creativity, Everyday Creativity, and Health*. Greenwich: Ablex.

Schiller, F. 1795 (2000). *Briefe über die ästhetische Erziehung des Menschen* [*Letters upon the Aesthetical Education of Man*]. Ditzingen: Reclam.

Segal, H. 1991. *Dream, Phantasy, and Art*. London: Routledge.

Unseld, S. 1996. *Goethe and his Publishers*, trans. by Kenneth J. Northcott. Chicago: University of Chicago Press.

Varela, F.-J., Thompson, E. and Rosch, E. 1991. *The Embodied Mind: Cognitive Science and Human Experience*. Cambridge, MA: MIT Press.

Wellbery, D. E. 1996. *The Specular Moment: Goethe's Early Lyric and the Beginnings of Romanticism*. Stanford, CA: Stanford University Press.

Wiethölter, R. 2005. "Just-ifications of a law of society", trans. by Iain L. Fraser. In *Paradoxes and Inconsistencies in the Law*, ed. by O. Perez and G. Teubner. Oxford: Hart Publishing, pp. 65–75.

Winnicott, D. W. 1971. *Playing and Reality*. London: Tavistock.

Zajonc, A. 1998. "Goethe and the science of his time". In *Goethe's Way of Science: A Phenomenology of Nature*, ed. by D. Seamon and A. Zajonc. New York: SUNY Press, pp. 15–30.

Goethe's works

FA: Johann Wolfgang Goethe. *Sämtliche Werke. Briefe. Tagebücher und Gespräche*. Frankfurter Ausgabe, ed. by Dieter Borchmeyer et al. 40 volumes. Frankfurt: Deutscher Klassiker Verlag, 1985–1999.

HA: *Goethes Werke*. Hamburger Ausgabe, ed. by Erich Trunz, 10th edition, revised. Munich: C. H. Beck'sche Verlagsbuchhandlung,1981.

HA Letters *Briefe von und an Goethe. Hamburger Ausgabe*, ed. by K. R. Mandelkow. Munich: C. H. Beck'che Verlagsbuchhandlung, 1988.

WA: *Goethes Werke*. Weimarer Ausgabe, ed. by Hermann Böhlau (and successors), 1887–1919, Munich, 1987.

Works: The Works of J.W. von Goethe, ed. by Nathan Haskell Dole.14 vols. London and Boston: Francis A. Niccolls & Co., 1900.

Amelung, H. (ed.) 1914. *Goethes Briefwechsel mit einem Kinde*. Berlin: Bang & Co.

Appelbaum, S. (ed. and trans.) 1999. *103 Great Poems: A Dual-Language Book = 103 Meistergedichte*/Johann Wolfgang von Goethe. Mineola, NY: Dover Publications.

Arnim, B. v. 1920. *Goethes Briefwechsel mit einem Kinde*, ed. by W. Oehlke. Berlin: Propyläen.

Arnim, B. v. 1861. *Goethe's Correspondence with a Child*. Boston: Ticknor and Fields.

Bell, E. (trans.) 1884. *Early and Miscellaneous Letters of JW Goethe, Including Letters to his Mother*. London: George Bell & Sons.

Beutler, E. (ed.) 1949. *Johann Wolfgang Goethe Gedenkausgabe*. Düsseldorf: Artemis.

Bode, W. (ed.) 1999. *Goethe in vertraulichen Briefen seiner Zeitgenossen*. 2 vols. Berlin: Aufbau.

Boerner, P. 2005. *Goethe*, trans. by N. Boerner. London: Haus Publishing.

Bowring, E. A. (trans.) 1874. *The Poems of Goethe: Translated in the Original Metres*, second edition,revised and enlarged. London: George Bell & Sons.

Boyesen, H. H. (ed.) 1885. *Goethe's Works*, 5 vols. Philadelphia: G. Barrie.

Calvert, G. H. (trans.) 1845. *Correspondence between Schiller and Goethe from 1794 to 1805*. Vol. 1 (1794–1797). New York and London: Wiley & Putnam.

Carlyle, T. (trans.) 1907. *Wilhelm Meister's Apprenticeship and Travels* (3 vols in one). London: Chapman and Hall.

Coleridge, A. D. (trans. and ed.) 1892. *Goethe's letters to Zelter, with extracts from those of Zelter to Goethe.* London and New York: George Bell & Sons.

Eastlake, C. L. (trans.) 1840. *Goethe's Theory of Colours.* John Murray: London.

Ezust, E. (trans.) n.d. "Saucy and cheery". Accessed at www.lieder.net/lieder/get_text. html?TextId=6400.

Farie, R. (trans.) 1849. *Campaign in France in the Year 1792.* London: Chapman and Hall.

Gibbs, Alfred S. (trans.) 1880. *Goethe's Mother: Correspondence of Catharine Elizabeth Goethe with Goethe, Lavater, Wieland, Duchess Anna Amalia of Saxe-Weimar, Friedrich von Stein, and Others.* New York: Dodd, Mead & Co.

Goethe, J. C., Goethe, C. and Goethe, C. E. 1960. *Briefe aus dem Elternhaus.* Stuttgart: Artemis.

Goethe, J. W. v. "Roman Elegies", anonymous translator. n.d. Accessed at www.gutenberg. org/files/7889/7889-h/7889-h.htm.

Gräf, H. G. (ed.) 1916. *Goethes Briefwechsel mit seiner Frau.* 2 vols. Frankfurt: Rütten & Löning.

Grosche, S. (ed.). 2001. *"Zarten Seelen ist gar viel gegönnt" – Naturwissenschaft und Kunst im Briefwechsel zwischen C.G. Carus und Goethe.* Göttingen: Wallstein.

Hamburger, M. (trans.) 1958. "Roman elegies". In *Great Writings of Goethe*, ed. by S. Spender. New York and Toronto: The New American Library, pp. 222–223.

Herzfeld M.von, and Sym, M. (trans.) "Letters from Goethe". In *Great Writings of Goethe*, ed. by S. Spender. New York and Toronto: The New American Library, pp. 26–41.

Kirby, M. (trans.) 2015. *Faust: The First Part of the Tragedy.* Indianapolis: Focus.

Köster, A. 1904. *Die Briefe der Frau Rath Goethe.* Leipzig: Poeschel.

Krebs, S. (trans.) n.d. "To Luna". Accessed at www.lieder.net/lieder/get_text.html? TextId=111055.

Mann, T. (ed.) 2006. *The Goethe Treasury: Selected Prose and Poetry.* Mineola, NY: Dover Publications.

Morrison, A. J. W. and Nisbet, C. (trans.) 1885. *Goethe's Travels in Italy: Together with his Second Residence in Rome and Fragments on Italy.* London: George Bell and Sons.

Oxenford, J. (trans.) 1850. *Conversations of Goethe with Eckermann and Soret.* 2 vols. London: Smith, Elder, and Co.

Page, G. A. (trans.) 1913. *Wilhelm Meister's Theatrical Mission.* New York: Bretano's.

Saunders, T. B. (trans.) 1908. *The Maxims and Reflections of Goethe.* Second revised edition. London: Macmillan and Co.

Schmitz, L. D. (trans.) 1845. *Correspondence between Schiller and Goethe from 1794 to 1805.* Vol. 2 (1798–1805). New York and London: Wiley and Putnam.

Schmitz, L. D. (ed. and trans.) 1885. *Miscellaneous Travels of J.W. Goethe.* London: George Bell & Sons.

Smith, M. S. (rev. and trans.) 1908. *Poetry and Truth: From My Own Life*, Volumes 1 and 2. London: George Bell & Sons.

Whaley, J. (trans.) 1998. *Goethe: Selected Poems.* Evanston, IL: Northwestern University Press.

Williams, J. R. (trans.) 2007. *Faust: A Tragedy in Two Parts and the Urfaust.* London: Wordsworth Editions.

Index